STUDIES IN LABOUR
AND SOCIAL LAW

GENERAL EDITORS
BOB HEPPLE
Professor of English Law in the
University of London, at Unversity College
PAUL O'HIGGINS
Regius Professor of Laws,
Trinity College, University of Dublin

Strikes in Essential Services

Strikes in Essential Services

GILLIAN S. MORRIS

MANSELL PUBLISHING LIMITED
LONDON AND NEW YORK

First published 1986 by Mansell Publishing Limited
(A subsidiary of the H.W. Wilson Company)
6 All Saints Street, London N1 9RL, England
950 University Avenue, Bronx, New York 10452, U.S.A.

British Library Cataloguing in Publication Data
Morris, Gillian S., *1953—*
Strikes in essential services. — (Studies in labour and social law)
1. Strikes and lock-outs — Public utilities — Law and legislation — Great Britain
I. Title II. Series
344.104'189201 KD3076

ISBN 0–7201–1791–7

Library of Congress Cataloging-in-Publication Data
Morris, Gillian S.
Strikes in essential services.

(Studies in labour and social law)
Based on author's thesis (Ph.D.) — University of Cambridge, 1977.
Bibliography: p.
Includes index.
1. Strikes and lockouts — Law and legislation — Great Britain. 2. Strikes and lockouts — Civil service — Law and legislation — Great Britain. I. Title.
II. Series.
KD3076.M67 1986 344.41'01892 86–12768

ISBN 0–7201–1791–7 (U.S.) 344.1041892

Printed in Great Britain

CONTENTS

For my parents,
Eve and Edgar Morris

PREFACE

Strikes in essential services have attracted enormous publicity and concern in Great Britain in recent years. How to deal with the problems they present has become a prominent issue of political debate, with a wide range of strategies being advocated. Some see the introduction of further legal restrictions on the freedom to strike as the solution; for others, voluntary self-restraint is the only answer. The aim of this book is to analyse the role which the law has played so far in relation to industrial action in essential services, to examine the industrial relations practices which have governed the conduct of disputes, and to assess the viability of the various proposals for reform which have been made.

My research in this area began with a doctoral dissertation submitted to the University of Cambridge in 1977. This book draws on that study, but subsequent developments and further research and reflection have resulted in a book which bears little resemblance to the dissertation and which is, in effect, an entirely new work.

My thanks are due to a number of individuals who have helped me with my research. I owe a particular debt of gratitude to Bob Hepple, both for his careful supervision of the initial research and for his invaluable advice and constant support ever since. I would also like to thank Peter Wallington for his generous provision of time and help in guiding the dissertation through its final stages of preparation. Special thanks are also due to Paul O'Higgins for his unfailing willingness to provide advice and encouragement over the years.

The development of the ideas contained in this book was furthered considerably by a research project on industrial action in the National Health Service which I conducted in the period 1982–3. I would like to thank the Polytechnic of North London for its generosity in providing me with a Research Assistant, Stephen Rydzkowski, to work on this project and to thank Stephen for his committed and tireless efforts in carrying out the study. I would also like to thank Christopher Champness and other members of the Law Department at the Polytechnic of North London for their general support and encouragement. Finally, I would like to thank the many individuals who work for organizations referred to in this book for their assistance in providing information to which I would otherwise not have had access.

The law is stated in the light of information available on 1 May 1986.

List of Abbreviations

A.C.A.S.	Advisory, Conciliation and Arbitration Service
A.P.A.P.	Association of Professional Ambulance Personnel
A.S.L.E.F.	Associated Society of Locomotive Engineers and Firemen
A.S.T.M.S.	Association of Scientific, Technical and Managerial Staffs
A.U.E.W.	Amalgamated Union of Engineering Workers
B.H.D.F.	British Hospital Doctors Federation
B.M.A.	British Medical Association
C.C.S.U.	Council of Civil Service Unions
C.C.U.	Civil Contingencies Unit
C.E.G.B.	Central Electricity Generating Board
C.O.H.S.E.	Confederation of Health Service Employees
C.P.S.A.	Civil and Public Services Association
D.H.S.S.	Department of Health and Social Security
E.E.T.P.U.	Electrical, Electronic, Telecommunication and Plumbing Union (formerly the E.T.U.: Electrical Trades Union)
E.M.A.	Engineers and Managers Association
E.P.E.A.	Electrical Power Engineers Association
F.A.P.	Federation of Ambulance Personnel
F.B.U.	Fire Brigades Union
F.N.P.	Federation of Nursing Personnel
G.C.H.Q.	Government Communications Headquarters
G.M.B.A.T.U.	General, Municipal, Boilermakers and Allied Trades Union (formerly the G.M.W.U.: General and Municipal Workers Union)
H.C.S.A.	Hospital Consultants and Specialists Association
H.D.A.	Hospital Doctors Association (formerly the J.H.D.A.: Junior Hospital Doctors Association)
I.L.O.	International Labour Organisation
M.P.	Member of Parliament
M.P.U.	Medical Practitioners' Union

N.A.F.O.	National Association of Fire Officers
N.A.L.G.O.	National and Local Government Officers Association
N.C.B.	National Coal Board
N.G.A.	National Graphical Association
N.I.C.E.	Nationally Integrated Caring Employees
N.H.S.	National Health Service
N.U.P.E.	National Union of Public Employees
N.U.R.	National Union of Railwaymen
N.U.S.	National Union of Seamen
O.M.S.	Organisation for the Maintenance of Supplies
P.O.E.U.	Post Office Engineering Union
R.A.F.	Royal Air Force
R.C.M.	Royal College of Midwives
R.C.N.	Royal College of Nursing
S.C.P.S.	Society of Civil and Public Servants
S.L.A.D.E.	Society of Lithographic Artists, Designers and Engineers
S.O.G.A.T. 82	Society of Graphical and Allied Trades 1982
S.T.C.	Supply and Transport Committee
T.G.W.U.	Transport and General Workers Union
T.U.C.	Trades Union Congress
U.C.W.	Union of Communication Workers (formerly the U.P.O.W.: Union of Post Office Workers)
U.R.T.U.	United Road Transport Union

1

A Survey of the Issues

During the 1970s British industrial relations were transformed by a growth in militancy in the public sector. A number of public sector workers, including local authority manual workers, gasworkers, health service ancillary staff, doctors, nurses, Post Office workers and civil servants, embarked on nation-wide campaigns of industrial action for the first time. Other groups for whom industrial action was less of a novelty, coalminers, electricity power workers, and firemen, also brought home in no uncertain terms the strength of their industrial muscle. Many of these disputes affected essential services for which there was no alternative source of supply. For the Royal Commission on Trade Unions and Employers' Associations,[1] reporting in 1968, disputes in monopolistic essential services were hardly an issue. A decade later, how to deal with the problems they present had become a major topic of political debate, with strong pressure for reform of the law from a number of quarters. This book examines the existing legal provisions relating to industrial action in essential services and the use which has been made of them; the practices which have applied to the conduct of disputes in selected services; the strategies which respective governments have pursued to minimize disruption; and the implications of the reforms which have been proposed.

Unlike many other legal systems, British law has never prohibited or restricted strikes in the public sector in general, nor has it attempted to enumerate specific 'essential services' which should always be safeguarded against disruption. Individual groups of workers (the police, the armed forces, merchant seamen, and postal and telecommunications workers) are subject to special restrictions, but these restrictions were imposed at different times for differing reasons rather than as the product of an integrated strategy. The British approach to labour disputes in essential services has traditionally centred upon taking measures to secure supplies by alternative means once they have been disrupted rather than using the law to forestall disruption in the first place. The most far-reaching powers to achieve this are granted by the Emergency Powers Act 1920. This Act enables the Government, on proclaiming a state of emergency, to take extensive measures to 'secure the essentials of life to the community' when the supply and distribution of food, water, fuel, or light, or the means of locomotion, are put at risk. These measures can include employing troops on work left undone by strikers, but the Act does not allow strikers to be ordered back to work or restrictions to be imposed on the freedom to withdraw labour. Since 1939 the Government has also had a standing power to deploy troops on 'urgent work of national importance' without a proclamation of emergency

The 1920 Act is useful to the Government when the supplies which are disrupted can be rationed, stored or directed. Food, medical supplies, electricity and petrol are examples of such commodities. The power to use troops is also significant when the work-force which soldiers are required to replace is relatively unskilled and small in number. Where, however, disruption affects technologically complex areas, such as electricity and water supply, or industrial action is taken by highly trained professional groups such as doctors and nurses, the ability of troops to replace strikers is limited or non-existent. The disputes of the 1970s highlighted these limitations and laid the foundations of pressure for change.

Why did public sector workers become more militant? There is no single answer to this question, but one key factor was undoubtedly the impact of Government incomes policies on established principles of pay determination. Before the late 1960s, the public sector was seen as 'one of the few jewels in the crown' of the industrial relations system.[2] From 1919 onwards the Government had assumed the role of a 'model' employer. Centralized collective bargaining machinery was set up for the civil service, and later for local government, the nationalized industries, and the National Health Service, and workers were actively encouraged to join trade unions, Union density was high; 83 per cent in 1974, as compared with 38.6 per cent in the private sector.[3] From the mid-1950s, the principle of fair comparison with outside staffs sustained relatively stable pay relationships and arbitration was available to settle any disputes which did arise. In short:

> [f]or two decades after World War II, the stability of public sector industrial relations was based on an implicit understanding that as long as government and senior management discharged their responsibility to be 'good' employers, then employees and their

union representatives would accept a reciprocal obligation to avoid industrial conflict.[4]

This 'implicit understanding' was shattered by a series of incomes policies, designed to reduce the rate of inflation, which seemed often to hit hardest at the public sector. Two of these policies affected only public sector workers: an eight-month 'pay pause' introduced by the Macmillan Conservative Government in 1961–2; and the 'n— 1' policy of the Heath Conservative Government in 1970–2, an informal policy which aimed to reduce successive pay settlements below the level of the preceding ones. In each case the private sector was exhorted to follow suit but was under no compulsion to do so. A statutory incomes policy imposed by the Wilson Labour Government between 1965 and 1969 also discriminated against many public sector groups, partly because of its emphasis on productivity, which in non-manual areas could not easily be measured and in the public service in general could not be quickly introduced, and partly because the public sector was more susceptible to government control.[5] In 1972 the Conservative Government also adopted a statutory incomes policy, but this in turn produced further anomalies, with its first stage, a pay freeze, frustrating a number of public sector claims. Although it is simplistic to present a picture of uniform decline in public sector pay,[6] the effect of these policies, which disturbed traditional relativities and undermined the principle of comparability, was to destabilize established systems of pay determination and produce a mounting sense of grievance among the workforce. In the early 1970s this anger was translated into action. Groups for whom more than a token protest would once have seemed unthinkable embarked on fiercely fought campaigns.

A number of these disputes could be won only if the restraints of incomes policy were overcome. Public sector workers were thereby in direct conflict with the Government rather than with their immediate employers. Invoking the Emergency Powers Act did not prevent a Government defeat on two crucial occasions. The fragile 'n — 1' policy was finally shattered by a coalminers' strike in 1972 which drastically disrupted electricity supplies; the Government was ultimately forced to establish a Court of Inquiry to end the dispute and this recommended increases way beyond the policy's limits. A second miners' campaign in 1973–74 culminated in a General Election which the Government lost. This time the Government had no hesitation in presenting the crisis as political; according to ministers the miners were challenging legislative limits and thereby the will of Parliament and the democratic process. This was not the first time a government had dubbed trade union power an attack upon the State; Lloyd George, Baldwin and Wilson had made similar assertions in the face of a coalminers' strike in 1921, the 1926 General Strike, and a seaman's strike in 1966 respectively. The difference lay in the fact that in 1974 the union won.

The election of a Labour Government in March 1974 brought relative peace to the public sector; there was no formal incomes policy, and between mid-1975 and 1977 the T.U.C. voluntarily agreed to pay restraint. Towards the end of its term of office, however, the picture changed completely. In 1978 the Government attempted unilaterally to impose a 5 per cent limit on all pay settlements. Following major breaches of this guideline in the private sector, local government workers, health service workers, civil servants and teachers mounted campaigns to break the limit. Private sector lorry drivers also went on strike. During the 1978–79 'winter of discontent' the media were full of tales of uncollected refuse, untreated patients, undelivered food, and neglected children, and the unpopularity which this brought the unions also rubbed off on the Government. It was defeated on a motion of 'no confidence' in the House of Commons and thrust out of office in the Election which followed. The outgoing Prime Minister, Mr James Callaghan, attributed the Tory victory to 'a vote against the events of last winter'.[7]

The 'winter of discontent' disputes heralded widespread publicity for the view that strikes in essential services should be prohibited or restricted. This was not the first time that such ideas had been mooted in peace-time; the Lloyd George Government had considered measures along these lines in 1920 and the Society of Conservative Lawyers had pressed for a 'cooling-off' period in the 1960s.[8] Although strikes in essential services were not then a major problem, the Heath Government's ill-fated Industrial Relations Act 1971 had allowed a 'cooling-off' period and compulsory ballot of the workers involved in 'emergency disputes'. These procedures were introduced after a narrow and ill-informed debate and were discredited after only one dispute. They were repealed with the rest of the Act in 1974. Since 1979 rather more wide-ranging proposals have been made.

The Conservative election manifesto of 1979 contained a pledge to restrict industrial action in essential services without specifying how this might be done. A Green Paper on Trade Union Immunities,[9] issued by the Department of Employment in 1981, demonstrated waning enthusiasm for this idea. It pointed out that existing legal provisions had been little used and that workers in key industries generally exercised their power with restraint, and emphasized the problem of identifying the groups to be restricted, the damage to industrial relations that the imposition of restrictions would cause, and the difficulties of enforcing sanctions. It concluded that voluntary 'no-strike' agreements, where these could be negotiated, seemed the best course to follow. The House of Commons Employment Committee, which considered the Green Paper, disagreed. A majority of the Committee decided that 'industrial action which puts public health or public safety at risk poses a very serious problem, which must be tackled without delay' and recommended introducing legislation 'at an early date'.[10] The Government remained unmoved. In a debate on the 1982 Employment Bill in the House of Lords, the Lord Advocate, Lord Mackay of Clashfern informed the House that consultations on the Green Paper had indicated that '[m]ost people agreed that. . . [strikes in such services]. . . were highly undesirable, but most people also acknowledged the diffiiculty of preventing them by legislation'.[11]

Industrial action by civil servants in 1981 and by health service workers the following year, taken in response to a *de facto* pay policy enforced through the mechanism of cash limits, brought no further plans for change. A water strike in 1983, however, revived the Conservative Party's commitment to reform. Its 1983 election manifesto stressed the need for essential services to be governed by 'adequate procedure agreements' and promised consultations on removing immunity from civil liability for industrial action taken in breach of such agreements. Ministers reiterated this commitment after the election, but once again the Government has not been in any great hurry to implement its pledge. Another essential service stoppage may well lend a greater sense of urgency to the process of reform. Meanwhile, trade union power in the public sector has been weakened in less direct ways by other aspects of Government policy. These include the contracting-out of some health and local government services to private enterprise, the relaxation of public sector monopolies in posts, telecommunications and electricity; and the banning of membership of national civil service unions at Government Communications Headquarters, allegedly on the ground that this was necessary to prevent industrial action which could endanger national security.

The case for reform of the law is still being strongly pressed upon the Government by two organizations with considerable influence within the Conservative Party: the Institute of Directors and the Centre for Policy Studies. The Institute of Directors sees strikes in essential services as 'the most crucial' industrial relations problem of the day. It advocates the imposition of compulsory binding arbitration, possibly on a 'final offer' basis, as the concluding stage of disputes procedures in these services, and agrees with the Government's suggestion that industrial action in breach of procedure should be deprived of immunity.[12] It also favours decentralizing collective bargaining in the public sector monopolies and establishing separate employer units, thus confining disputes to a local level, together with substantial elements of privatization.[13] All these policies would reduce the ability of unions in the public sector to organize effective campaigns.

The Centre for Policy Studies exhorts a more direct approach. It proposes that strikes in the fire, health, nuclear power and sewerage services and in the public utilities should be prohibited altogether, with particularly severe punishment where withdrawal of the service leads to death or serious injury. It suggests linking the pay of workers in these services to the retail price index and compulsory arbitration for disputes over other matters.[14] The Social Democratic Party also advocates reform in the shape of compulsory arbitration where industrial action threatens life and limb.[15]

The imposition of legislative restrictions on the freedom to take industrial action in essential services is unequivocally opposed by the trade union movement. This does not mean, however, that trade unions have ignored the problems presented by essential service stoppages. A consultative document published by the T.U.C. in January 1986 recognises that 'whichever Government is in power, special steps have to be taken to avoid disruption to services on which the community relies' and suggests that these may 'include a major emphasis on arbitration as a way of reaching decisions when disputes cannot be resolved through negotiation and conciliation'.[16] Lord McCarthy, the Labour Party's front bench spokesman on Employment in the House of Lords, proposes that all public sector trade unions should be given the opportunity to enter agreements providing for independent binding arbitration in pay and conditions disputes, thus excluding, on a voluntary basis, industrial action over these matters during the currency of the agreement.[17] The desire of trade unions to minimize disruption to essential services has also been reflected by the pursuit of a strategy of self-restraint and joint regulation. In the disputes of the 1970s unions commonly formulated Codes of Conduct for their members to follow and in 1979 the T.U.C. issued guidelines exhorting affiliated unions to co-operate with employers in maintaining supplies and services essential to health or safety or otherwise required to avoid serious hardship or exceptional pollution.[18] Such co-operation is usually conditional on management refraining from implementing certain sanctions against those workers who do take action or from otherwise acting to undermine the effectiveness of the workers' campaign, for example by introducing substitute labour. The efficacy and implications of the self-restraint and joint regulation approach to disputes, and a comparison with alternative methods of tackling disruptive action, is one of the major themes of this book.

THE CONCEPT OF 'ESSENTIAL SERVICES'

The idea that certain services require particular protection against disruption is reflected in the law of most countries, although the methods adopted to safeguard them vary greatly. Sometimes the need for an uninterrupted service is felt to be so strong that workers in that service are not permitted to withdraw their labour under any circumstances. (Many countries have also denied the right to strike to all public service workers, regardless of the service they provide.)[19] Alternatively, the legality of industrial action may depend upon observance of particular procedures, such as a minimum period of notice, a 'cooling-off' period to allow more time for a peaceful settlement, or agreement that specified workers should remain at work to maintain a basic service. In general these procedures are the product of legislation, but in a few countries, such as Sweden, Germany and, most recently, Italy, trade unions have voluntarily agreed to comply with them. The problems of enforcing restrictions on essential service strikes are discussed in Chapter 7.

The services which are deemed to be 'essential' also vary greatly between different legal systems. In some countries the definition is confined to services necessary for public health and safety; in others, it extends to 'all activities which the government may consider appropriate or all strikes that may be contrary to public order, the general interest or economic development'.[20] The developing nations, in particular, have tended to take a broad view of the concept. In the Philippines, for example, the definition includes 'companies engaged in the generation or distribution of energy, banks, hospitals, and export-orientated industries'. In 1983 the 'semi-conductor electronics industry' was added to the list.[21] South Korea, too, includes 'stock transaction and banking business'.[22] The list in Malaysia is extremely extensive, covering

> banking services; any section of any service, on the working of which the safety of the employees therein or of the establishment relating thereto depends; postal, telegraph, telephone and telecommunications services; transport services by land, water or air; public health services; any industry or government undertaking which generates or supplies electricity, gas or water to the public; port, deck, harbour and airport services and undertakings, including stevedoring, lighterage, cargo-handling and pilotage; any service provided by any of the Government Departments such as Chemistry, Civil Aviation, Customs and Excise, Immigration, Marine, Meteorology, Printing, and Fire Services; services which are connected with or related to, or which assist towards the

> maintenance and functioning of the Armed Forces and the Royal Malaysian Police Force; and business and industries which are connected with the defense and security of Malaysia.[23]

The inclusion of services which affect the economy is not confined to developing countries; in 1976 the New Zealand definition was extended to 'export slaughterhouses' and 'various countries, both industrialised and developing, have recently included in their list of essential services certain financial operations such as those carried out by banks and foreign exchange offices'.[24]

Essential services may be defined specifically or by reference to a general concept. Countries in Asia, Africa, Latin America and the Caribbean have tended to adopt the enumeration method. By contrast, Western countries generally allow special provisions to be invoked if industrial action is deemed by a particular person or body to threaten particular consequences. In the United States special procedures come into effect if the President considers that a dispute affecting 'an entire industry or a substantial part thereof' would imperil 'the national health or safety' and a court agrees with this assessment.[25] In France the Government can requisition strikers 'employed in a service or an enterprise regarded as indispensable to provide for the needs of the nation'.[26] The self-restraint procedures adopted by the German unions refer to 'plants vital to sustain life'.[27] The enumeration method has the advantage of certainty and it removes the need to decide whether to apply procedures to particular strikes. It has the disadvantage that it restricts industrial action regardless of its scope and the character of the participants, who may not be needed to provide a basic service. It could also prove unduly rigid. In practice, however, most countries which adopt the enumeration approach also enable the government to expand their list by means of a highly expeditious procedure'. In addition, 'many of these countries have other provisions of a very general nature enabling the government to intervene in any dispute which it sees as endangering the national economy or the national interest in general'.[28] Further discussion of the merits of each approach appears in Chapter 7.

Even a cursory survey of different systems clearly demonstrates that there is no consensus view as to which services are essential and which are not. This is partly explained by the fact that the necessity for continuous provision of a service in any given country depends upon a variety of geographical, environmental and technological factors.

> What is an emergency in one country is not necessarily an emergency in another; one of the most dire threats to the life of the community in. . . [the United Kingdom] . . . is a dock strike, but the

United States can contemplate a strike of the 'longshoremen' with slightly greater eqaunimity.[29]

The availability of accessible substitutes is also a crucial consideration; a rail strike will have far less impact if traffic can be diverted with ease onto the roads. More fundamentally, however, there is no consensus as to the appropriate yardstick of essentiality which should be adopted. This lack of agreement is reflected in international provisions. Article 31 of the European Social Charter 1965 allows restrictions on the right to strike which are prescribed by law and 'necessary in a democratic society for the protection of the rights and freedoms of others or for the protection of the public interest, national security, public health or morals'. The Freedom of Association Committee of the International Labour Organisation takes a narrower view; it emphasizes that strikes should be proscribed only if interrupting a service would endanger 'life, personal safety or health'.[30] Legislation in many countries clearly goes well beyond the boundaries of that definition, and on receiving complaints to that effect the Committee has ruled that banking, agricultural activities, transport, the metal, petrol, tobacco and printing industries, and teaching are not essential activities.

Consideration of the concept of 'essential services' must also involve the question: 'essential to whom?'. Terms such as the 'public at large' or 'the community' are rhetorically potent but they may disguise the fact that it is often the interests of particular groups which are at stake.[31] Disputes which jeopardize the 'national economy' may cause loss and inconvenience to financiers and investors but leave most of the population untouched. Even on a narrow view of essentiality, not all are equally indispensable to every person. To those dependent on State social security benefits, disruption of the payments system may be more important than uninterrupted policing, to others it is irrelevant. For those with access to private medicine, a strike by public sector health care workers is of little concern. Moreover, as this book shows, the 'national' or 'public' interest may easily become confused with the political interests of the government of the day. In the words of Benjamin Aaron, 'the concept of essentiality is not an absolute, capable of being defined by purely objective criteria; rather, its meaning varies according to subjective group interests and political expediency'.[32] The considerations which may influence the decision to proscribe a particular dispute are discussed in greater detail in Chapter 7.

THE STRUCTURE OF THIS BOOK

The next three chapters describe the legal and administrative provisions which currently exist in Great Britain to counter the dislocation of particular supplies and services. (The extensive powers which were bestowed on the executive during the two world wars lie outside the scope of this book.)[33] Chapter 2 looks at provisions which attempt to prevent disruptive action from ever taking place. As well as laws which seek directly to inhibit industrial action in particular occupations, there are also a number of means by which industrial action, or at any rate its effectiveness, can be inhibited indirectly. These include restrictions on trade union membership, limitations on the scope of statutory immunities against civil liability, the discretion of the courts to grant interlocutory injunctions, restrictions on picketing, protections against union discipline, and restrictions imposed by professional organizations. As the chapter indicates, these indirect methods may be more effective in limiting industrial action in particular services than any direct restrictions.

Chapter 3 analyses the scope of the special powers which the British Government possesses to mitigate the impact of disruptive action and examines the situations in which these have been invoked. In fifty per cent of disputes during which the Emergency Powers Act 1920 has been invoked the Government had an interest in the terms of settlement, either directly or because its incomes policy was in jeopardy. The chapter shows the difficulty of separating the protection of essential supplies from the protection of Government policies in situations where the Government is committed to resisting the workers' claim.

Chapter 4 discusses the use of substitute labour during disputes and traces the development of Government contingency planning for industrial emergencies. The Armed Forces have been the most widely used source of replacement labour, but the police have also been deployed during disputes and the use of civilian volunteers has sometimes been considered. Although troops cannot be employed to advantage in all disputes, the power to call on them still remains significant. The deployment of substitute labour has always been central to Government contingency plans for emergencies. At one time governments questioned the political wisdom of maintaining a standing organization to counter industrial disruption; such an organization now has a permanent place in the bureaucracy of the State. In recent years this organization, the details of which are shrouded in secrecy, has become increasingly sophisticated. The chapter assesses the implications of the adversarial approach to tackling industrial action in essential services which is manifested by this form of contingency planning.

The only measure of the scale of disruption to particular services reflected in official statistics is the number of working days lost over a given period. To look exclusively at numbers of working days lost can be misleading, however. Sanctions short of a strike can sometimes cause damage equivalent to that of a total strike and many public sector campaigns have been based on such tactics. Calling out small numbers of key workers can also have an impact which is far more severe than their numbers would suggest. What is material in disputes in essential services is not so much the numbers taking disruptive action but the areas in which action is taken and, in particular, whether or not emergency cover is maintained. Chapters 5 and 6 look at the conduct of disputes in five sectors which furnish services which are 'essential' according to the most restrictive definition in that they affect the health and safety of a substantial proportion of the British population: the fire service, the electricity, gas and water industries, and the National Health Service. It shows that in many disputes the self-restraint and joint regulation ('Queensberry Rules') approach advocated by the unions has been put into practice, although there have also been times when the 'rules' were not observed. The implications of the 'Queensberry Rules' approach to disputes are examined in greater detail in a discussion of responses to industrial action at local level in the N.H.S., based on a survey of administrators which was carried out in 1983.

The final chapter considers the range of strategies available to deal with industrial action in essential services and considers their implications and viability in the light of experience in Britian and elsewhere. It concludes by looking at some recent developments which may influence the conduct of disputes in essential services in Britain in the future.

NOTES

1. Cmnd. 3623 (1968).
2. P.A. Beaumont and D.A. Heald, 'Public Employment' in *Government Policy Initiatives 1979–80: Some Case Studies in Public Administration* ed. P.M. Jackson, R.I.P.A., London, 1981, p.19.
3. Robert Price and George Sayers Bain, 'Union Growth Revisited: 1948–74 in Perspective', *British Journal of Industrial Relations* XIV (1976), table 2, p. 342.
4. David Winchester, 'Industrial Relations in the Public Sector' in *Industrial Relations in Britain* ed. George Sayers Bain, Blackwell, Oxford, 1983, p. 176.
5. R. Undy, V. Ellis, W.E.J. McCarthy and A.M. Halmos, *Change in Trade Unions*, Hutchinson, London, 1981, p. 222.
6. See generally A.W.J. Thomson and P.B. Beaumont, *Public Sector Bargaining: A Study of Relative Gain*, Saxon House, Farnborough, 1978.
7. Eric Wigham, *Strikes and the Government 1893–1981*, Macmillan, London, 1982, p. 205.
8. See the Royal Commission on Trade Unions and Employers' Associations 1965–8, as above, note 1, para. 419.
9. Cmnd. 8128 (1981), paras. 330–8.
10. House of Commons, Second Report from the Employment Committee, Session 1980–1, p. ix, paras. 24 and 29.
11, H.L. Deb., Vol. 434, col. 629 (August 2, 1982). The results of these consultations are contained in the Report referred to in note 10, above.
12. Institute of Directors, *Settling Disputes Peacefully*, I.O.D., London, 1984.

13. Institute of Directors, *Democracy and Competitiveness: Further Steps Towards Trade Union Reform*, I.O.D., London, 1983.

14. Centre for Policy Studies, *The Right to Strike in a Free Society*, C.P.S., London, 1983.

15. Social Democratic Party, *Reforming the Trade Unions*, S.D.P., London, 1982.

16. Trades Union Congress, *Industrial Relations Legislation*, T.U.C., London, 1986, para. 4.31.

17. William McCarthy, *Freedom at Work: Towards the Reform of Tory Employment Laws*, Fabian Society, London, 1986, p. 44–5.

18. Annex to the 'Social Concordat': The Economy, the Government and Trade Union Responsibilities: Joint Statement by the T.U.C. and Government, H.M.S.O., London, 1979.

19. See Efren Córdova, 'Strikes in the Public Service: Some Determinants and Trends', *International Labour Review* 124 (1985), p. 163.

20. International Labour Office, *Freedom of Association and Collective Bargaining*, I.L.O., Geneva, 1983, para. 213.

21. Cicero D. Calderon, 'Labour Relations in Essential Services' in the Second Asian Regional Congress of Labor Law and Social Security, September 14–16, 1983, pp. 33–4.

22. As above, note 19.

23. As above, note 19, p. 32.

24. A. Pankert, 'Settlement of Labour Disputes in Essential Services', *International Labour Review* 119 (1980), p. 723 at p. 728.

25. Taft-Hartley Act 1947; see Chapter 3 for details of this provision. Interstate railroads and airlines are covered by the Railway Labor Act 1934.

26. See K.W. Wedderburn, 'Industrial Action, the State and the Public Interest' in *Industrial Conflict: A Comparative Legal Survey* ed. B. Aaron and K.W. Wedderburn, Longman, London, 1972, pp. 351–3.

27. As above, note 24, p. 349.

28. As above, note 22, pp. 727–8.

29. Paul Davies and Mark Freedland, *Kahn-Freund's Labour and the Law*, Stevens, London, 1983 (3rd ed.) pp. 305–6.

30. International Labour Office, *Freedom of Association*, I.L.O., Geneva, 1985 (3rd ed.), para. 400.

31. For further discussion of this point, see essays by Lord Wedderburn, Richard Hyman, Colin Crouch, William McCarthy and Jon Clark in *Labour Law and the Community: Perspectives for the 1980s* eds. Lord Wedderburn of Charlton and W.T.Murphy, Institute of Advanced Legal Studies, London, 1982.

32. Benjamin Aaron, 'Strikes in Essential Services: Reflections on the Western Experience' in the Second Asian Regional Congress of Labor Law and Social Security, as above, note 19, p. 17.

33. For an account of the powers which were available during the First World War see Gerry R. Rubin, *War, Law and Labour, 1915–1921*, O.U.P., Oxford, forthcoming.

2

Legal Restrictions on Industrial Action in Essential Services

Provisions which directly inhibit industrial action by particular groups of workers in Britain are a piecemeal collection rather than the product of an integrated strategy. They divide into those which curtail industrial action in specific occupations and those which proscribe industrial action having specified effects. The first part of this chapter discusses these direct restrictions, which vary considerably in their nature, purpose and impact. Five groups of workers are currently singled out for special treatment under legislation: the police, the armed forces, merchant seamen, postal workers and telecommunications workers. (Restrictions on gas, water and electricity workers, dating back to 1875, were repealed in 1971.) In addition, there is no statutory immunity against liability in tort for those who organize industrial action by staff at the Houses of Parliament. Unlike civil servants in many other countries, British civil servants are free from statutory restraints on industrial action, but the Government has recently warned them that withdrawing their labour in some circumstances may result in disciplinary sanctions being imposed.

Section 5 of the Conspiracy and Protection of Property Act 1875 is the major provision to restrict industrial action in terms of its consequences. Broadly speaking, this section makes it an offence to take certain industrial action which puts at risk life, health or property. Health and safety legislation may also be relevant in this connection.

As well as these direct restrictions, there are also a number of other means by which industrial action in essential services may be inhibited or its effectiveness undermined. These include restrictions on trade union membership, limitations on the scope of the immunities against civil liability, interlocutory injunctions, restrictions on picketing, protections against union discipline and restrictions imposed by professional bodies. These indirect methods of imposing limitations, which may be just as important in practice as direct restrictions, form the subject of the second section of the chapter.

DIRECT RESTRICTIONS ON INDUSTRIAL ACTION

The Police

Collective action by the police is restricted on two levels; they are barred both from striking and from joining trade unions. (A new recruit may retain existing union membership if his Chief Officer of Police agrees.)[1] These proscriptions date back to the Police Act 1919. Police trade unionism began in London in 1913 and spread rapidly through the force when the National Union of Police and Prison Officers was formed the following year.[2] Strenuous opposition from the Government and local police authorities, including threats that trade unionists would be dismissed, failed to crush the union. A strike in London in August 1918 was supported by the majority of police, and it compelled the Government to grant substantial concessions, including an agreement to allow union membership on condition that the union did not attempt to interfere with the regulations or discipline of the service or to organize industrial action. The union then broke this agreement in pursuit of its desire for recognition and its conduct in so doing provoked the decision to expunge trade unionism entirely from the force. The Government appointed a committee to enquire into police conditions, and following its report, introduced legislation which, on the one hand, established machinery to implement the committee's recommendations for improving pay and allowances [3] and on the other prohibited trade union membership. The union called a strike in protest, but only 2,365 out of a total of 60,000 policemen took part; they were all dismissed and the union ceased to exist shortly afterwards.

To provide an alternative channel for collective representation, the Police Act 1919 set up the Police Federation, the membership of which is confined to the service and to which all policemen below the rank of superintendent automatically belong. Its function, now laid down in section 44 of the Police Act 1964, is to represent members in matters affecting their welfare and efficiency, other than questions of discipline and promotion affecting individuals. The Federation may not associate with any person or body outside the service. Successive governments have justified this isolation on the ground that any external affiliation could compromise the duty of the police to uphold the law.

The 1919 Act did not make industrial action unlawful as such; rather, it penalized the incitement of unrest among the police. The substance of the offence was re-enacted in section 53(1) of the Police Act 1964. 'Any person who causes, or attempts to cause, or does any act calculated to cause, disaffection amongst the members of any police force, or induces or attempts to induce, or does any act calculated to induce, any member of a police force to withhold his services or to commit breaches of discipline' is liable to a maximum of two years' imprisonment, an unlimited fine, or both. Those organizing industrial action by the police would certainly commit this offence. It could probably be argued that participants were also guilty of it in doing an act 'calculated to induce' other members of the force to do the same. The section prohibits the provocation of any acts of 'disaffection', so that even industrial action not involving a breach of police regulations, such as collective resignation or overloading the system by enforcing the law to the letter (a tactic used by some American forces) would fall within it. No guilty intention is required; the offence covers conduct objectively likely to engender a state of unrest among the police. The only recorded prosecutions under section 53(1) and its predecessor involved persons connected with the National Unemployed Workers' Movement between 1921 and 1932; no policemen have been charged.[4] In addition to attracting criminal liability, campaign organizers would also face liability in tort; the statutory immunities against certain heads of tortious liability do not apply to disputes involving the police.[5]

Participation in industrial action by a police officer could also infringe the statutory disciplinary code (which includes offences of disobeying orders, neglecting duty and discreditable conduct).[6] A chief constable could impose penalties ranging from a caution, reprimand or fine up to reduction in rank or dismissal. It is most unlikely, however, that the code would be applied to any mass campaign. The fire service is governed by a similar disciplinary code, outlined in Chapter 5;[7] disciplinary charges were brought in many brigades against firemen who took industrial action in 1951, but the penalties imposed were, in general, rescinded, and no attempt has been made to apply the code to disputes since 1954.

Another set of provisions, in force until 1964, made it a criminal offence for a constable to act in 'neglect or violation of his duty in his Office', or to resign or withdraw from his duties without one month's notice or the permission of his superintendent.[8] Five constables who encouraged a collective refusal to go on duty at three London stations in 1872 were charged with violation of duty.[9] No reference was made to these offences during the strikes of 1918 or 1919; they had probably been overlooked.

In general, the police have acquiesced in the argument that industrial action would be incompatible with their role as a disciplined force whose members are pledged to uphold the law. There was a break in this tradition in 1976–7, however, when the Police Federation was compelled by grass-roots pressure during a pay dispute to support a call for the right to strike. The Government established a Committee of Inquiry to review the service's negotiating machinery, and subsequently also pay, and in its evidence to the Committee the Federation urged the repeal of all restrictions on industrial action, subject to a ballot before any withdrawal of labour. The Police Superintendents' Association and the Association of Chief Police Officers were strongly opposed to this, but both stressed the need for adequate compensation for these restrictions. The Inquiry accepted their argument and recommended substantial pay increases, combined with a formula for annual uprating linked to the monthly index of average earnings.[10] It appears that support for a change was 'more of a gesture, an expression of frustration and discontent, than a permanent shift to the left. The police still seem to prefer being a special case, with appropriate treatment, to any identification with the working class'.[11]

In recent years there has been a trend towards employing civilian staff, paid on lower local government salary scales, alongside police officers on clerical, communications and forensic work. These staff are not subject to any specific restraints on taking industrial action. The Police Federation drew attention to the dangers of this situation after a six-day strike over their grading structure by fingerprint specialists in West Yorkshire in July 1985. The Home Office denied having considered no-strike agreements for these staff in the past, but clearly more extensive disruption by these workers may provoke a review of this position.

The armed forces

As in the case of the police, the criminal law barring industrial action by members of the armed forces aims to punish those who incite unrest. It is an offence punishable by life imprisonment under section 2 of the Incitement to Mutiny Act 1797 'maliciously and advisedly' to endeavour to seduce a serviceman from his duty and allegiance to the Crown or to incite him to mutiny. 'Maliciously and advisedly' means that the prosecution must prove intention to commit the offence; this involves showing that the accused knew that the object of his endeavours was a member of the forces. In 1934, section 1 of the Incitement to Disaffection Act created the much broader offence of 'maliciously and advisedly' endeavouring to seduce a serviceman from his duty *or* allegiance (punishable by up to two years' imprisonment and a £200 fine). 'A relatively trivial offence, such as persuading a soldier to overstay his leave, is . . . within the later Act, but not the earlier'.[12] Section 2 of the 1934 Act also makes it an offence to possess a document whose dissemination would constitute an offence under section 1 with intent or commit, or to further the commission of, such an offence.

Charges were successfully brought under the Incitement to Mutiny Act in 1912 and 1925 in connection with publications urging soldiers not to shoot strikers, and in 1931, the printer of the *Daily Worker* was convicted under the Act after the paper had exhorted sailors to join a fight against pay cuts which began at Invergordon when sailors refused to fall in for work.[13] The Incitement to Disaffection Act has not been used in the context of industrial disputes, but it clearly could be, either in the case of industrial action by servicemen themselves or if troops were acting as substitute labour for strikers, and attempts were made to dissuade them from this course. Prosecutions under the 1934 Act require the consent of the Director of Public Prosecutions.

Servicemen taking any form of industrial action would inevitably commit offences under military law,[14] and those who organised it would have no protection against liability in tort.[15] Servicemen are permitted to join trade unions as individuals 'provided this does not involve them in activities which would conflict with their military duties',[16] but unlike in some European countries, there is no form of recognized collective representation.

Merchant Seamen

Industrial action by merchant seamen is restricted in order to protect the safety of ships and the interests of employers rather than the welfare of the public at large. Before 1970 a merchant seaman could not take industrial action during the currency of his contract without committing a criminal or disciplinary offence. Section 42(2) of the Merchant Shipping Act 1970 now permits a seaman employed in a ship registered in the United Kingdom to terminate his employment in contemplation or furtherance of a trade dispute after giving the master a minimum of forty-eight hours' notice (regardless of the terms of his contract), provided that the ship is in the United Kingdom and securely moored in a safe berth when notice is given.[17] Unless these conditions are satisfied, a seaman taking industrial action could be prosecuted; any seaman who 'persistently and wilfully' neglects his duty or disobeys lawful orders or, at any time when a ship is at sea, combines with other seamen employed in it to disobey lawful commands, neglect any duty, or impede its progress or navigation, is liable to a maximum penalty of two years' imprisonment and a fine.[18] Alternatively, he could be faced with proceedings under the statutory disciplinary regulations.[19]

Since 1980 it has been union practice to advise members to sit on board ships, wherever they are, rather than terminate their employment during disputes, in order to prevent the ships being moved. Despite the illegality of this action, which was a tactic in the

1981 national dispute, the shipowners have not pressed charges. One reason which has been suggested for this forbearance is that using the law in this context would be 'flatly contradictory' to the trend of 'treating seamen like shore-based workers'.[20] The law is far from being a dead letter, however. In 1982 the Natural Environment Research Council threatened to prosecute seamen who participated in a ban on non-essential overtime at sea to protest against the alleged victimization of the ship's union convenor. The threat was ultimately withdrawn.

Postal workers

Restrictions on postal workers derive from provisions enacted in the reign of Queen Anne which were intended to deter individual acts of interference with the royal mail. The current legislation provides that any officer who 'contrary to his duty, wilfully detains or delays, or procures or suffers to be detained or delayed' any postal packet is liable to a maximum penalty of two years' imprisonment and an unlimited fine, and any person who solicits or endeavours to procure such action is liable to up to two years' imprisonment (Post Office Act 1953, ss.58, 68).[21] In *Gouriet* v. *U.P.O.W.*[22] in 1977 the House of Lords held that these provisions made unlawful a proposed boycott of communications between England and South Africa, rejecting the view of the union's General Secretary that they were appropriate to deal with 'highwaymen and footpads' but were now obsolete.[23] This ruling, which followed an (unsuccessful) application by a private individual for an injunction to restrain the threatened boycott, came as some surprise. Postal workers had taken national industrial action four times during the thirteen years preceding the Gouriet decision, including a seven-week strike in 1971 and a boycott of mail to South Africa in 1973, but legal proceedings had never been threatened. After *Gouriet* the then Labour Government promised to amend the legislation, but a Private Members' Bill,[24] introduced with Government and union support, failed for lack of time and the law has remained unchanged. (The Bill would have removed criminal liability for striking, but granted immunity to other industrial action only if it was in contemplation or furtherance of a trade dispute and did not discriminate against individual customers. The union — now the U.C.W. — seeks an unfettered freedom to take industrial action but backed this Bill in the hope that it would enlist sufficient support.)

The judgements in *Gouriet* left the legal position of Post Office workers who take industrial action extremely unclear. The only statement which can be made with confidence is that discriminatory action against particular customers is illegal.[25] In 1981 the Conservative

Attorney-General, Sir Michael Havers, said that striking could not be an offence because the statutory restrictions are directed against particular acts, omissions or breaches of duty concerning one or more postal packets, which would be too remote a consequence of a strike, and that they deal only with misconduct while at work. However, he considered that industrial action short of a strike might be an offence if it were in breach of contract.[26] The House of Lords judgments in *Gouriet* do not support such a distinction, and the Attorney-General's construction of the legislation is open to question. The arguments which he applied to striking would apply equally to a ban on contractual overtime, and limiting the provisions to particular acts of misfeasance would seem to exclude other forms of industrial action not involving deliberate discrimination between customers. The Attorney-General stressed that the action must be 'wilful', but even on the assumption that the sections are limited to particular acts as he suggests, the case-law is inconsistent as to whether 'wilful' applies to all elements of the offence; there is authority for the view that it is sufficient that the proscribed conduct is committed as the result of an intentional act.[27] Industrial action will generally be intended to disrupt communications to further an external objective; that workers do not specifically intend to disrupt any particular postal packet may not be necessarily fatal to conviction under the legislation.

In 1981, the Minister for Industry and Information Technology Mr. Kenneth Baker, expressed the view that postal workers should be free to strike but not to impose discriminatory measures.[28] There is a strong case for legislative clarification of the position. Recent industrial action by postal workers has not brought the threat of prosecution, but it is clearly most undesirable that their campaigns should be conducted in an atmosphere of legal uncertainty.

Telecommunications workers

The Interception of Communications Act 1985, section 1, makes it an offence, punishable by an unlimited fine and up to two years' imprisonment, for any person intentionally to intercept a communication in the course of its transmission by means of a public telecommunications system unless the interception takes place in circumstances authorized by the Act. Under previous legislation, telecommunications workers were liable to prosecution if they 'wilfully or negligently' failed to transmit or deliver, or delayed, any message or if, contrary to their duty, they intercepted a telephone call.[29] The Attorney-General interpreted these earlier provisions in a similar way to those which still apply to Post Office workers; that is, that they could not be used against strikers but could cover discriminatory action or other industrial action in breach of contract.[30] The Government claimed that the Telecommunications Act 1984, discussed below, removed the possibility of criminal liability attaching to industrial action by telecommunications workers.[31] In the absence of any statement to that effect in either statute, it is by no means clear that the offence set out in section 1 of the 1985 Act could not be committed in the course of a dispute, although no criminal proceedings can lie against any person who commits, conspires to commit, or incites others to commit, a breach of an enforcement order issued under the 1984 Act of the type described below (Telecommunications Act 1984, s.18(4)). Prosecutions under the Interception of Communications Act 1985 require the consent of the Director of Public Prosecutions (s.1(4)).

More important than any possible criminal liability from now on is likely to be the new forms of civil liability for industrial action created by the Telecommunications Act 1984, liabilities against which there is no statutory immunity. This Act, which abolished the exclusive privilege of running telecommunications systems previously conferred on British Telecommunications, requires those operating telecommunications systems to obtain a licence. If an operator contravenes any of the conditions of the licence, the Director-General of Telecommunications, who oversees the industry, must issue an enforcement order. Once such an order has been issued, the operator is under a statutory duty to comply with it, and if he fails to do so, any person affected by the non-compliance who sustains 'loss or damage' as a result may sue for breach of that duty (s.18(6)(a)). The person sued can defend such a claim by proving that he took 'all reasonable steps and exercised all due diligence to avoid contravening the order' (s.18(7)). It is hard to predict whether the fact that his business is being disrupted by industrial action would constitute a defence to an operator sued under this provision or whether he would be required to demonstrate that he had taken steps to counteract or terminate the disruption. Where non-compliance with the enforcement order is due to industrial action the Act also specifically enables an affected person to sue the organizer for any act which, by inducing breach of the operator's duty to obey the order or interfering with its performance, 'causes that person to sustain loss or damage and which is done wholly or partly for the purpose of achieving that result' (s.18(6)(b)). Customers of telecommunications operators can therefore obtain damages or seek an injunction against the union or other organizers of industrial action where they suffer loss or damage from disruption to the service.

The Government maintained that this provision was designed to grant a remedy for selective industrial action against particular customers but would not jeopardize strikes to improve pay and conditions which led incidentally to an enforcement order being breached because the defendant's purpose must include a desire to damage the plaintiff, although this need not be the main purpose.[32] As Opposition spokesmen pointed out, this is a very fine distinction to draw in practice, given that a successful strike would almost certainly interfere with an enforcement order and cause disruption to customers and, indeed, is intended to achieve that result to put pressure on the employer.[33] 'At the very least the Government should have required harm to the plaintiff to be the dominant purpose'.[34] As the legislation stands, it is not surprising that unions with members in the telecommunications industry are concerned that any form of industrial action in the industry is put at risk.

Gas, water and electricity workers

At one time workers in the gas, electricity and water industries were also singled out for special legislative treatment. Section 4 of the Conspiracy and Protection of Property Act 1875 (as amended by the Electricity Act 1919) made it a criminal offence, punishable by a maximum fine of £20 or three months' imprisonment, for an employee in these industries 'wilfully and maliciously' to break his contract of service 'knowing or having reasonable cause to believe' that the probable consequences of his so doing, either alone or in combination with others, would be to 'deprive the inhabitants wholly or to a great extent of their supply'. This section 'frequently led to strike notices being given by unions in these three industries in the form of notice to terminate employment contracts',[35] although there were also a number of occasions when the section must have been breached. The only prosecution ever brought under it, however, was in 1950 when the Labour Attorney-General, Sir Hartley Shawcross, initiated proceedings against leaders of an unofficial gas strike, described in Chapter 5. The section 4 charge was dropped after the men pleaded guilty to a second charge of contravening a wartime order which had continued in force.[36] In 1970 the Central Electricity Generating Board considered that a work-to-rule imposed by manual workers involved breaches of contract but decided that 'the situation would not have been helped by prosecution', and the Court of Inquiry which followed endorsed that view.[37]

Despite the lack of prosecutions, both the Gas Council and the Electricity Council told the Donovan Commission that section 4 was a useful reminder of the importance of these industries to public safety, although both employers thought their workers' sense of responsibility a more influential brake on major lightening industrial action.[38] The majority of Labour witnesses thought it unfair to single out these groups. The Donovan Commission recommended keeping the section on the ground that these public utilities had the special quality of affecting every household and 'a stoppage without warning . . . may have serious consequences as regards the health and safety of the population'.[39] The subsequent Conservative Government, however, agreed with Mr Andrew Shonfield who, in a Note of Reservation to the Commission's Report, argued that liability should attach to the likely consequences of a sudden stoppage rather than to particular industries.[40] The Government considered that section 5 of the 1875 Act, described below, together with their fresh proposals for dealing with emergency disputes, discussed in Chapter 3, made it 'unnecessary and unjustifiable' to retain these selective provisions,[41] and section 4 was repealed by the Industrial Relations Act 1971.

Staff of the Houses of Parliament

It is not a statutory offence for staff of the Houses of Parliament to take industrial action, but those who organize campaigns by staff employed by the House authorities have no immunity against actions in tort.[42] Recently the T.U.C. complained to the I.L.O. that this exclusion infringed the principle of freedom of association. The Government replied that 'the workings of the Houses of Parliament must not be impeded by the activities of other bodies'.[43] The I.L.O. Committee of Experts on the Application of Conventions and Recommendations found no basis for this discrimination in I.L.O. Conventions, and invited the British Government to consider extending the immunities to industrial action by these staff.[44]

Civil servants

There are no statutory restrictions on industrial action by civil servants but, as described below, members of security and intelligence agencies are forbidden from joining national trade unions and cannot in practice organize collective action. In accordance with the Government's traditional desire to appear a 'model' employer (a desire which over the last twenty years has been progressively eroded),[45] trade union membership for civil servants in general was actively encouraged from 1919 onwards and in 1979, over 90 per cent of civil servants belonged to a union.[46] The Trade Disputes and Trade Unions Act 1927, which followed the Labour movement's defeat in the General Strike, isolated civil servants from other trade unionists for over twenty years. (Although civil servants did not participate in the strike, many civil service unions gave financial support to the strikers.) Section 5 prohibited established civil servants from joining any organization whose primary object was 'to influence or affect the remuneration and conditions of employment of its members' unless its membership was confined to Crown servants, it was independent of, and not affiliated to, any organization whose membership was not so confined, and it had no political object or association. The penalty for flouting this restriction was disqualification from membership of the civil service. The Act was repealed by the Labour Government in 1946, and all the nationally recognized civil service trade unions are now affiliated to the T.U.C.

Although there is no statutory bar, successive governments have consistently affirmed that industrial action by civil servants is a disciplinary offence, leaving them 'perfectly free to take any disciplinary action that any strike situation that might develop demanded'.[47] When moving the repeal of the 1927 Act, the Attorney-General warned that in the event of a strike the Crown 'would exercise the right, as an employer, to instant dismissal without hope of reinstatement'.[48] Another drastic penalty which could be imposed is loss of established status and consequent loss of pension rights. In practice, formal sanctions against participants in industrial action traditionally were restricted to loss of pay for the period of absence. Whole days of absence do not qualify for superannuation, pay increments or higher leave allowances, and staff who refuse to work normally may be temporarily relieved from duty until they are prepared to resume normal working. By convention, when civil servants returned to work they were given an undertaking that participation in industrial action would not be recorded in their personal file.

In recent years, however, there have been indications of a tougher response. The first instance came in 1982 when the Conservative Government warned civil servants who took industrial action in support of a campaign by health service workers that, if they did so again, they would face disciplinary proceedings. 149 did take sympathetic action a second time, and apart from those who already had disciplinary action outstanding, all these staff received a common penalty, a letter of displeasure. Like all disciplinary penalties, this was recorded on the individual's promotion dossier. A Circular issued in October 1982 stated that individual warnings would not henceforth be issued before disciplinary proceedings were taken in connection with absence related to a non-civil service dispute. Industrial action within the civil service has also attracted official disapproval. In December 1983 a number of staff in a managerial grade (that of principal) were told that participation in a day of action in support of D.H.S.S. workers in Birmingham and Oxford was incompatible with their status. In 1985 the Minister of State at the Treasury made clear that participation in industrial action may be 'one of the factors' taken into account in deciding questions of promotion, although it would not constitute an absolute bar.[49] The T.U.C. alleged that threats of this nature were a breach of I.L.O. Convention Number 151 on Protection of the Right to Organize and Procedures for Determining Conditions of Employment in the Public Service. This Convention provides that public employees should enjoy the same rights as other workers which are 'essential for the normal exercise of freedom of association, subject only to the obligations arising from their status and the nature of their functions.'[50] The Government replied that 'managers should subordinate their personal feelings about the merits of any industrial dispute to their obligations as managers', obligations which included maintaining 'the work of their department when there is a threat to the normal functioning of the service for whatever reason'.[51] The Committee of Experts on the Application of Conventions and Recommendations turned down the T.U.C.'s complaint, stating that, in the case of public officials, the principle of freedom of association 'does not necessarily imply the right to strike'.[52] Clearly the kind of pronouncements which Government and civil service spokesmen have made of late about the consequences of taking industrial action may deter ambitious civil servants from giving their active support to campaigns. Moreover, in 1984 the Government imposed a complete ban on membership of national civil service trade unions by the workforce at Government Communications Headquarters with the declared aim of preventing the recurrence of any form of industrial action. The details of this ban and its aftermath are discussed below.

Restrictions in terms of the consequences of industrial action

Section 5 of the Conspiracy and Protection of Property Act 1875 makes it an offence 'wilfully and maliciously' to break 'a contract of service or of hiring, knowing or having reasonable cause to believe that the probable consequences of . . . so doing, either alone or in combination with others, will be to endanger human life, or cause serious bodily injury, or expose valuable property . . . to destruction or serious injury'. The penalty is a maximum of three months' imprisonment or a £50 fine. Unlike the repealed section 4, section 5 applies to both parties to a contract of service (or hiring), and the Donovan Commission suggested that an employer who broke a contractual obligation and thereby provoked a stoppage having the specified probable consequences could be guilty of the offence.[53] Clearly, industrial action by a number of workers, such as firemen, and workers in the health service and public utilities, could come within this provision. As any industrial action, except a strike preceded by notice of termination of employment (or ban on non-contractual working) involves a breach of contract, [54] there has been no shortage of disputes where it could have been invoked. There is no record of any prosecutions under it, however. The Donovan

Commission recommended leaving the section 'undisturbed' on the ground that its repeal might be seen as condoning what it prohibited, but it had no strong views on the issue.[55] The right-wing Centre for Policy Studies suggested in 1980 that section 5 should be given wide publicity and the penalties under it increased,[56] but this seems unlikely after over a century of dormancy.

Another provision which may be relevant to industrial action is section 7(b) of the Health and Safety at Work etc. Act 1974. This makes it the duty of every employee while at work 'as regards any duty or requirement imposed on his employer or any other person by or under any of the relevant statutory provisions, to co-operate with him so far as is necessary to enable that duty or requirement to be performed or complied with'. Breach of this duty is an offence, punishable by up to two years' imprisonment or an unlimited fine (s.33). Any employees who blacked essential safety work could arguably be guilty of the offence. To date there have been no prosecutions arising out of industrial action.

Between 1927 and 1946, strikes and lockouts having any object other than or in addition to the furtherance of a trade dispute within the strikers' trade or industry and 'designed or calculated to coerce the Government either directly or by inflicting hardship upon the community' were declared illegal by section 1 of the Trade Disputes and Trade Unions Act 1927. Anyone organizing or acting in furtherance of such a strike or lockout, otherwise than by merely ceasing to work or refusing to accept employment, was liable to up to two years' imprisonment. There was no detailed consideration by the courts of the range of strikes and lockouts declared illegal by this broadly phrased provision before the Act was repealed.[57]

INDIRECT RESTRICTIONS ON INDUSTRIAL ACTION

Restrictions on trade union membership

Limiting freedom of associations is clearly a very effective way of making it difficult for workers to organize collective action. Reference has already been made to restrictions on the police. In addition, workers in most state security and intelligence agencies have traditionally been unable to join trade unions,[58] and in 1984 the Conservative Government extended this ban to workers at Government Communications Headquarters (G.C.H.Q.), an institution which safeguards the security of the United Kingdom's military and official communications and provides signals intelligence for the Government. Although previously encouraged to join appropriate national unions, in common with other civil servants, workers at G.C.H.Q. are now permitted to belong only to a departmental staff association approved by their director.[59] The Association is not permitted to affiliate to the T.U.C. or any other political or trade union organization, and industrial action is prohibited. The Government claimed that banning union membership was essential to ensure the necessary continuous operation of G.C.H.Q., which had been threatened seven times by industrial action between February 1979 and April 1981, mostly in furtherance of national civil service disputes. Ministers pointed in particular to a one-day strike in March 1981 when 25 per cent of staff had taken action and national union officials had apparently ignored appeals to protect particular areas. Although there had been 'no serious threats to the nation's security' on that occasion,[60] the Government wished to ensure there could be no future conflicts of loyalty for G.C.H.Q. staff during national campaigns.

The Government's decision was taken without any prior consultation with trade unions or staff at G.C.H.Q., a course which was unanimously condemned by the House of Commons Select Committee on Employment.[61] The Committee urged the Government to consider whether its objectives could be achieved in some other way and, in particular, to investigate whether proposals by the national unions, designed to reconcile the Government's requirements with continuing union representation, were adequate to safeguard national security. The unions' proposals included making it a condition of service of G.C.H.Q. staff that they would take no action which might interfere with the uninterrupted operation of essential security and intelligence services, such services to be designated by the Government after consultation with local union representatives. The Government rejected this idea on the ground that no distinction between essential intelligence and other services could be entertained and workers could still be subject to external pressures leading to conflicts of loyalty.[62]

After the failure of negotiations, the unions challenged the Government's decision in the courts. The High Court held that the absence of prior consultation made the Prime Minister's instruction to revise the conditions of service of G.C.H.Q. staff – the means by which the ban had been effected — invalid.[63] The Court of Appeal and the House of Lords disagreed. The House of Lords accepted that workers at G.C.H.Q. had a legitimate expectation, based on past practice, of prior consultation before their terms and conditions of employment were significantly altered but ruled that this duty to consult could be outweighed by considerations of national security. The decision as to whether this was the case rested with the Government. Here there was evidence to show that consultation had been avoided to prevent the risk of provoking industrial action at G.C.H.Q. which would have threatened national security, and the court was therefore unable to intervene.[64]

The union case met with greater success on the international plane. In June 1984 the I.L.O. Governing Body adopted the recommendation of its Freedom of Association Committee that the Government action at G.C.H.Q. violated Convention No. 87 on Freedom of Association and the Right to Organize.[65] This Convention guarantees the right to form and join organizations of their own choosing to all workers 'without distinction whatsoever', the police and the armed forces being the only permitted exceptions. The Committee ruled that the ban on trade unions at G.C.H.Q. infringed this right, which was not affected by other Conventions which accepted that certain categories of public servants (including those in highly confidential positions) could be exempted from protections against anti-union discrimination.[66] It urged renewed efforts by the Government and unions to reach a satisfactory agreement, but the Government did nothing to implement this recommendation. The civil service unions are currently referring the ban to the European Commission of Human Rights. Article II of the European Convention on Human Rights establishes the right to form and join trade unions, subject to such restrictions as are 'prescribed by law and are necessary in a democratic society in the interests of national security or public safety'. The unions may be expected to argue that the outright ban on union membership was not proportionate to the Government's aims, which could have been met by a no-disruption agreement or in some other way. Article II also allows 'lawful restrictions' on the exercise of the right to union membership by 'members of the armed forces, or the police or of the administration of the State'. The position of civil servants under this provision is uncertain.

The vast majority of workers at G.C.H.Q.[67] accepted the new conditions offered by the Government (and a payment of £1,000 as compensation for having been deprived, at the same time, of most of their statutory employment protection rights).[68] About seventy workers, however, did not accept these terms and, although the Government threatened them with disciplinary action, measures against this group have been confined to bars on promotion and foreign postings and the denial of special pay rises awarded to other G.C.H.Q. staff. These workers, whose numbers at the time of writing have fallen to thirty-five, are currently being encouraged to transfer to other Government departments or accept early retirement. By contrast, staff who initially accepted the new conditions but subsequently rejoined a trade union, of whom there are about twenty, are now facing disciplinary measures. The Government has stated that the penalties to be imposed will fall short of dismissal,[69] a decision which may have been influenced by undertakings from many trade unions, including some with members in the electricity supply industry, to ballot their members on taking industrial action should any G.C.H.Q. worker be dismissed for union membership. The main Opposition parties have said that they will rescind the ban should they attain Governmental office. Meanwhile, the Conservative administration has confirmed that it has no intention of introducing similar limitations on trade union organization outside the field of security and intelligence.[70]

The scope of the immunities

The freedom to strike in Great Britain depends upon statutory immunities, without which almost all industrial action would render the organizers liable to civil proceedings. To attract immunity, industrial action must be taken 'in contemplation or furtherance of a trade dispute', the so-called 'golden formula'.[71] Since the Employment Act 1982, a 'trade dispute' must be between workers and their own employer.[72] As far as subject-matter is concerned, before 1982 a dispute had only to be 'connected with' one of the objects of 'collective bargaining' as legislatively defined to constitute a 'trade dispute'.[73] At one time, the courts ruled that if disputes were primarily to further purposes other than collective bargaining matters, the 'golden formula' would not apply, an approach which gave the judges great discretion. In 1979, however, the House of Lords affirmed that it was sufficient that a collective bargaining matter was at issue; it need not be the predominant object of the dispute.[74] This decision provoked the Government to change the statutory definition, and the Employment Act 1982 now requires a dispute to relate 'wholly or mainly' to one of these matters.[75] The Government intended this amendment to direct inquiry into the predominant object of a dispute and to make unlawful those which are judged primarily personal or political, despite being linked with a collective bargaining matter.

Strikes solely designed to influence Government policy or proposed legislation unconnected with industrial matters have always stood outside the 'golden formula', both because of their subject-matter and because, with certain exceptions, the Government cannot be a party to a trade dispute other than as an employer.[76] In 1971 a one-day strike against the Industrial Relations Bill was held not to be a trade dispute, despite its connection with labour relations.[77] Trade union leaders did not even try to argue that a national strike called in 1980 to protest against the Government's economic policies attracted immunity.[78] In many situations, however, the dividing line between industrial and political matters is very hard to draw. In Kahn-Freund's words:

> Whatever the political colour of the Government, it is involved in industry, and the organisations of both sides of industry are involved in Government. Is not every major industrial problem a problem of governmental economic policy? Is it not true that, not only in publically owned industries, governmental decisions on wages policies — whether statutory or not — on credits and on subsidies, on the distribution of industry and on housing and town planning, and on a thousand other things, affect the terms and conditions of employment at least as much as decisions of individual firms? Where is the line between a strike to induce an employer to raise, or not to reduce, wages, and a strike to press the government for measures which would enable the employer to do so?[79]

The issues raised by this last question were exemplified by stoppages in the coalmining industry in 1921 and 1926, where, as discussed in Chapter 3, any concessions to the miners required a Government subsidy. A High Court decision that the General Strike in sympathy with the miners in 1926 was illegal did nothing to resolve the issue.[80] Astbury J. merely affirmed that there was no trade dispute in any of the unions affected other than the miners', and there could be no trade dispute between the T.U.C. and the Government; he failed to consider whether there was indeed a trade dispute involving the miners, and if so, whether other workers were acting in furtherance of it.[81] (Sympathetic action of this nature would now fall outside the immunities).[82]

The requirement that a dispute must now relate 'wholly or mainly' to a collective bargaining matter may make it particularly difficult to predict the lawfulness of industrial action in the public sector where disputes over wages or job cuts, for example, may involve challenging broader government policies such as incomes policies or privatization. Would these be 'trade' or 'political' disputes? The only case to address this issue to date has been *Mercury Communications Ltd* v. *Scott-Garner and the P.O.E.U.*[83] As part of its campaign against the Government's policies of liberalizing and privatizing the telecommunications industry, the P.O.E.U. instructed its members not to connect Mercury Communications to the British Telecommunications network. The union argued that it was taking this action in furtherance of a dispute between British Telecommunications and its employees over job security, which, the union claimed, would be put at risk if Mercury were connected, and it was therefore protected against liability in tort by the 'golden formula'.[84] The Court of Appeal rejected this argument; the dispute did not relate 'wholly or mainly' to the fear of future redundancies but was concerned with the union's opposition to government policies and was, therefore, outside the 'trade dispute' definition.

In reaching its conclusion, the Court of Appeal in the Mercury case was influenced heavily by evidence of a Job Security Agreement between British Telecommunications and the union to which the union had not made reference during the dispute; this seemed to point away from concern about the threat to jobs. The decision in this case does not mean that all disputes over privatization, a key issue in the health service and local government at present, are outside the 'golden formula', but it does illustrate the kind of balancing exercise which the courts are required to carry out. Although Government ministers denied that the 1982 amendment would threaten the lawfulness of those disputes over pay and conditions or jobs which challenge government policy, such statements are not admissible before a court, and in the frenzied atmosphere of interlocutory proceedings, described below, postulating the argument that a public sector dispute is primarily political may be sufficient to persuade a court to grant an interlocutory injunction to halt it.

Another danger facing dispute organizers in the public sector is that of being held liable for wrongs not protected by the immunities. In the late 1970s the Court of Appeal opened up the possibility of liability for action which prevented employers from discharging their statutory duties. In *Meade* v. *Haringey London Borough Council*[85] the plaintiff parents argued that, by closing its schools during a strike by school caretakers, the authority was breaching its statutory duty under the Education Act 1944 to provide education. The majority of the Court of Appeal refused to decide this issue conclusively in interlocutory proceedings, but it was suggested that if the authority were in breach, the trade unions, by calling on the employer to close the schools, could be inducing the authority to breach its statutory duty, a wrong for which there is no protection. This idea was developed in *Associated Newspapers Group Ltd* v. *Wade*[86] where it was argued that leaders of the print unions N.G.A. and S.L.A.D.E. were interfering with a health authority's and water board's performance of their respective statutory duties by blacking newspaper advertising from them. Lord Denning considered that merely hindering the performance of statutory duties could be sufficient to found liability. The other judges were more circumspect; Lawton L.J. was open to the argument that this might be so but declined to offer a definitive view on the issue; Geoffrey Lane L.J. refused to express any opinion at all.

Many public sector employers, including health and water authorities, British Gas and the Electricity Council, operate under statutory duties, and if the wrongs suggested in *Meade* and *Wade* were developed, the lawfulness of industrial action by most of their workers would be put in jeopardy. These two cases should be treated with considerable caution, however. Both arose out of interlocutory proceedings where there was little opportunity to consider the issues in detail. Moreover, since the recent House of Lords decision in *Lonrho Ltd* v. *Shell Petroleum Ltd*,[87] it seems that, in order for the plaintiff to proceed, a court may now have to find either that the statutory obligation was imposed for the benefit or protection of the class of individuals to which the plaintiff belongs or that the statute creates a public right and the plaintiff is a member of the public who has suffered special damage. This issue was not addressed at all by the court in *Wade*. Whether a statutory duty is independently actionable depends upon the language and purpose of the statute. Whether independent actionability will indeed be required depends upon whether the wrongs suggested in *Meade* and *Wade* are treated as torts for which breach of the statutory duty in question constitutes 'unlawful means' or an 'unlawful act',[88] in which case it will be, or whether they form some new head of liability, in which case it may not.[89] The fact that the Conservative Government felt it necessary to introduce a specific remedy for inducing breach of a telecommunications' operator's duty to obey an enforcement order is indicative of the uncertainty surrounding the present state of the law.

Interlocutory injunctions

Interlocutory injuntions prevent the defendant to an action carrying out an allegedly unlawful activity pending a full trial of the case where the lawfulness or otherwise of that activity can be probed in detail. They can be granted at a very early stage of an action, at short notice, after a brief hearing, which is often conducted on the basis only of affidavit (written) evidence. Non-compliance with the terms of an interlocutory injunction is contempt of court, exposing individuals and unions to imprisonment or fines as appropriate.

For employers faced with industrial action, interlocutory injunctions can constitute a very useful remedy. Employers in this situation want immediate relief; by the time a case reached full trial the dispute would probably be over and seeking an injunction would be otiose. They could still claim damages from the dispute organizers (and, since 1982, damages can be claimed from a trade union) were the action ruled unlawful, but up to now this has rarely been done. For workers to be subject to an interlocutory injunction is disastrous, however. They need to be able to use their industrial muscle at the appropriate moment, and it is impossible to quantify the loss they may suffer from being enjoined from doing so should it ultimately be decided that their campaign was not, after all, unlawful. Although the general function of interlocutory injunctions is to preserve the status quo pending a full hearing, in industrial disputes, granting an injunction usually decides the issue.

> [I]t is the nature of industrial action that it can be promoted effectively only so long as it is possible to strike while the iron is still hot; once postponed it is unlikely that it can be revived.[90]

The interlocutory stage is therefore crucial. According to what principles do the judges grant or refuse these orders? There is some guidance given by legislation, as outlined below, but the judges have maintained a residual discretion to look at the circumstances of the individual case, a discretion which means that industrial action in essential services may be enjoined even though it appears to fall within the ambit of the statutory immunities.

At one time a plaintiff seeking an interlocutory injunction had to establish a *prima facie* case; that is, the court had to be satisfied 'that if no further evidence were led at the trial the plaintiff would be likely to succeed on the legal and factual issues at stake'.[91] In addition, the plaintiff had to (and still has to) satisfy the 'balance of convenience'. This means that:

> The court must be of the opinion that on the assumption that the plaintiff will succeed in establishing his case at the trial, the harm he is likely to suffer in the interim if the interlocutory injunction is denied will exceed that likely to be suffered by the defendant if the interlocutory injunction is granted and it turns out at the trial that the plaintiff fails to establish his case.[92]

In 1975, however, the House of Lords ruled that instead of the plaintiff having to show a *prima facie* case, a court had only to be satisfied that there was a 'serious question to be tried', whereupon the decision as to whether or not to grant the injunction could be made largely according to the balance of convenience.[93] This formulation spelt defeat for most defendants in cases arising out of industrial action, where there was usually a serious question at issue, and the balance of convenience test was traditionally applied so as to take greater account of the interests of employers. 'The loss of production and revenue to the employer totally overshadowed the prohibition of the industrial action, which was often seen as merely a temporary inconvenience to the organisers of it'.[94] The statutory immunities against tortious liability could clearly be set at nought if this approach prevailed. In order to prevent this happening, the Labour Government introduced legislation requiring a court, in exercising its discretion as to whether to grant an injunction, to 'have regard to the likelihood' that the defendant will establish a defence of statutory immunity at the full trial where such a defence is claimed.[95] In *NWL Ltd* v. *Woods*[96] the House of Lords stated that normally an interlocutory injunction would be refused where the defendant had shown that a defence of statutory immunity was likely to succeed, but emphasized that the court still retained a discretion to grant it regardless of this factor. Cases may exist, said Lord Diplock:

> where the consequences to the employer or to third parties or the public and perhaps the nation itself, may be so disastrous that the injunction ought not to be refused, unless there is a high degree of probability that the defence will succeed.[97]

In a later decision Lord Fraser affirmed that even where the defence seemed highly likely to succeed, 'if the probable result of the threatened act would be to cause immediate serious danger to public safety or health and if no other means seemed to be available for averting the danger in time', it would not be wrong to grant the injunction.[98]

The residual discretion left to judges in granting interlocutory injunctions means that even industrial action which clearly falls within the statutory immunities may be restrained should its consequences be deemed to warrant it, let alone action whose lawfulness is uncertain because of the vagueness surrounding the definition of a 'trade dispute' and the ambit of newly created wrongs described in the previous section. Given the nature of their impact on the public at large, campaigns in essential services are particularly vulnerable to judicial discretion being exercised so as to prevent the continuation of industrial action.

Could industrial action be enjoined on the ground that it contravenes a penal statute such as section 5 of the Conspiracy and Protection of Property Act 1875? The Attorney-General has a discretion to seek an injunction to prevent the commission of a criminal offence as part of his general power to enforce public rights, but this power is very rarely used. In the words of Lord Diplock, it has been

> confined by the consistent practice of successive Attorney-Generals to statutes whose objects are to promote the health, the safety or the welfare of the public and to particular cases under such statutes either where the prescribed penalty for the summary offence has proved to be insufficient to deter the offender from numerous repetitions of the offence...; or where the defendant's

> disobedience to the statutory prohibition may cause grave and irreperable harm[99]

In *Gouriet* v. *U.P.O.W.*[100] the House of Lords made clear that it is a power which should be exercised in only highly exceptional circumstances. The Attorney-General need give no reason for his decision not to apply for an injunction and the courts will not subject his decision to judicial review.[101]

As far as private citizens are concerned, they cannot apply for an injunction to prevent the commission of a statutory offence merely because the Attorney-General has declined to do so.[102] It now appears to be the case that an individual has a right of action based on breach of a penal statute in only two situations. The first is where 'upon the true construction of the Act it is apparent that the obligation or prohibition was imposed for the benefit or protection of a particular class of individuals' and the plaintiff is a member of this class.[103] It is extremely improbable that section 5 or other penal statutes in this area fall within this category. (In *Gouriet*, Viscount Dilhorne expressed the view that breaches of sections 58 and 68 of the Post Office Act 1953, described above, did not give rise to private wrongs.)[104] The second situation is where the statute creates a 'public right' and the plaintiff 'suffers special damage peculiar to himself from the interference with the public right'. To constitute a public right, '[a] mere prohibition upon members of the public generally from doing what it would otherwise be lawful for them to do, is not enough'; there must be 'a legal right to be enjoyed by all of Her Majesty's subjects who wish to avail themselves of it'.[105] Again it is hard to see how an individual plaintiff could have a cause of action on this ground in the context of an essential service dispute. It appears that breach of a penal statute can only constitute 'unlawful means' for the purposes of torts which rely upon proof of an unlawful act threatened or employed by the defendant[106] where the breach itself gives rise to a civil action.[107]

Code of Practice on Picketing

The Code of Practice on Picketing issued by the Secretary of State for Employment under the Employment Act 1980 imposes special restrictions on pickets involved in disputes in essential services. It states that pickets should ensure that 'the movement of essential goods and supplies, the carrying out of essential maintenance of plant and equipment and the provision of services essential to the life of the community are not impeded'[108] and urges prior agreement on arrangements to guarantee this between unions and employers. Examples of supplies to be protected include heating fuel for schools, residential institutions and private residences; goods and services necessary for the maintenance of plant and machinery; supplies for the production, packaging, marketing and distribution of food, animal feeding stuffs and pharmaceutical products; and supplies to health and welfare institutions and those needed in the interests of public health and safety.[109] This represents, to say the least, a broad interpretation of the concept of essentiality. Failure to comply with the Code does not of itself render an individual liable to legal proceedings, but it must be taken into account in any proceedings to which it appears relevant.[110] Having said that, these particular provisions do 'not seem to impinge very closely on the legal obligations of pickets',[111] although the courts may consider non-compliance with them relevant to the exercise of their discretion to grant interlocutory injunctions preventing pickets from continuing their activities.[112]

Protection against union discipline

Workers in essential services who are instructed by their union to take industrial action may feel concerned about the legal and/or ethical consequences of doing so. On the one hand, they may fear that the union will take disciplinary action against them should they not comply with an instruction, a measure which could have particularly serious implications where union membership is compulsory. There are a number of provisions which seek to prevent employees being faced with this dilemma. In doing this, they may also make it more difficult for unions to organize effective campaigns.

First, a code of practice issued under the Industrial Relations Act 1971, which has remained in force, deals specifically with the position of professional employees. Paragraph 22 states that a professional employee should not be called upon by his trade union to take action which would conflict with the standards of work or conduct laid down by the profession if that action would endanger (1) the public health or safety; (2) the health of an individual needing medical or other treatment; or (3) the well-being of an individual needing care through the personal social services.

The Code of Practice on the Closed Shop, issued by the Secretary of State for Employment under the Employment Act 1980, is more far-reaching. Paragraph 61 provides that unions should not threaten disciplinary action against members who refuse to take part in industrial action where, among other things, there were reasonable grounds for believing that the action was unlawful, involved a breach of statutory duty or the criminal law, or constituted a serious risk to public safety, health or property, or where the member believed that it contravened his professional or other code of ethics. 'Unlawful' here means not protected by the statutory immunities. Given the uncertainty surrounding the application of the definition of a 'trade dispute' and the breadth of section 5 of the Conspiracy and Protection of Property Act 1875, this provision could be invoked by non-participants threatened with disciplinary action in most essential service disputes. Members of unions specified in closed shop agreements (which make union membership compulsory) have a statutory right not to be 'unreasonably expelled' from such unions,[113] and paragraph 61 is clearly relevant in determining whether or not an expulsion is reasonable.

Paragraph 61 may also be used by the common law courts, which have the power to ensure that unions exercise their disciplinary powers strictly in accordance with the union rules. The courts have traditionally been inclined to interpret union rules in favour of union members and are likely to wish to protect the individual who refuses to take industrial action which comes within the terms of paragraph 61. Disciplinary action in this context is generally pursued under some broadly phrased rule which proscribes acts contrary to the interests of the union. The courts would probably say that disobeying a union instruction to take industrial action coming within the terms of paragraph 61 could not be seen as contravening the union's interests or that the member was justified in believing the union was abusing its powers by issuing an instruction of this nature.[114] Disciplinary action against the member allegedly in default would then be rendered void.

An indication of the courts' desire to protect the individual is the decision in *Partington* v. *N.A.L.G.O.*[115] which concerned a dispute in the gas industry. Here the defendant union's power to order members to take industrial action was held by the court to be limited by a tripartite agreement between the employers, unions and individual employees which, as interpreted by the court, allowed the employers to order employees to return to work during disputes in order to provide safety cover. The union rules could not be applied so as to frustrate this agreement, and Mr Partington's expulsion from the union for returning to work without permission was therefore held to be void. This case is discussed in greater detail in the section on the gas industry in Chapter 5.

The position of professional employees

The last section discussed the ways in which professional workers and others in essential services are protected against union discipline. There are also provisions which protect professional workers against the operation of closed shop agreements. Where a closed shop is in force, it is automatically fair for an employer to dismiss an employee who is not a member of one of the unions specified in the closed shop agreement, provided the agreement has been approved in a secret ballot within the five years preceding the employee's dismissal, unless the employee is within one of the statutorily exempted categories.[116] (In practice, most non-members probably will be in one of these categories.) The Code of Practice on the Closed Shop advises employers who are considering agreeing to a closed shop to pay special regard to the interests of members of professional associations which have codes of ethics or conduct who might object to joining a union whose rules do not respect their professional obligations.[117] The Employment Act 1982 introduced increased protection for professional employees where a closed shop is in operation. If employees holding qualifications relevant to their employment and subject to a written code of conduct are expelled from a specified union for refusing to take part in industrial action because it would breach this code (or if they refuse to become or remain a union member because they would be required to take part in such industrial action), then their dismissal for non-membership is automatically unfair (s.58(8)). Should the employer refuse to take them back, they will be entitled to substantial financial compensation (at least £12,600, provided that they seek re-employment).[118]

Professional associations can play an important role in inhibiting their members from taking industrial action. Most reserve the right to expel members who are judged guilty of professional misconduct, and two bodies which have the power to prevent their members from continuing in practice have issued warnings about the risk of taking industrial action in recent years. In 1979 the General Nursing Council for England and Wales stated that if nurses put the health, safety or welfare of patients at risk by taking industrial action, this could constitute professional misconduct. After an outcry from T.U.C.-affiliated unions with nursing members, the Council emphasized that this statement was merely a reminder that industrial action was not immune from disciplinary proceedings, but whether it amounted to professional misconduct would depend on the circumstances. Large numbers of nurses have, in fact, taken industrial action without disciplinary charges being brought against them.[119] Only seven allegations of professional misconduct arising out of industrial action went before the Council's Investigating Committee before the Council's abolition in 1983, and of these, only two proceeded to a hearing by the Disciplinary Committee. These charges resulted in the nurses in question being cautioned. However, three other nurses involved in the same dispute, which was at a hospital for handicapped children, were removed from the Northern Ireland nurses' register.

Since mid-1983, responsibility for the nursing profession (and midwives and health visitors) has been in the hands of the United Kingdom Central Council for Nursing, Midwifery and Health Visiting. This Council has issued a Code of Professional Conduct which states that a member of these groups shall:

> At all times act in such a way as to promote and safeguard the well being and interests of patients/clients for whose care she is professionally accountable and ensure that by no action or omission on her part their condition or safety is placed at risk.[120]

The Secretary to the Professional Conduct Committee, Mr Reginald Pyne, considers that if a nurse gives adequate notice of her intention to withdraw her labour, it is then up to management to ensure the necessary cover, and she should not fear disciplinary action. The length of notice required would depend on the circumstances.[121] This is helpful, but not definitive advice, and part of the problem for professional employees contemplating industrial action lies in the lack of clear guidelines. Solicitors are in a similarly difficult situation. The Council of the Law Society starts from the position that for solicitors employed in local government or industry, striking for the purpose of bringing pressure to bear on their employers could be a disciplinary offence.[122] Where, however, such solicitors consider that failing to respond to a strike call by their union could result in their careers being 'seriously blighted', going on strike may be justified provided that they comply with any personal undertakings they have given and take appropriate steps to deal with any urgent business and to avoid inconveniencing other members of the profession or the public.[123] At the end of the day:

> Whether or not disciplinary proceedings would be taken against a solicitor who engaged in strike action would depend upon the individual circumstances of the case and the conduct of the solicitor concerned.[124]

Given the power of many professional associations to remove a person's source of livelihood, it might be thought appropriate to introduce some form of legal protection against internal disciplinary proceedings for employees who feel compelled to take industrial action. The freedom to strike can clearly be set at nought if workers fear that exercising it may have drastic consequences for the remainder of their working lives.

CONCLUSION

Traditionally the law has not played a prominent role in inhibiting workers in essential services from taking industrial action. The British response to industrial action in essential services has generally centred upon taking measures to secure supplies by alternative means rather than attempting to use the law to prevent it in the first place. The provision which in theory could restrict industrial action by many essential service groups, section 5 of the Conspiracy and Protection of Property Act 1875, has been widely ignored and has never been enforced. Restrictions on gas, water and electricity workers were repealed in 1971 on the ground that they were unnecessary and unjustifiable in view of section 5 and, perhaps more importantly, the introduction of legislation enabling the Government to impose a cooling-off period and ballot of the workforce in 'emergency disputes'. (These powers, described in the following chapter, have now themselves been repealed.) Of the groups which remain subject to specific restrictions, varying comments can be made. The police do not object in principle to being denied the freedom to withdraw their labour; their concern is that they are fairly treated as regards their pay and other conditions. The armed forces lack the collective representation to make their voices heard, but there is no evidence of pressure from that quarter for a change in the law. Restrictions on merchant seamen, designed to protect ships and employers rather than essential supplies, have not prevented action being taken by seamen. Restrictions on postal workers, originally intended to deter misconduct by individuals but recently declared applicable to industrial disputes, should be reformed. Their scope is unclear and there seems little logic in singling out this group for special treatment in an age of sophisticated communications by means other than the mail. This argument is reinforced by the repeal of similar limitations on workers in the telecommunications industry, although the civil liabilities which have replaced them may, in practice, prove more significant. These provisions, too, require amendment; they are widely drawn and put in doubt the lawfulness of industrial action of any kind.

The increasing use of indirect means to restrict industrial action in essential services reflects a change in the traditional pattern of the non-involvement of the law. Uncertainties which surround the application of the definition of a 'trade dispute' — the concept on which the freedom to strike depends — to disputes in the public sector makes it difficult to predict the lawfulness of many campaigns. The willingness of the courts to contemplate new wrongs beyond the scope of the immunities adds to this uncertainty. Even if industrial action is considered lawful, the discretion allowed to the judges to grant an interlocutory injunction should the harmful consequences of a dispute be deemed to warrant it enables the courts to subvert those freedoms which the legislation does afford without a full trial of the issues of fact and law. The unlimited powers of professional associations to discipline members who commit acts of professional 'misconduct' when taking industrial action can deprive individuals of their freedom to withdraw labour. Restrictions on industrial action in essential services are at present imposed in an *ad hoc*, haphazard way. There is a need to reassess the necessity for each of these restrictions; if they are necessary, alternative dispute resolution mechanisms must be found while, at the same time protecting, so far as possible, the freedom of individuals to withdraw their labour. The various ways in which the issues presented by strikes in essential services may be approached are discussed at greater length in the concluding chapter.

NOTES

1. Police Act 1964, s.47(1).
2. Gerald W. Reynolds and Anthony Judge, *The Night the Police Went on Strike*, Weidenfeld and Nicolson, London, 1968; and V. L. Allen, 'The National Union of Police and Prison Officers', *The Economic History Review* XI:1 (1958), 133, provide full accounts of the history and activities of the union.
3. Report of the Committee on the Police Service, Part 1, Cmd. 253 (1919).
4. David Williams, *Keeping the Peace*, Hutchinson, London, 1967, pp. 193–4; Thom Young *Incitement to Disaffection*, Cobden Trust, London, 1976, pp. 35, 58–9.
5. Trade Union and Labour Relations Act 1974, as amended, ss.13, 29, 30. Neither would protection against liability for conspiracy under section I of the Criminal Law Act 1977 apply.
6. The Police (Discipline) Regulations 1985 S.I. 1985 No. 518.
7. The Fire Services (Discipline) Regulations 1985, S.I. 1985 No. 930.
8. Metropolitan Police Act 1839, ss.14 and 15; County Police Act 1839, ss.12 and 13, later the County and Borough Police Act 1859, s.4; Municipal Corporations Act 1835, s.80.
9. Reynolds and Judge, above note 2, pp.202–12
10. Committee of Inquiry on the Police, Cmnd. 7283 (1978), Ch.6.
11. Robert Reiner, *The Blue-Coated Worker*, Cambridge University Press, Cambridge, 1978, p.276.
12. J.C. Smith and Brian Hogan, *Criminal Law*, 5th edn, Butterworths, London, 1983, p.787.
13. T. Young, *Incitement to Disaffection*, as above, note 4, pp.14–18, 46–7, 53–4.
14. See the Army Act 1955, ss.31–41; Air Force Act 1955, ss.31–41; Naval Discipline Act 1957, ss.8–18.
15. See above, note 5.
16. Francis Pym, Secretary of State for Defence, H.C. Deb., vol. 970, col. 248 (July 10, 1979).
17. S.5 of the Conspiracy and Protection of Property Act 1875 does not apply to merchant seamen.
18. Merchant Shipping Act 1970, s.30 (as amended by the Merchant Shipping Acts of 1974 and 1979).
19. Merchant Shipping (Disciplinary Offences) Regulations 1972, S.I. 1972, No. 1294.
20. Peggy Kahn, Norman Lewis, Rowland Livock and Paul Wiles, *Picketing: Industrial Disputes, Tactics and the Law*, Routledge and Kegan Paul, London, 1983, p.184.
21. See also Post Office Act 1953, s.59, and Interception of Communications Act 1985, s.l.
22. [1978] A.C. 435.
23. Quoted by Lord Wilberforce at p.473.
24. The Post Office Workers (Industrial Action) Bill
25. This was affirmed by the Court of Appeal in *Harold Stephen Co. Ltd* v. *Post Office* [1977] 1 W.L.R. 1172

26. H.C. Standing Committee B, cols. 581–5 (March 3, 1981).
27. See Smith and Hogan, *Criminal Law*, above, note pp.111–12.
28. H.C. Deb., Vol. 2, col. 313 (April 1, 1981).
29. Telegraph Act 1863, s.45, as amended; Telegraph Act 1868, s.26, as amended.
30. See note 26, above.
31. Lord Mackay, H.L. Deb., Vol. 448, col. 598, (February 20, 1984).
32. Kenneth Baker, H.C. Deb., Vol. 58, col. 140 (April 9, 1984); Lord Mackay, H.L. Deb., Vol. 448, col. 599 (February 20, 1984); H.L. Deb., vol. 449, col. 1010 (March 19, 1984); and H.L. Deb., Vol. 450, col. 378 (March 29, 1984).
33. Lord Donaldson, H.L. Deb., Vol. 448, col. 599 (February 20, 1984); Lord Wedderburn, H.L. Deb., Vol. 450, col. 378 (March 29, 1984).
34. Hazel Carty, 'Telecommunications Act 1984', *Industrial Law Journal* 13 (1984), 166.
35. K.W. Wedderburn 'Industrial action, the State and the public interest' in *Industrial Conflict: A Comparative Legal Survey* ed. B. Aaron and K.W. Wedderburn, Longman, London, 1972, p.360.
36. Conditions of Employment and National Arbitration Order (S.R. & O. 1940, No. 1305).
37. Report of a Court of Inquiry into a dispute between the parties represented on the National Joint Industrial Council for the Electricity Supply Industry, Cmnd. 4594 (1971), para 11.12.
38. Royal Commission on Trade Unions and Employers' Associations 1965–1968, Minutes of Evidence Nos. 11 and 12.
39. Royal Commission on Trade Unions and Employers' Associations 1965–8 Cmnd. 3623 (1968), para. 838.
40. Note of Reservation to the Royal Commission, above, note 39, paras. 9 and 10.
41. Consultative Document on the Industrial Relations Bill, para. 73.
42. Trade Union and Labour Relations Act 1974, as amended, ss.13, 29, 30. Parliamentary staff appear not to be protected by legislation which does not specifically include them: see G.F. Lock, 'Labour Law, Parliamentary Staff and Parliamentary Privilege, *Industrial Law Journal* 12 (1983), 28.
43. Decision of the Committee of Experts on the Application of Conventions and Recommendations, I.L.O., Geneva, 1985, p.353.
44. *Ibid.*
45. See Bob Hepple, 'Labour Law and Public Employees in Britain' in *Labour Law and the Community*, ed. Lord Wedderburn of Charlton and W.T. Murphy, Institute of Advanced Legal Studies, University of London, London 1982.
46. George Sayers Bain and Robert Price, 'Union Growth: Dimensions, Determinants and Destiny' in *Industrial Relations in Britain*, ed. George Sayers Bain, Blackwell, Oxford, 1983, p.15.
47. *Staff Relations in the Civil Service*, 4th edn. (5th imp.), H.M.S.O., London, 1978, para. 73.
48. H.C. Deb., Vol. 419, col. 213, (February 12, 1946).
49. Barney Hayhoe, H.C. Deb., Vol. 73, col. 729 (February 18, 1985).
50. Article 6.
51. *Decisions of the Committee of Experts on the Application of Conventions and Recommendations*, I.L.O., Geneva, 1985, p.355.
52. *Ibid.*
53. As note 39, above, para. 841.
54. *Simmons* v. *Hoover Ltd* [1977] I.C.R. 61.
55. As note 39, above, para. 846.
56. *Liberties and Liabilities: The case for Trade Union Reform*, Centre for Policy Studies, London, 1980, p.19.
57. In *R.* v. *Trease* [1945] 2 All E.R. 403, the issue on appeal was whether the defendants could be acting in furtherance of a strike which had not yet begun. There was no appeal against the decision of the Assize Court that the strike, whose purpose was to secure the exemption of apprentices from liability to work in the mines, was illegal.
58. Margaret Thatcher, H.C. Deb., Vol. 53, col. 120 (January 31, 1984) (written answer).
59. This change was effected by an oral instruction issued by the Prime Minister, as Minister for the Civil Service, on December 22, 1983, under Article 4 of the Civil Service Order in Council 1982. In addition, the Foreign Secretary signed certificates exempting persons employed at G.C.H.Q. from those provisions of the Employment Protection Act 1975 and Employment Protection (Consolidation) Act 1978 which apply to persons in Crown employment on the ground

that this was necessary 'for the purpose of safeguarding national security' (EPA, s.121(4); EPCA 1978, s.138(4)). This meant, in particular, that workers at G.C.H.Q. could no longer complain to an industrial tribunal if they were dismissed, or if action short of dismissal were taken against them, because of their membership of an independent trade union or participation in its activities. For a fuller description of the decision to ban trade unions and responses to it, see Gillian S. Morris, 'The Ban on Trade Unions at Government Communications Headquarters', *Public Law* (1985), 177.

60. Sir Geoffrey Howe, Foreign Secretary, H.C. Deb., Vol. 55, col. 27 (February 27, 1984).

61. House of Commons, First Report from the Employment Committee, Session 1983–4.

62. Sir Geoffrey Howe, H.C. Deb., Vol. 55, cols. 29, 31 (February 27, 1984).

63. *R.* v. *Secretary of State for Foreign and Commonwealth Affairs, ex parte Council of Civil Service Unions and another* [1984] I.R.L.R. 309.

64. *Council of Civil Service Unions* v. *Minister for the Civil Service* [1984] 3 W.L.R. 1174. The argument that national security had been at stake was introduced by the Government in the hearing before the Court of Appeal.

65. Case No. 1261.

66. Right to Organise and Collective Bargaining Convention, 1949 (No. 98); Conditions of Service in the Public Sector Convention, 1978 (No. 151).

67. Over 98 per cent by the end of April 1984: Sir Geoffrey Howe, H.C. Deb., Vol. 59, col. 42, (April 30, 1984) (written answer). A small percentage of staff requested transfer to another Government department: Sir Geoffrey Howe, H.C. Deb., Vol. 55, col. 392 (March 2, 1984) (written answer).

68. G.C.H.Q. staff still have access to industrial tribunals for complaints of sex and race discrimination unless a Minister certifies that the act complained of was done for the purpose of safeguarding national security: Sex Discrimination Act 1975, s.52; Race Relations Act 1976, ss.42, 69(2). In addition, some of the individual rights lost, including maternity rights and time off for public duties, continue to be available under the Civil Service Pay and Conditions Code and Principal Civil Service Pensions Scheme, and the Civil Service Appeals Board can hear complaints about dismissal.

69. Sir Geoffrey Howe, H.C. Deb., Vol. 94, col. 293 (March 19, 1986).

70. Sir Geoffrey Howe, H.C. Deb., Vol. 52, col. 1917, (January 25, 1984).

71. Trade Union and Labour Relations Act 1974, as amended ss.13, 29.

72. Trade Union and Labour Relations Act 1974, as amended, s.29(6).

73. Trade Union and Labour Relations Act 1974, s.29(1) (and see also the Trade Disputes Act 1906).

74. *NWL Ltd* v. *Woods* [1979] I.C.R. 867.

75. Trade Union and Labour Relations Act 1974, s.29(I), as amended by the Employment Act 1982, s.18(1) (c).

76. A dispute between a government minister and any workers relating to matters which require him to exercise a statutory power will be treated as a dispute between those workers and their employer: Trade Union and Labour Relations Act 1974, as amended, s.29(2).

77. *Associated Newspapers Ltd* v. *Flynn* (1971) 10 K.I.R. 17.

78. *Beaverbrook Newspapers Ltd and another* v. *Keys and others* [1980] I.R.L.R. 247.

79. Paul Davies and Mark Freedland, *Kahn-Freund's Labour and the Law*, 3rd edn., Stevens, London, 1983, p.317.

80. *National Sailors' and Firemen's Union* v. *Reed* [1926] 1 Ch. 536.

81. See A.L. Goodhart, 'The Legality of the General Strike in England', *Yale Law Journal* 36 (1926–7), 464.

82. Employment Act 1980, s.17.

83. [1983] I.R.L.R. 494.

84. Fear of future redundancies is a protected object: see *Hadmor Productions Ltd* v. *Hamilton* [1982] I.R.L.R. 102.

85. [1979] I.C.R. 494.

86. [1979] I.C.R. 664.

87. [1981] 3 W.L.R. 33.

88. The torts of conspiracy to use unlawful means, indirect procurement of breach of contract, intimidation, and unlawful interference with business.

89. Cf. *Clerk and Linsell on Torts*, Sweet and Maxwell, London, 1982, p.738, note 12, p.782.
90. Lord Diplock in *NWL Ltd* v. *Woods*, above note 74, at 879.
91. Paul Davies and Mark Freedland, *Labour Law: Text and Materials*, 2nd edn., Weidenfeld and Nicholson, London, 1984, p.767.
92. *Ibid.*
93. *American Cyanamid Co.* v. *Ethicon Ltd* [1975] A.C. 396.
94. Davies and Freedland, *Labour Law*, as above, note 91, p.768.
95. Trade Union and Labour Relations Act 1974, s.17(2) (added by the Employment Protection Act 1975).
96. Above, note 74.
97. As above, note 74, at 881–2. (The correction of the phrase cited was approved by Lord Diplock: see note [1980] I.C.R. 167).
98. *Duport Steels Ltd* v. *Sirs* [1980] I.C.R. 161 at 187.
99. *Gouriet* v. *U.P.O.W.*, above, note 22, at 500.
100. As above, note 22.
101. *Gouriet* v. *U.P.O.W.*, as above, note 22.
102. *Ibid.*
103. Lord Diplock in *Lonrho Ltd* v. *Shell Petroleum Co. Ltd*, above, note 87 at 38.
104. As above, note 22, at 493.
105. As above, note 103, at 39.
106. See note 88, above.
107. *Lonrho Ltd* v. *Shell Petroleum Co. Ltd*, above, note 87; *RCA Corporation and another* v. *Pollard* [1982] 3 All E.R. 771, and see W(edderburn), 'Rocking the Torts', *Modern Law Review* 46(1983), 224 at 229.
108. Para. 37.
109. Para. 38.
110. Employment Act 1980, s.3(8).
111. Paul Davies and Mark Freedland, *Labour Law: Text and Materials*, above, note 91, p.885.
112. Roy Lewis and Bob Simpson, *Striking a Balance? Employment Law after the 1980 Act*, Martin Robertson, Oxford, 1981, p.174.
113. Employment Act 1980, s.4.
114. See *Esterman* v.*N.A.L.G.O.* [1974] I.C.R. 625 and Richard Kidner, *Trade Union Law*, 2nd edn., Stevens and Sons, London, 1983, p.43.
115. [1981] I.R.L.R. 537.
116. Employment Protection (Consolidation) Act 1978, s.58, as substituted by the Employment Act 1982, s.3.
117. Para. 24.
118. Employment Protection (Consolidation) Act 1978, s.72, as substituted by the Employment Act 1982, s.3.
119. See Chapter 6.
120. *Code of Professional Conduct for Nurses, Midwives and Health Visitors*, United Kingdom Central Council, London, 1983, para. 6.
121. Conversation with the author.
122. *A Guide to the Professional Conduct of Solicitors*, The Law Society, London, 1974, Ch.11, para. 4.
123. Decision of the Professional Purposes Committee of the Council dated April 17, 1980, quoted in *The Law Society's Gazette* October 31, 1984, pp.2992–3.
124. As above, note 122. For a critique of this position, see *The Law Society's Gazette*, January 30, 1985, pp.267–8.

3

Emergency Powers

British governments have had recourse to a variety of special peacetime powers in order to mitigate the consequences of disruption to the operation of particular services and industries. This chapter looks at the scope of these powers, the extent to which they have been used, the considerations which have influenced the decision of governments to invoke them, and their likely application in future disputes.

The most extensive powers to ameliorate disruption are granted by the Emergency Powers Act 1920, and a discussion of this legislation forms the first and largest section of this chapter. The Emergency Powers Act enables the executive, on proclaiming a state of emergency, to introduce measures to 'secure the essentials of life to the community' when the supply and distribution of specified commodities is interrupted or when transport is dislocated. There have been twelve separate states of emergency under the Act, the most recent in 1973–4. The section begins with a brief account of the background to the Act which indicates that the Government of the day originally contemplated the introduction of much more far-reaching legislation. There follows a detailed examination of the use of the Act, starting with an overview of the disputes which have occasioned its use and the nature of the powers taken. In most disputes, the Government has assumed many more powers than it could realistically have expected to require to deal with the instant emergency. There is then a discussion of the factors which governed the timing of proclamations of emergency and the use which was made in practice of the powers which were taken. Intrinsic to this discussion is an analysis of the Government's attitude towards the merits of the disputes in question; this makes clear that on a number of occasions the decision to declare a state of emergency cannot be separated from broader aspects of goverment policy. Consideration of the alternative strategies for dealing with disputes which have been adopted since 1974 reinforces this point. Finally, there is a short investigation of the extent to which Parliament and the courts would be capable of restraining the excesses of a government which attempted to abuse the wide powers which the Act bestows on it.

Since late 1973, the Government has had at its disposal an alternative source of emergency powers, albeit of a more limited nature, when energy supplies are put at risk. These powers are now contained in the Energy Act 1976. The second section considers this Act, which enables the Government to avoid the political repercussions of declaring a state of emergency and the requirement of regular parliamentary debate of the reasons for taking powers which the 1920 Act imposes. The Energy Act has not so far been used in the context of industrial action, although powers under its predecessor, the Fuel and Electricity (Control) Act 1973, were invoked during the 1973–4 miners' dispute.

Post-war governments have been able to deploy troops on 'urgent work of national importance', including work left undone by strikers, without declaring a state of emergency under the 1920 Act. This power, and the use which has been made of it, is discussed in detail in Chapter 4.

In addition to relying upon standing emergency legislation, governments have also introduced *ad hoc* measures to deal with industrial action which lay outside the scope of their permanent powers. This was done on three occasions in recent years, during disputes involving civil servants, prison officers and registrars of births, marriages and deaths. The penultimate section of this chapter outlines these provisions.

The chapter concludes with a discussion of the emergency procedures which were available under the Industrial Relations Act 1971. These provisions marked a significant departure from the traditional British approach to 'emergency disputes'; by enabling the Government to seek from the courts orders for a cooling-off period and compulsory ballot of the work-force taking industrial action, they allowed direct interference in the conduct of disputes rather than simply authorizing measures to cushion their effect. Although these powers have now been repealed, they remain worthy of consideration because of the lessons they may contain for the future.

THE EMERGENCY POWERS ACT 1920

The Emergency Powers Act 1920 enables a proclamation of emergency to be issued if

> at any time it appears to Her Majesty that there have occurred, or are about to occur, events of such a nature as to be calculated, by interfering with the supply and distribution of food, water, fuel, or

> light, or with the means of locomotion, to deprive the community, or any substantial portion of the community, of the essentials of life. . . [s.1(1)]

By convention, the Queen exercises a power of this nature only on the advice of the Government. Once a proclamation of emergency has been issued, Her Majesty in Council is empowered to make regulations 'for securing the essentials of life to the community' (S.2(1)). These regulations may confer or impose on a minister or government department, or any other persons acting on behalf of the Crown.

> such powers and duties as Her Majesty may deem necessary for the preservation of the peace, for securing and regulating the supply and distribution of food, water, fuel, light, and other necessities, for maintaining the means of transit or locomotion, and for any other purposes essential to public safety and the life of the community. . . [s.2(1)].

Provisions may also be made which 'appear to Her Majesty to be required for making the exercise of those powers effective'. The Government cannot force strikers to go back to work, however; it is specifically stated that regulations may not impose compulsory military service or industrial conscription, nor may they make it an offence to strike or peacefully persuade others to do so. The maximum penalty which may be imposed for contravening a regulation, after summary trial, is three months' imprisonment, a £2,000 fine, or both.[1] The regulations may not alter existing criminal procedure nor confer any right to punish by fine or imprisonment without trial (S.2(3)).

The Emergency Powers Act allows the government to take and implement emergency powers without prior sanction by Parliament. It also provides for consideration by Parliament of the decision to invoke the Act at an early stage. The occasion of a proclamation of emergency must be communicated to Parliament 'forthwith', and if Parliament is not due to meet within five days of the proclamation being issued, it must be summoned within five days (S.1(2)). Regulations are to be laid before Parliament 'as soon as may be' and require approval by both Houses within seven days of being laid in order to continue force (S.2(2)). A fresh proclamation and set of regulations must be issued once a month and the same procedure followed (S.1(1)). Should the Government fail to comply with these procedures (which has never so far happened), this would probably not result in the powers taken becoming legally invalid but it would undoubtedly have serious political repercussions.[2]

The background to the Emergency Powers Act

The Emergency Powers Act was the final product of prolonged debate within the Lloyd George (Liberal–Unionist) Coalition Government as to how the problems raised by strikes in essential services should be tackled. During the period of industrial unrest which followed the First World War many such services were threatened with disruption. There was a General Strike in Glasgow in January 1919, and stoppages of London's power stations and underground and in the mines were also threatened. Yorkshire miners went on strike in July and a nine-day railway strike began in September. The Triple Industrial Alliance of miners, railwaymen and transport workers, formed in 1915, was seen as a constant source of potential trouble. Against a background of revolutionary feeling and social unrest throughout Europe, the Government feared that industrial action could be used as a revolutionary weapon and issued frequent warnings against the 'Bolshevik' menace. A reflection of these fears was the Aliens Restriction (Amendment) Act 1919, which was directed against foreign agitators. Section 3 of this Act, which remains in force, made it an offence for an alien to attempt to cause sedition or disaffection among the armed forces or civilian population or to attempt to promote unrest in any industry in which he had not been bona fide engaged in the United Kingdom for at least two years. Official propaganda portrayed strikes in essential services as attacks upon the State, and Government control of the mines and railways, assumed during the war and continued until 1921, facilitated the representation of wage claims in these industries as political demands.

Initially the Government was able to rely upon the extensive administrative machinery established during the war to deal with any dislocation of essential supplies. The necessary legal powers to control supplies and requisition property also remained available. Section 1 of the Defence of the Realm (Consolidation) Act 1914 had empowered the King 'during the continuance of the present War to issue regulations for securing the public safety and defence of the realm', and the war continued for legislative purposes until August 1921.[3] The 1914 Act was sufficiently wide to permit the proscription of industrial action. Ministers considered arresting leaders of the Glasgow strike under existing wartime regulations,[4] and a new regulation was issued to enable the organizers of the London electricity strike to be arrested should the stoppage take place.[5]

To meet the threatened coal strike the Government contemplated new legislation, however. The provisions of the Strikes (Exceptional Meaures) Bill[6] were intended to become operative if a coal strike began or was threatened whose object was to withhold supplies 'essential to the life of the whole community', action which was deemed to be 'a conspiracy against the State'. (Its operation could also be triggered by strikes in other industries if Parliament so resolved.) Once one of these events had occurred, it would then become illegal to organize a strike in the mines or in any other essential industry or service or to pay strike pay. The assets of trade unions with members in those areas would be frozen and those which were not deposited in banks could be confiscated. The stoppage which precipitated this far-reaching measure was averted and the Bill never reached the stage of being published.

By January 1920 the Home departments had begun to prepare drafts of standing emergency legislation. The use of troops to replace strikers was a crucial element in Government contingency plans for countering disputes in essential services, and there was doubt as to whether troops employed on civilian work of this kind were covered by military discipline.[7] Moreover, special powers were also required to operate the permanent administrative machinery which the Government had by then resolved to establish to meet any threats to supplies. The early drafts of legislation linked disruption of supplies and challenges to the constitutional process.[8] An emergency situation arose if the monarch considered that the 'safety of the Realm or any part' was endangered

> by the action of any persons who by force, threats, or terrorism or by injury or threats of injury to persons or property or by depriving or threatening to deprive. . . the community of the means of subsistence or of any essentials of life, attempt to destroy settled government, or to put compulsion on Parliament or His Majesty's Government to yield to their demands. . .

Once a state of emergency had been declared, organizing strikes in essential industries and services would become illegal and, as in the Strikes (Exceptional Measures) Bill, disposal of union funds would be restricted. A wide range of executive and police powers would become available automatically, and regulations could be made for 'securing the public safety', subject only to a negative resolution in either House of Parliament.

These early drafts were replaced in July 1920 by a draft closer in form to the Bill as published.[9] It is unclear why the more extensive proposals were abandoned; ministers may have considered them too provocative. The Government was in a dilemma as to whether to introduce a Bill during time of industrial peace or whether to wait for a crisis.[10] This dilemma was rapidly resolved. A national miners' strike began on October 16 and on October 21 the railwaymen decided to strike in sympathy unless the dispute was settled within two days. It was widely believed that other groups of workers would also come out in sympathy. The Emergency Powers Bill was given its first reading in the midst of this crisis on October 22. The miners subsequently accepted an invitation to meet the Prime Minister on October 25 and asked the railwaymen to suspend their strike to avoid imperilling negotiations. Miners' leaders and Labour MPs appealed to Lloyd George to withdraw the Bill, and even *The Times* agreed that this was 'plainly the least opportune [moment] for a measure which is designed to vest the government with powers only likely to be needed in the last extremity of an industrial conflict. . .'.[11] The Government remained unmoved, however; the need for powers was considered to be urgent and, Lloyd George informed miners' leaders, Parliament might not in the future be so receptive to such legislation.[12] Moreover, one minister explained:

> A Bill of this kind will never be admitted to be opportune. If it was introduced in a time of peace, someone would be certain to say 'Why cannot you let sleeping dogs lie?' But if it were introduced when trouble was imminent, it was certain to be called provocative and calculated to inflame passion.[13]

The Government initially intended to steer the Bill through all the remaining stages of its Parliamentary passage in one day. After protests from MPs, however, it agreed to allow debate over two, and finally three, days in the Commons. It passed through the House of Lords on one day and received the Royal Assent on October 29. By the time the Act came into force, the miners had reached a settlement and so the legislation was not required on that occasion.

Government spokesmen presented the Emergency Powers Bill as an innocuous, non-partisan measure which was designed only to ensure the equitable distribution of essential supplies should they be disrupted. Being for the benefit of the whole community, it could not be considered provocative or anti-union. However, Lloyd George belied this non-combative stance when he posed the question 'Are the Triple Alliance to make arrangements in advance and the Government to make none?'[14] In general, M.P.s of all parties agreed that the Government should possess exceptional powers to meet emergencies. Mr. J.R. Clynes, vice-chairman of the Parliamentary Labour Party, acknowledged that '[t]he striker would not like to be compelled to live in a state of semi-starvation any more than the rest of the community'.[15] Labour M.P.s argued, however, that powers could always be made available as and when an emergency arose; there was no requirement for standing legislation. They were also highly critical of the speed with which the Government was planning to enact the Bill and suggested a Select Committee of Inquiry or a series of conferences to examine the issue at leisure. The Government was not impressed by these proposals.

Despite the restricted opportunity for debate, a number of crucial amendments were proposed, and accepted by the Government, during the legislation's parliamentary passage. The three specific limitations on the regulation-making power which have already been referred to were inserted. (The Government denied having ever intended to prohibit industrial action or impose industrial conscription under the Act,[16] but there is no evidence that its earlier plans to proscribe the organization of strikes during emergencies had been abandoned.) Important changes in procedure were also made: Parliament was to be summoned within five, and not fourteen, days on an emergency being proclaimed; the regulations required approval within seven, and not fourteen, days of being laid, and the duration of a proclamation was limited to a month.

An 'emergency' under the 1920 Act embraced interference with the designated supplies and services by human action only. Section 1 of the Emergency Powers Act 1964 extended the definition to interference by any agency. In proposing this extension, the Conservative Home Secretary, Mr Henry Brooke, gave as examples of other possible causes abnormally bad weather conditions, natural disasters and the interruption of vital supplies from abroad.[17] Man-made technological disasters would also be covered. Labour M.P.s opposed this amendment in debate, maintaining that Parliament could grant the extended power if and when it became necessary to use it, but the Bill passed through both Houses without a vote being taken on it.

The use of the Emergency Powers Act

States of Emergency

A state of emergency has been proclaimed under the 1920 Act on twelve separate occasions, all industrial disputes, including nine since 1945 and five during the Heath Government of 1970–4.[18] The last of these occasions was in 1973–4. The majority of these disputes involved coal-miners and dockers; others involved railwaymen, electricity supply workers, seamen and London busmen and tramwaymen. Table 1 outlines the course of each emergency. In 1924 and 1948 the dispute in question was settled before regulations were issued (although in 1948 the proclamation was not revoked; it continued in force until it expired). Of the remaining emergencies, six lasted for one month or less and one (in 1966) for six weeks. In 1921, 1926 and 1973–4 three, seven and five successive proclamations, respectively, were issued during the course of

TABLE 1. *The use of the Emergency Powers Act 1920*

Year	Workers involved	Industrial action	Dispute began	State of emergency proclaimed	Dispute ended	State of emergency ended	Government in office
1921	Coalminers	Strike	March 31 (last shift)	March 31	July 1	July 26	Liberal–Unionist Coalition
1924	Tramwaymen and busmen	Strike	March 22	March 27	April 1	April 1	Labour
1926	Coalminers (General Strike, 4–12 May)	Strike	May 1	April 30	December 22	December 19	Conservative
1948	Dockers	Strike	June 14	June 28	June 29	July 27	Labour
1949	Dockers	Strike	June 23	July 11	July 23	July 26	Labour
1955	Railwaymen	Strike	May 29	May 31	June 14	June 21	Conservative
1966	Seamen	Strike	May 16	May 23	July 1	July 6	Labour
1970	Dockers	Strike	July 13	July 16	July 31	August 4	Conservative
1970	Electricity manual workers	Work-to-rule and overtime ban	December 7	December 12	December 14	December 17	Conservative
1972	Coalminers	Overtime ban then strike	November 1 1971 (strike January 9 1972)	February 9	February 25	March 8	Conservative
1972	Dockers	Strike	July 28	August 3	August 18	September 2	Conservative
1973	(i) Electricity power engineers; (ii) Coalminers (iii) Railwaymen	(i) Ban on 'out of hours' work; (ii) overtime ban then strike; (iii) ban on Sunday, rest-day and overtime work.	(i) November 1; (ii) November 13 (strike Feb 10, 1974); (iii) December 12.	November 13	(i) December 28; (ii) March 8, 1974; (iii) February 11, 1974.	March 11, 1974	Conservative

the dispute. With two exceptions, the industrial action occasioning the declaration of an emergency took the form of a total stoppage. The leaders of these two other disputes, which involved electricity manual workers (in 1970) and coalminers (in 1973), forecast at the outset that their members' action would quickly have the same impact as that of a strike.

What interpretation have governments placed on the scope of the enabling power by declaring a state of emergency in these situations? The power to issue a proclamation under section 1(1) of the Act is limited in three important respects. First, the 'events' which occasion the emergency must interfere with the 'supply and distribution of food, water, fuel or light, or with the means of locomotion'. On the face of it, industrial action by all the groups whose disputes have occasioned states of emergency falls within the definition. Disputes involving other workers who are generally considered to furnish 'essential' services such as doctors, nurses and other health service workers, are clearly excluded, and disruption to the fire service could be included only by arguing that this would eventually threaten the listed supplies. A police strike is also *prima facie* outside the definition, although again it could be argued that the state of lawlessness and consequent interference with the designated supplies and services this would sooner or later entail, would bring it within the Act.

The second and third limitations arise from the necessity for the 'events' in question to deprive the community, or any substantial portion, of the essentials of life. The 'essentials of life' are nowhere defined in the legislation. On three occasions the Government has interpreted this phrase as covering damage to the economy, a view which seems inordinately wide. The 1948 and 1949 proclamations were stated to be necessary to protect external trade as well as essential food supplies,[19] and in 1966 the need for powers was based on economic grounds alone.[20] In each case the (Conservative) Opposition supported the Government's action; in 1966, a spokesman merely pointed out that damage to the economy was not currently within the Act but urged extending the definition of an emergency so that it was so covered.[21] Although this would be a significant extension of the scope of the Act in theory, if interference with the listed supplies and services were still required, it would probably not expand greatly the range of situations to which the Act can be applied in practice. (An 'emergency' under the Industrial Relations Act 1971, discussed below, did extend to economic damage.)

The concept of a 'substantial portion' of the community has also received a generous interpretation. During the legislation's parliamentary passage, the Attorney-General, Sir Gordon Hewart, stated that the Act was intended primarily to deal with 'national' emergencies; the words above were present merely to prevent objections to its use because 'although the greater part of the community were deprived the whole community was not'.[22] All but three states of emergency have been caused by national industrial action. The 1949 dock strike, however, involved little more than half the dockers at the Port of London.[23] Whilst the impact of this dispute doubtless spread beyond its immediate location, and the use of the Act can therefore be justified on that ground, it is hard to argue that the 1924 stoppage of London transport workers conformed to Hewart's understanding of a 'substantial portion of the community'. Localized disputes involving energy supplies which do not have repercussions for a 'substantial portion of the community' could now be dealt with under the Energy Act 1976, discussed below.

Emergency regulations

For the first state of emergency in 1921, the Government introduced regulations containing 'the large majority of powers that are ever likely to be required',[24] and ever since then (apart from in 1949 and 1955) governments have followed the practice of issuing a corpus of regulations, to which additions and alterations are occasionally made, regardless of the exigencies of the immediate situation. Sometimes ministers have argued that the seemingly otiose powers may eventually be needed should the emergency last for some time.[25] On other occasions, however, they have justified a regulation's presence on the ground that it may be necessary to deal with some future emergency. In 1972, for example, the Home Secretary, Mr Robert Carr, acknowledged that a new regulation allowing the procedures involved in importing drugs and essential medicines to be 'short-circuited', was unlikely to be used on the instant occasion but stated that 'experience in the last one indicated. . . that. . . [it] should be added to the corpus'.[26] This policy of issuing a complete code has been generally followed and accepted by representatives of all major parties. It is not a practice of which governments should be proud. Article 15 of the European Convention on Human Rights permits derogation from particular obligations 'in time of war or other public emergency threatening the life of the nation' only 'to the extent strictly required by the exigencies of the situation'. Commissions of Inquiry established by the I.L.O. to examine alleged violations by Greece and Poland of the Freedom of Association and Protection of the Right to Organise Convention, 1948 (No. 87) and the Right to Organise and Collective Bargaining Convention, 1949 (No. 98) adopted a similarly restrictive approach. Neither Convention expressly allows for any derogation and the Commissions concluded that international custom required

> the plea of emergency to justify restrictions on the civil liberties that are essential to the proper exercise of trade union rights can be advanced before an international authority only in circumstances of extreme gravity constituting a case of *force majeure* and provided that any measures affecting the application of the Convention are limited in scope and in duration to what is strictly necessary to deal with the situation in question.[27]

Article 31 of the European Social Charter permits limitations on the right to strike which are 'prescribed by law and are necessary in a democratic society for the protection of the rights and freedoms of others or for the protection of the public interest, national security, public health or morals'. British Governments should apply the same test of necessity to emergency regulations even if they do not touch on matters within the scope of these international provisions. Additional powers can be taken at any stage of an emergency should they be required; there is no justification for adopting superfluous powers at the outset. In most emergencies (other than the four coal disputes) only a small proportion of the regulations have been put to use.

The 1921 and 1926 regulations reflected greater fears of civil disturbance than those which have been issued since the Second World War, although in some cases the powers taken during the earlier emergencies were later given permanent statutory force, making special provision unnecessary. In all codes of regulations the powers to interfere with property rights have been more extensive than the powers to restrict individual civil liberties. The pre-war regulations applied military discipline to troops employed on work which a Secretary of State declared 'of vital importance to the community';[28] since the start of the Second World War, separate legislation, described in Chapter 4, has provided for this. The regulations have always laid down the maximum permitted penalties for their infringement or for that of instruments made under them. (The maximum fine permitted stood for many years at £100 and was raised only in 1982 to £2,000.)[29] A detailed account of the regulations would cover many pages; the broad survey which follows is intended to give only a general idea of the scope of the powers which the Government has assumed.[30]

Inteference with property and the production, disposition and use of goods and supplies. The 1921 and 1926 regulations, and those issued since 1966, contained a general power to take possession of land and requisition chattels, with appropriate compensation, where possession was considered 'necessary or expedient' by any Government minister.[31] Codes issued in 1926, 1949, 1966 and 1970[32] also enabled troops to be billeted on the civilian population. In 1921 the executive was given extensive powers to control the production, disposition and use of coal and coal products, and in 1926 these powers were extended to all articles essential to the life of the community or required for their production.[33] Since the war, powers to direct consumption and supply have been limited to fuel, electricity, gas, water, food and animal feeding stuffs.[34] There were no powers to control production until 1972, when a regulation was introduced enabling the appropriate Secretary of State to direct production of liquid fuel and refinery products.[35] Power in 1926 to impose maximum prices on all essential articles[36] has been confined since the war to food for human and animal consumption.[37]

Control of public services (other than transport) All regulations, other than in 1949, have empowered the executive to direct and regulate the supply and consumption of gas and electricity.[38] A similar power in relation to water was introduced in 1966.[39] Since 1972 the appropriate minister has also been empowered to prohibit consumption of gas and electricity in particular premises and to sever supplies altogether if this appears 'necessary or expedient' to make the best use of available resources.[40] Since 1966 sewage authorities have been empowered to disregard restrictions on discharging water when draining their districts and dealing with sewage.[41] There has been no equivalent provision concerning refuse.

Before 1966 all codes empowered the Postmaster-General to direct that particular telegraphic messages should not be accepted for transmission,[42] and in 1949 this power was extended to telephone messages and postal packets.[43] The Post Office Act 1969, which established the Post Office as a separate corporation, now allows the Post Office to restrict services in case of emergency and the Minister of Industry and Information Technology could probably direct it to impose restrictions under his general powers.[44] Section 94 of the Telecommunications Act 1984 enables the Minister to give such directions to telecommunications operators as appear to him requisite or expedient in the interests of national security.

Control of transport and ports The pre-war regulations gave the appropriate ministers extensive powers of control over all forms of transport.[45] The 1949 regulations omitted these powers and the 1955 code was confined to provisions (included in subsequent codes) allowing the Minister of Transport to relax restrictions on the use of vehicles and those who could drive them in order to maximize the availability of road transport.[46] Regulations were introduced during the 1966 seamen's strike empowering the appropriate ministers to direct persons using goods vehicles for business purposes to carry particular goods and air transport operators to carry particular passengers and cargo.[47] The 1970 regulations allowed similar instructions to be given to public service vehicle operators,[48] and in 1972 this power was extended to the railways.[49]

The pre-war regulations empowered the Board of Trade to control the traffic into, or close altogether, any port or harbour.[50] The post-war codes (other than in 1955) have enabled the appropriate minister to give directions to ensure that the best use is made of port facilities, and such directions override any proprietary interests in berths or storage accomodation. (This power can be delegated to an Emergency Committee.)[51] The Minister has also been authorized to permit persons other than registered dockworkers to perform dock work without this constituting a breach of the statutory scheme.[52]

Public order There is no comprehensive common law power to prohibit the holding of meetings and demonstrations and no general statutory power to do this existed before 1936.[53] The 1921 and 1926 regulations empowered the Home Secretary, or any mayor, magistrate or chief officer of police authorized by him, to prohibit the holding of a meeting or procession if there was reason to apprehend that such an assembly could lead to a breach of the peace and thereby cause undue demands to be made upon the police or promote disaffection.[54] Any gathering held in breach of such a prohibition could be dispersed.[55] No corresponding power has been included in any post-war regulations. Processions, but not meetings, can now be banned under section 3 of the Public Order Act 1936 where a Chief Officer of Police believes that they may result in 'serious public disorder', provided that the relevant local authority and the Home Secretary consent.[56] This power has not so far been exercised in the context of 'emergency disputes'. (The Public Order Bill which is before Parliament at the time of writing significantly extends the powers of the police to impose conditions on marches and also gives them statutory powers to impose conditions relating to the location, duration and size of meetings in public places.)

The 1921 and 1926 regulations gave the Government extensive powers of control over firearms, ammunition, and explosives, including power to prohibit dealing in, and carrying, such materials.[57] It was an offence to attend a public gathering carrying one of these articles or substances 'or any stone or dangerous missile'.[58] The carrying of firearms is now regulated by the Firearms Act 1968.

Offences and police powers The pre-war regulations laid down a comprehensive offence of inciting disaffection and impeding the operation of essential services, some elements of which merely enabled existing offences to be dealt with in the magistrates courts, others for which there was no provision in the ordinary law.[59] No proof of guilty intention was required. It was an offence for any person to do or attempt to do any act calculated or likely to cause mutiny, sedition or disaffection among any of His Majesty's forces[60] or among members of any police force[61] or any fire brigade, or among the civilian population,[62] or to impede, delay or restrict any measures taken for securing and regulating essential supplies and services or 'for any other purposes essential to the public safety or the life of the community'. The 1926 regulations also made it an offence to print, produce, publish or distribute any document containing a statement which could constitute the above offence, or to possess any such document without lawful authority or excuse, unless the defendant could prove that he did not know, and had no reason to suspect, that the document contained such material or that he had no intention of distributing it.[63] Another regulation made it an offence to obstruct or otherwise interfere with any person performing a duty under the regulations.[64] The post-war regulations have divided the offences in this area into two categories: (1) acts endangering, obstructing or interfering with servicemen, constables and other persons performing essential services and (2) inducing members of the armed or police forces to withhold their services or commit breaches of discipline.[65]

The 1921 and 1926 regulations made it an offence to do any act calculated to injure various properties used in connection with the maintenance of essential services.[66] Codes issued since the war have included the offence of sabotage, which is defined as doing:

> any act with intent to impair the efficiency or impede the working or movement of any vessel, aircraft, vehicle, machinery, apparatus, or other thing used or intended to be used in the performance of essential services, or to impair the usefulness of any works, structure or premises used or intended to be [so] used.[67]

They have also made it an offence to trespass on premises used for essential services or on premises in their vicinity.[68]

All codes have given the police power to arrest without warrant any person they have reasonable cause to believe is guilty of an offence under the regulations. The codes up to 1949 also gave the police wide powers of entry and search to obtain evidence of such offences;[69] there have been no such powers in later regulations.

The timing of proclamations and the use of emergency regulations

The stage of a dispute at which a state of emergency has been declared ranges from before industrial action started to three-and-a-half months into it. As Table 2 indicates, the timing of the proclamation has bourne no direct relation to the industry group involved nor to the nature of the industrial action.

TABLE 2. *The stage of a dispute at which a state of emergency was proclaimed* [70]

Stage	*Dispute*
Before industrial action had begun	Coalmining: strike 1926. Coalmining: strike 1921.
In the first week of industrial action.	Coalmining: overtime ban. Electricity power engineers: ban on 'out of hours' working 1973. Railways: strike 1955. Docks: strike 1970. Tramwaymen and busmen (London): strike 1924. Electricity supply manual workers: work to rule and overtime ban 1970. Docks: strike 1972.
In the first fortnight of industrial action.	Seamen: strike 1966.
In the first three weeks of industrial action.	Docks (London, Merseyside): strike 1948. Docks (London): strike 1949.
After three-and-a-half months of industrial action.	Coalmining: overtime ban, later strike 1972.

On three occasions, in 1966, July 1970 and August 1972, the Government said that it was taking emergency powers as a precautionary measure in case the level of disruption should increase. These powers were not, in the event, required. In 1966 the Prime Minister, Mr Harold Wilson, warned on the first day of the seamen's strike that a state of emergency would be declared if it should continue,[71] and decided seven days later to advise a proclamation 'so that regulations made under it could be debated by Parliament before the [Whitsun] recess'.[72] The Attorney-General predicted that the armed forces would need to requisition port facilities,[73] and port emergency committees were established a month after the first proclamation,[74] but compulsory action to prevent congestion was never required. Port emergency committees were also established during the 1970 and 1972 dock strikes, but again they were not required to exercise any compulsory powers.

In 1949 troops were sent into the London docks to unload food supplies four days before the proclamation. The Government gave no specific reason for the decision to take emergency powers during the debate on the regulations, but subsequently stated that this had been necessary to resolve doubts as to whether servicemen could work in the ports (the dock labour scheme restricted employment to registered dockworkers) and to enable ships to be dealt with in an order which served 'national requirements' rather than 'the commercial needs of the port'.[75] Identical action had been taken before the proclamation, however, and Jeffery and Hennessy suggest that its main purpose was to give moral support to those dockworkers who had remained at, or wished to return to, work.[76] In 1948 as well, troops had been working in the docks five days before the proclamation. On that occasion the dispute ended before the regulations were issued.

In the case of the remaining emergencies, the Government took powers with the intention of putting at least some of them to immediate use. Had the 1924 London transport strike continued, the Government planned to use emergency regulations to harness 'all available and suitable facilities' to transport hospital patients,[77] government employees and workers in other emergency services,[78] and to employ troops to man the power stations should electricity supply workers withdraw their labour in sympathy. In 1955 the footplatemen's strike initially paralyzed the railway system, and regulations relaxing or suspending some restrictions on the use of road transport were put into effect. Regional transport commissioners were given power to requisition tippers, but as a sufficient number were made available voluntarily, this proved unnecessary.[79] Provincial police forces were directed to send reinforcements to London to assist with traffiic problems arising from the strike.[80] Service aircraft and lorries were used to carry essential mail, and the Minister of Transport concluded an agreement with insurance companies to allow the use of private cars for giving lifts under existing insurance policies.[81]

The electricity manual workers' work-to-rule and overtime ban in December 1970 brought immediate voltage reductions and disconnections, and the electricity authorities took steps to maintain supplies to priority users. The electricity workers' unions warned that supplies could cease altogether within a couple of weeks, and the Government acknowledged that troops would not be capable of taking over the running of the power stations.[87] As soon as a state of emergency had been declared, an Order was issued prohibiting electricity consumption for the purposes of advertising, display and floodlighting, other than with the consent of the Secretary of State,[83] but the dispute ended on the day this restriction took effect.

Only in the case of the four coal stoppages was any extensive use made of emergency regulations. In both the pre-war disputes the Government feared that the stoppage would spread, in 1921 to the other Triple Alliance unions (the railwaymen and transport workers) and in 1926 to the whole trade union movement. The emergency administrative machine was ready to spring into action from the outset, and the Government also took steps to counter the danger of civil disturbance. In 1921 troops were sent to the mining areas to undertake peace-keeping duties at the beginning of the stoppage, and about 12,000 soldiers remained stationed there throughout the dispute.[84] When the Triple Alliance decided on April 8 to come out in support of the miners, the Prime Minister announced that the Armed Forces Reserves would also be mobilized and a 'Defence Force' of patriotic citizens formed 'to aid the civil power in protection duties and the prevention of disorder'.[85] By April 18, when recruiting was halted, the Triple Alliance unions having withdrawn their threat, some 75,000 men had enlisted for this newly-created organization.[86]

Emergency regulations authorizing control of the movement, supply and consumption of coal and power supplies were also given immediate effect; restrictions, administered by local authorities, were imposed on the acquisition of coal for business and domestic premises, and it was made unlawful to use lighting for advertising or display.[87] One month into the dispute the Cabinet considered introducing more stringent restrictions on energy consumption but decided that, given these could bring mass unemployment and increased pressure for a settlement, they should be avoided if possible,[88] and no further measures of this kind were needed. At the start of the stoppage the Government also invoked powers under the Ministry of Food (Continuance) Act 1920 to control food supplies and requisition road transport, but when the threat from the Triple Alliance receded, these powers were no longer required. Servicemen were authorized to perform a number of tasks under military discipline, including those essential to prevent serious damage to the mines,[89] but it seems that their activities were probably confined to protecting civilian volunteers.

In 1926 'the basic policy was to use police supported by the various volunteer organizations to maintain public order'.[90] The Home Secretary was authorized to increase the number of special constables and also to enrol a 'Civil Constabulary Reserve'. As a precautionary measure, however, troops were moved to Scotland, South Wales and Lancashire at the beginning of the stoppage, and naval vessels were stationed at strategic ports.[91] As in 1921, restrictions on the supply and consumption of coal, gas and electricity, again supervised largely by local authorities, were introduced immediately; Coal Emergency Committees were also established to regulate the distribution of coal under the direction of the Secretary of State for Mines, and the export and movement of coal coast-wise or inland from ports could be done only with ministerial approval.[92] These restrictions remained in force for most of the stoppage. During the nine-day General Strike – when workers in the railway and transport services, and the gas, electricity, building, printing, metals and heavy chemicals industries withdrew their labour in support of the miners – the successful operation of carefully-laid voluntarist plans largely obviated the need for Government officials to use their compulsory powers to regulate the supply and distribution of food and other essential commodities.[93] (The background to these plans is described in Chapter 4.) The Government took direct charge only of the distribution of milk; Orders were issued directing all milk producers within the Metropolitan Police Area to put their supplies at the disposal of the London Milk Committee.[94] Volunteers were used to unload food supplies at various docks around the country, and there was no need for any rationing of food. Naval ratings worked in power stations and unloaded petrol imports,[95] and submarines maintained electricity supplies to the refrigeration plant at the London docks.[96] Naval vessels carried yeast to the mainland from the Scottish and Irish distilleries and mail across the Irish Sea.[97]

Official propaganda portrayed the General Strike as an attack upon the constitution; the Prime Minister, Mr Stanley Baldwin, declared that union leaders were 'going nearer to proclaiming Civil War then we have been for centuries past'.[98] The T.U.C. vigorously denied having any such object, and 'there is evidence that alarm about the usurpation of constitutional authority was deliberately fostered'[99] in order to legitimate taking drastic counter-measures. One of these measures was the blocking of overseas aid for the strike. On May 3 a new emergency regulation was introduced which gave ministers the power to prohibit banks from dealing in 'monies, securities or credits' transmitted from abroad or applied under foreign instructions except under licence where they had reason to believe that the money would be used 'for a purpose prejudicial to the public safety or the life of the community'.[100] The regulation was aimed primarily at donations from Russia, and the Home Secretary ordered a London bank to return £100,000 which the All-Russian Central Council of Trade Unions had asked to be sent to the T.U.C.[101] The Government also contemplated more drastic action. On May 8 the Cabinet resolved to put before Parliament the Illegal Strikes Bill. This Bill 'declared' illegal any sympathetic strike 'calculated to intimidate or coerce the Government or the community', gave the Home Secretary power on the suit of the Attorney-General to prevent the use of trade union or co-operative funds to support such a strike, and provided that no worker who refused to participate in one could be deprived of his union membership or any benefits of membership.[102] A further emergency regulation would have prevented bank deposits being withdrawn in advance of these restrictions coming into force.[103] Before the Bill was introduced, however, the Government Chief Whip informed the Cabinet that most Conservative M.P.s were against taking 'provocative action against the trade unions' at a moment when the strikers appeared to be beaten, and the Bill was at first postponed and then finally withdrawn.[104]

Much greater use was made of the 'public order' regulations in 1926 than in any of the other emergencies. A total of 7,960 people were prosecuted for offences connected with the General Strike and coal stoppage, 4,656 for offences under the ordinary law and 3,304 for breaches of the regulations.[105] The majority of charges brought under the regulations were for one of three offences: injuring property used to produce essential supplies or furnish essential services; acts likely to cause mutiny, sedition or disaffection; and obstruction of officers acting in accordance with their duties. Although the conduct of the General Strike itself was, on the whole, relatively peaceful, there were disturbances in some mining areas and in London, and 1,389 of the 1,760 charges brought under the regulations during this period were for offences involving violence and disorder.[106] The police made several raids on local offices of the Communist Party and the left-wing Minority Movement, and a number of people were prosecuted for producing, distributing or possessing militant strike bulletins.[107] Some sources suggest that as many as 20 to 25 per cent of the membership of the Communist Party was arrested during the General Strike.[108]

Once the General Strike had ended, the Government based its case for keeping emergency powers primarily on considerations of public order. Ministers stressed initially the deterrent value of the regulations in preventing disorder,[109] and later the need to protect from intimidation those miners who had started to drift back to work.[110] Up to mid-September, the power to prevent meetings and processions being held was exercised eighteen times,[111] and in mid-October the Home Secretary empowered chief constables to ban such gatherings without reference to him in order to counter a campaign by the Communist Party opposing a return to work.[112] Between October 19 and November 14 sixty-three meetings were banned under this extended power.[113]

In 1972 and 1973 the Government's main concern was the conservation of electricity supplies, and restrictions on electricity consumption, particularly in 1973, had an enormous impact on industrial and commercial life. In 1972 the Government delayed taking powers until a very late stage. A ten-week overtime ban was followed by the first national coal strike since 1926. This campaign was unexpectedly damaging.[114] Coal stocks were high before the dispute began, and once the action started the Government did nothing apart from implementing a voluntary system of preferential treatment for priority users of coal. They had reckoned without the activities of pickets, who were able to halt the movement of coal and prevent power stations from using much of the coal they had stockpiled.[115] By the time a state of emergency was declared on February 9, coal stocks for domestic and generating use stood at only two weeks' normal supply.[116] Drastic restrictions were introduced immediately. Rota power cuts of up to four hours' duration were ordered; with certain exceptions, the use of electricity for advertising, display and floodlighting was prohibited;[117] restrictions on heating non-domestic premises were imposed;[118] and 20,000 medium-sized industrial concerns (excluding certain essential services and producers) were put onto a three-day week.[119] By the time the restrictions were revoked on March 2, thousands of workers had been laid off.[120]

The Prime Minister, Mr Edward Heath, later acknowledged that his Government had rightly been 'bitterly criticised' for not acting sooner on that occasion,[121] and in 1973 it went to the other extreme, taking powers on the first day of an overtime ban by miners, when power station stocks stood at twelve weeks' supply.[122] A ban on out-of-hours working by electricity power engineers, then on its thirteenth day, was also cited in the proclamation, although this action had had little serious impact.[123] Restrictions on the use of electricity for advertising and display[124] and heating non-domestic premises,[125] which the Government estimated would save 5 per cent of normal consumption,[126] were introduced immediately, and the Government pursued a policy of preventative action towards electricity supplies throughout the dispute. On December 7, when coal stocks still stood at nine to ten weeks' supply, the Government announced that industrial and commercial users of electricity, with some exceptions, would be allowed to use electricity for trade or business purposes for only five days during the two-week period from December 17, and henceforth on only three specified days in any week.[127] The Government rejected calls from the T.U.C. to postpone these restrictions, maintaining that they were essential to ensure that priority power supplies could be guaranteed until the spring. By January 7, 1974, 885,000 workers had been laid off because of these restrictions.[128]

During the debate on the first set of emergency regulations, Opposition M.P.s alleged that the real reason for the proclamation was not the miners' action, which was being given the blame for political reasons, but a 25 per cent cut in deliveries of oil from Arab oil producers. Ministers denied these allegations, but only four days after this debate the Government directed oil companies to reduce deliveries of all main products by 10 per cent as compared with the previous year in order to conserve supplies.[129] The day after that, the method of supplying motor fuel was restricted under the emergency regulations in order to prevent hoarding,[130] and the Fuel and Electricity (Control) Bill received its first reading. This measure, which became law on December 6, gave the Secretary of State for Trade and Industry unrestricted powers to control by Order the production, supply, acquisition and use of fuel and electricity supplies without the need for a proclamation of emergency. There was also no general provision for regular parliamentary supervision of the exercise of these powers.[131] The maximum penalty for contravening the legislation was three months' imprisonment, a £400 fine, or both[132] – a financial penalty £300 greater than that then permitted by the Emergency Powers Act. The substantive provisions of the Fuel and Electricity (Control) Act 1973 were given effect for one year only, but they could be extended for a further year by an Order in Council provided that Parliament approved the extension.[133] In the event the Act was extended twice and remained in force until November 30, 1976, when the Energy Act 1976, discussed later in this chapter, took effect.

The Government claimed that the Fuel and Electricity (Control) Act 1973 was designed to provide the flexibility to deal with long-term energy problems which the Emergency Powers Act lacked, and it intended to use the Act to implement petrol rationing, for which four weeks' administrative preparation was required.[134] (The distribution of petrol coupons began at the end of November, but rationing was not ultimately required.) After the Fuel and Electricity (Control) Act become law, however, all further measures to deal with the general emergency situation, and not just those needing advance preparation, were taken under this Act rather than under the regulations, and orders already made under the regulations were revoked or reimplemented under the Act.[135] Although the state of emergency under the 1920 Act continued throughout the miners' dispute, with industrial action by railwaymen and the reduction in oil supplies to the country being added to the causes in the second proclamation, it seems that no further action was taken under the regulations. The Government justified maintaining them in force on the ground that they might still be needed in connection with transport services.[136]

On February 1, 1974, the miners gave their executive authority to organize an all-out strike, and on February 7 the Prime Minister called a General Election which resulted in the Government's defeat. The incoming Labour administration quickly facilitated the reaching of a settlement, and the three-day week was brought to an end the following day. The new Secretary of State for Energy estimated that the three-day week had cost the country £2,000,000,000;[137] although, since many firms had offered their employees the opportunity to work longer hours on the permitted working days, the fall in industrial output was less than originally expected.[138]

The impact of the 1972 and 1973-4 disputes in the mining industry stands in marked contrast to that of the 1984–85 miners' strike, discussed later in this chapter.

'Emergency disputes' and Government policy

Governments taking emergency powers have generally stressed that they are doing so purely to protect the 'national interest' and not to influence the course or outcome of the dispute in question. Nevertheless, with the exception of the Labour Government in 1924, governments have always denounced the stoppage which has occasioned the emergency and urged a return to work. Moreover, in seven of the twelve emergencies, the Government made clear its own position on the merits of the dispute and this in turn affected its role as peacemaker. All disputes, apart from the three dock strikes, concerned wages, and in six of these the Government had an interest in the terms of settlement, either directly or because the claim was a challenge to its incomes policy. Three of these latter six disputes, together with the 1949 dock strike, were presented as attacks upon the State.

In the 1921 and 1926 coal disputes, the Government had a direct vested interest in the outcome. Both stoppages began when the coal-owners terminated their workers' existing contracts of service and offered re-engagement on (generally) lower terms, determined on a district basis. In both cases any concession to the miners required a Government subsidy, and the Government was involved as a third party in negotiations. In 1921 the Government claimed that the miners' demand for a pooling of profits to finance a national settlement would require permanent Government control of the mines; this had been assumed during the war and later relinquished. They were therefore accused of putting in 'the forefront of. . . their demands a reversal of a decision arrived at by Parliament'.[139] At the outset of the stoppage the Prime Minister made a return to work by safety men a condition of Government good offices in further negotiations. The miners eventually agreed not to intefere with measures taken by the owners and Government to prevent flooding, thereby losing their most powerful weapon in return for talks which failed to produce a settlement.[140] The Government later offered a subsidy to lessen the wage reductions for a temporary period, but the miners continued to reject the proposals put forward until the end of June, when a district settlement on 'terms of defeat'[141] brought the stoppage to an end.

The 1926 dispute had been preceded by the threat of a miners' strike with the support of the railwaymen and transport workers in July 1925. Arrangements were made on that occasion for a state of emergency to be declared,[142] but the Cabinet finally decided that a subsidy to the industry, pending the report of a Royal Commission on its future, would be 'less disadvantageous' than a stoppage.[143] Meanwhile, the Government set in motion intensive administrative preparations, described in Chapter 4, to meet any future strike. The Commission's recommendations[144] were not acceptable to either side, and the Government did little to resolve the resulting deadlock between the parties. The Government responded to overtures from the T.U.C. for an eleventh-hour attempt to avert a General Strike, but then severed negotiations on the ground that instructions for a strike had already been issued and 'overt acts', including 'gross interference with the Press', had taken place, involving a 'challenge to the constitutional rights and freedoms of the nation'.[145] (These 'overt acts' consisted of a refusal by printers to print copies of *The Daily Mail* unless editorials denouncing the stoppage were changed.) The Government presented the General Strike as a challenge to the British constitution, despite T.U.C. protestations that it was simply an industrial stoppage, and ministers refused to countenance further negotiations with the miners until it was called off unconditionally. 'Unofficial' intervention by Sir Herbert Samuel, chairman of the Royal Commission, ended this impasse, and immediately the General Strike was over the Government attempted to settle the miners' dispute. Its proposals were rejected by both sides, however, and the Government took no further steps for another three months. The miners offered to renew negotiations on a national basis which accepted the need for wage reductions early in September, but the owners refused to consider a national settlement. Eventually 'the owners. . . won and the miners lost on all counts' as workers in individual districts sought agreements and the strike 'crumble[d] away'.[146]

The credibility of the Government's incomes policy was at stake in the emergency disputes of 1966, December 1970, January 1972 and 1973–4 (the miners' claim). In 1966, the N.U.S., for years a docile union, demanded the immediate introduction of a forty-hour week at sea and substantial increases in basic wage rates. In a broadcast on the first day of the strike the Prime Minister urged the seamen to accept the 'clear, effective and honourable alternative' of a full inquiry into the dispute and working conditions at sea.[147] He saw the strike as 'a test of Government determination' to preserve its incomes policy[148] and stated that were it to continue it would become 'a strike against the State — against the community'.[149] (In the light of large increases to judges, doctors and civil servants which had recently been approved, some members of the Cabinet found this 'quarrel with the seamen' hard to justify.)[150] The Government took the unusual step of establishing a Court of Inquiry while the strike continued in full swing, but the union executive immediately rejected its interim report, which recommended the introduction of a forty-hour week twelve months hence.[151] The Government made clear that it would oppose a settlement costing more than this report, and the union's General Secretary declared that this was now 'a fight with the Government'.[151] On June 20, Mr Harold Wilson made his famous allegation that the union executive was under the sway of a 'tightly knit group of politically motivated men',[153] and eight days later he named eight Communists whom he accused of using the strike to destroy the Government's incomes policy.[154] The day after these disclosures – 'whether or not because of them is a matter of debate'[155] – the union decided to call off the strike on terms marginally better than those recommended in the interim report.

There was no formal incomes policy in operation in 1970 or early 1972, but the Government was making strenuous attempts to reduce the level of wage settlements, and the electricity workers' and miners' claims ran counter to these efforts. On both occasions the Government denied that the respective employers were forbidden to increase their offers but acknowledged that ministers' concern about inflationary awards had been made known.[156] The electricity workers' action was taken in breach of the industry's agreed procedure, which required resort to arbitration, and the Government initially resisted Opposition demands for a Court of Inquiry but finally succumbed and the action was called off. In 1972 the N.C.B. insisted that its 7.9 per cent offer was the most it could afford, and the Government refused to provide the Board with any additional funds. The offer was increased substantially towards the end of January, however, after three weeks' of strike action. Eventually the Government once more gave in to pressures for a Court of Inquiry. The Court of Inquiry's report recognized the miners' claim for 'exceptional national treatment' and recommended an award which added £85 million to the wages bill.[157] The final terms of settlement added a further £5 million and necessitated an emergency Government grant. This result clearly demonstrated 'how the miners' strike power had been directed against the Government, who alone could meet their wage claim, and not against the N.C.B., which did not have the money'.[158]

There was a statutory incomes policy in force in 1973, and the Government stressed from the outset that the miners' claim was in breach of the terms of this policy and therefore challenged the democratic process.[159] (The miners argued that they simply sought treatment as a 'special case' within the terms of the policy.) A T.U.C. initiative recognized the 'distinctive and exceptional situation in the mining industry' and promised that other unions would not use a settlement outside the pay code as an argument in their own negotiations, but the Government rejected this proposal as containing insufficient guarantees. The Government finally agreed to refer the miners' claim to the statutory Pay Board under a relativities procedure provided for in the policy, but by that time a General Election had been called. On the return of a Labour Government the parties quickly reached a negotiated settlement.

In 1948 and 1949 the Labour Government refused to have any dealings with the leaders of the unofficial dock strikes which provoked states of emergency. The 1948 strike was over disciplinary action taken against eleven workers by the National Dock Labour Board. The Prime Minister, Mr Clement Attlee, urged the strikers to obey their unions' call to return to work and accused the strike organizers of having political motivations. The General Secretary of the T.G.W.U. agreed, alleging that 37 of the 48-strong strike committee were 'Communists or fellow travellers'.[160] The strike ended the day after the Prime Minister's appeal. The 1949 stoppage began when London dockers refused to unload two ships which had been declared 'black' by a Communist-dominated Canadian trade union. The employers refused to call on labour for other work until these ships had been attended to, and the men claimed to have been locked out. The Government denied this. The men were in breach of the dock labour scheme, which required them to take any work which was offered, and it was 'nothing but a Communist manoeuvre to pretend that there. . . was. . . any other explanation of the position'.[161] On announcing the proclamation of emergency, the Home Secretary declared that the Government faced 'a challenge to the whole authority of the State'.[162] Attempts to spread the strike to Tilbury a few days later were unsuccessful, however, and a mass meeting the following day voted to return to work.

Post-war Labour administrations, at least until 1974, seem to have been no less ready than Conservative Governments to take emergency powers. The 1924 Labour Government, however, was keenly embarrassed at having to contemplate the use of the Emergency Powers Act, and it went to considerable lengths to avoid doing so. Although anxious to assert that it was 'a national Government and not a class Government',[163] it did not want to take action which would bring 'a head-on collision with the unions and the party'.[164] The first crisis came with a national dock strike in February, shortly after the Government came into office. The Prime Minister, Mr Ramsey MacDonald, announced that a state of emergency would be declared should negotiations with the T.G.W.U. for the movement of essential supplies not succeed,[165] but the dispute was settled before this became necessary, on terms which conceded the workers' claim for increased wages and referred their other demand, for decasualization of labour, to a committee of both sides of the industry.

The second crisis came little over a month later, when the interim report of a Court of Inquiry into a claim by London tramwaymen[166] failed to terminate a strike they had started. Workers on the London underground threatened to join the stoppage, and the E.T.U. said that it would withdraw its members from power stations if 'blackleg' labour were used to run transport services. MacDonald held a series of conferences with union leaders in which he explained the Government's dilemma, but the T.U.C. General Council and Labour Party executive nevertheless passed a resolution 'deploring' the suggestion that the Emergency Powers Act might have to be invoked.[167] The Prime Minister announced a proclamation of emergency to the House of Commons the same evening, but a compromise settlement was reached the next day; the Government agreed to introduce an 'admittedly unsatisfactory Bill to reorganise London traffic',[168] and on the basis of this the employers felt able to grant a substantial part of the workers' claim. The proclamation was quickly revoked without ever having been published.

The Labour Government claimed that it had pursued a policy of neutrality in both these disputes, stating no opinion on the merits nor condemning the action of either side, but simply following 'the rule of protecting public convenience;. . . the rule that no Government and nobody in authority ought to do anything that makes divisions broader and deeper than, unfortunately, they are when the conditions of a strike have been created'.[169] Macdonald also acknowledged, however, that using emergency powers must inevitably 'interfere with the relationship of the parties to the dispute to secure the convenience of the public'.[170] This latter statement comes nearer to the truth. It is disingenuous and naive to pretend that invoking emergency powers does not affect the relative position of the parties, which, in many 'emergency disputes', have directly or indirectly included the Government. As the previous section indicates, there have been some disputes in which the Government declared a state of emergency at a much earlier stage than appeared strictly necessary. Alongside official explanations of the need to take precautions must be considered the Government's desire to underline the message that industrial action is harmful to the nation's interests. The decision to invoke the Emergency Powers Act cannot be looked at in isolation from broader aspects of a Government's policy.

'Emergency disputes' since 1974

The Emergency Powers Act 1920 has not been invoked since 1974, although, as Chapter 4 describes, the power to use troops without declaring a state of emergency has been exercised on several occasions. In addition, special legislation, which is outlined below, was enacted to deal with disruption in areas outside the scope of the 1920 Act. The non-use of the Emergency Powers Act is not, however, due to a lack of disputes falling within its terms; rather', it reflects the fact that governments since 1974 have preferred to adopt alternative strategies for safeguarding supplies.

The strategy of the Labour Government of 1974–9 one of co-operation with the unions. In 1979 a strike in the 'hire and reward' section of the road haulage industry, affecting about 35 per cent of all heavy goods vehicles, disrupted deliveries of food and other essential supplies. There was heavy picketing of docks and industrial concerns which employed their own drivers. The Government came under strong pressure from Opposition parties to declare a state of emergency at the outset. Mrs Thatcher maintained a proclamation would 're-establish the authority of Parliament'[171] and urged the Government to take powers immediately rather than waiting until the dispute had escalated.

The Government affirmed a readiness to declare a state of emergency or to send in troops should the need arise, but preferred to rely in the first instance on the operation of a code of practice it had drafted. This code listed priority supplies which should not be impeded and banned secondary picketing, and the unions in dispute – the T.G.W.U. and U.R.T.U. – agreed to recommend that their members should adhere to its provisions. Ministers argued that the 1920 Act should not be used for 'purely cosmetic reactions';[172] troops could move only 'a small fraction of the goods' which could be transported if the voluntary arrangements were successful,[173] and a proclamation would only serve to 'accentuate the dispute'.[174] Regional Emergency Committees, composed of civil servants from various government departments and representatives of local authorities, the police and the military, monitored the situation at local level and reported difficulties to Government officials in London. These officials held daily meetings with union leaders to identify problem areas. Although ministers admitted that adherance to the code of practice was far from uniform, with some local strike committees refusing to follow it, they continued to assert that the policy of co-operation maintained supplies more effectively than taking emergency powers would have done. This was probably correct; there were no prolonged shortages of any basic foodstuffs, and although shortages of raw materials led to some 235,000 workers being laid off and manufacturing production being reduced by about 10 per cent,[175] this situation would not have been improved significantly by using troops. The main consequence of the failure to invoke emergency powers was its effect on the Government's public image. One political commentator wrote that the Government 'seemed to have contracted the handling of the emergency to Mr Moss Evans' (the T.G.W.U. leader), whereas declaring a state of emergency would have been 'some sign of the Government's determination to stand up to the agents of coercion in the interests of the nation at large'.[176] This kind of argument reinforces the view that declaring a state of emergency may have more to do with strengthening resolve to 'fight' a dispute rather than with the real exigencies of the situation.

Despite Mrs Thatcher's exhortations in 1979, neither of her subsequent Conservative administrations has regarded the Emergency Powers Act as a first-line response to major disputes. The Government did not rush to proclaim a state of emergency when rail strikes began in 1982 (these proved short-lived) not when a water strike occurred in 1983. The water strike, described in detail in Chapter 5, did not produce the appalling consequences which contingency planners had feared, largely due to union self-restraint, and the Government was anxious not to jeopardize co-operation by strikers and by managerial and supervisory staff in maintaining supplies. The use of troops, and possibly a state of emergency, was on the agenda when an eleven-day dock strike began in July 1984, but the action ended before either of these steps were taken.

One-third of the emergencies declared under the 1920 Act have been occasioned by industrial action in the coalmining industry, and as earlier described, both the disputes of the early 1970s necessitated drastic restrictions on electricity consumption. In contrast, the year-long miners' strike which began in March 1984 had no significant impact on power supplies, and the Government was able to ride out the strike without invoking emergency measures. A number of factors contributed to this. First, preparations had been made for a stoppage in the mines for at least two years before the strike began. Coal stocks at pitheads were high, and the electricity authorities had been under 'steady pressure' to build up their coal stocks 'and to keep even heavily uneconomic oil-burning [generating] capacity in working order'.[177]

Once the strike began, the emphasis in electricity generation shifted from 'cost efficiency to coal-stock preservation',[178] and maximum use was made of nuclear and oil-burning stations. The Government was determined to avoid restrictions on electricity consumption, whatever the cost, and the decision by the Nottinghamshire miners to continue working facilitated this process. Another important factor was the extensive police operation which was mounted to prevent mass secondary picketing. Mutual aid between forces was co-ordinated by the 'National Reporting Centre' under the operational command of the President of the Association of Chief Police Officers. (This Centre was established after the 1972 miners' strike.) Lastly, a lack of practical support by other workers diminished the impact of the stoppage.

The effectiveness of the Conservative Government's strategy in dealing with the miners' strike has led to the suggestion that

> it will not be necessary either to use troops or even to invoke the Emergency Powers Act 1920 in any forseeable future dispute. In effect a more sophisticated pattern of response to major industrial disputes has been established, tested and (from the Government's point of view) vindicated.[179]

This seems too hasty a conclusion to reach. As Chapter 4 indicates, the post-1979 Conservative Governments have used or contemplated using troops on several occasions, and it is difficult to imagine how any police operation or contingency plan, however effective, could have prevented the circumstances which occasioned their deployment occurring. As far as the 1920 Act is concerned, manual workers in the electricity supply industry are certainly capable of disrupting normal supplies,[180] and there are many other situations where a government may wish to direct, ration or requisition supplies or equipment or to remove existing statutory restrictions on the maintenance of supplies. Moreover, it may be more difficult for a government of a different political complexion to condone the use of the police as the 'agency by which. . . [a] strike. . . [is] contained'.[181] For political or practical reasons, invoking the Emergency Powers Act may not be the most favoured response of a particular government to a dispute within its terms, but declaring a state of emergency enables the executive to take extraordinary measures which it could not effect lawfully by other means. As such it remains a highly significant governmental power.

Controlling the executive

The General Secretary of the National Council for Civil Liberties, writing in 1940, denounced the Emergency Powers Act as a 'constant menace' to British civil liberties, enabling the executive 'to weight the scales heavily against those who may be in active opposition to the government of the day'.[182] Defenders of the legislation would argue that Parliament can restrain any excesses by refusing to approve the continuance of offending regulations, and should a Government attempt to introduce measures which exceed the terms of the legislation, the courts could intervene to declare them invalid. This section considers briefly how effective either of these forms of control over the executive are likely to be in practice.

In the House of Commons, Opposition M.P.s have opposed the motion that emergency regulations should continue in force on several occasions; in 1921, 1926,[183] February 1972 and November 1973 the House was divided along party lines; in 1949 and July 1970 small groups of M.P.s voted against continuance. The House of Lords has been divided only once, in 1972. Sometimes opposition has been designed to protest against the way the Government has approached a dispute rather than specifically to oppose the taking of powers. In February 1972 the vote was to show displeasure at the Government's handling of the situation and because, if unequivocal approval of the powers had been given, there would have been no guarantee that the Government would not 'use them to prolong the strike rather than to settle it'.[184] In 1973 it was alleged that the true cause of the emergency was the reduction in oil supplies from the Arab states, and the Government was acting disingenuously in blaming the miners for the crisis.[185] In each case the Government's majority was sufficiently substantial not to put the regulations at risk.

The Emergency Powers Act provides that regulations may be 'added to, altered or revoked by resolution of both Houses of Parliament' (s.2(4)).[186] Opposition M.P.s in 1921 and 1926 attempted to force the exclusion of regulations restricting freedom of speech and assembly but without success, and no specific amendments have been put forward since the war. On only two occasions has debate in Parliament led to changes in the regulations: in 1921, when the Home Secretary agreed to omit two regulations and a part of a third, and in 1973. On the latter occasion the Joint Committee on Statutory Instruments had reported that a regulation which made it an offence to impair the efficiency or impede the working of any object used for performing essential services could infringe the spirit of the proviso preventing the proscription of strikes by making industrial action short of a strike an offence.[187] The regulation was redrafted to make clear that industrial action was not included in the activities prohibited.[188]

It seems fair to conclude that, while the Emergency Powers Act appears to guarantee parliamentary control over the exercise of the powers it bestows (when these powers are taken for any length of time), in practice the extent of this control is limited and compliance with the procedure is more a matter of form than an effective method of checking the executive. To some extent this has been the fault of Parliament itself. The Act obliges the Government to account for and justify its actions, and those who are concerned about civil liberties could take greater comfort if Parliament were to subject the powers taken to more rigorous scrutiny and to object to those which are not required, rather than simply to accept a full code of regulations on each occasion regardless of the nature of the emergency.

Control over the executive by the courts is likely to be equally limited. Broadly speaking, measures taken under the Emergency Powers Act are in theory open to challenge in the courts on the ground either that the executive has acted outside the terms of the substantive powers granted by the statute (or by an instrument made under it) or that it has failed to adhere to the prescribed procedures for retaining powers, although, as the discussion below explains, it is unlikely that these procedures would be found to be legally binding. A challenge could arise directly through an application for judicial review, through an action for damages, a declaration, or injunctive relief, or through an application for *habeas corpus* by or on behalf of a person detained under the regulations.[189] Alternatively, it could arise collaterally by way of a defence to criminal prosecution or a civil action against the State. In the absence of any challenge, administrative action is presumed to be valid, and the courts do not act of their own motion. On two occasions high-ranking ministers have argued that the chances of challenge were sufficiently slight to justify taking powers which were outside the scope of the Act. The 1926 regulations conferred powers on local authorities which the Law Officers decided in 1936 were not authorized by section 2(1) of the Emergency Powers Act because local authority workers are not 'in Her Majesty's service or acting on Her Majesty's behalf'. This meant that there was no legal authority for food and coal distribution schemes which local authorities had operated during the General Strike. The Home Secretary in 1936, Sir Herbert Samuel, decided that it was preferable to risk an action in the courts in any future emergency rather than to amend the Act to extend powers to local authorities. He argued:

> if the Regulations were challenged it would be during an emergency and the challenge would not be well received by the House of Commons so that the conditions for getting amending legislation would be more favourable.[190]

An equally sanguine approach was adopted in 1949 by the Labour Attorney-General, Sir Hartley Shawcross, when he proposed taking the 'risk' of introducing regulations covering

> matters on which action is required without undue regard to the niceties of the law. In an emergency the Government may have, in matters admitting of legal doubt, to act first and argue about the doubts later, if necessary obtaining an indemnification Act.[191]

This rather relaxed attitude to the law was probably not unrealistic, although of questionable constitutional propriety; on only one occasion, discussed below, has action taken under the Emergency Powers Act been challenged in the courts.

There are a number of grounds on which a court may conclude that a person or body entrusted with discretionary powers by statute has acted outside these powers (or acted *ultra vires*). The principles which the bearer of discretion must adhere to have been summarized as follows:

> In general, a discretion must be exercised only by the authority to which it is committed. That authority must genuinely address itself to the matters before it: it must not act under the dictation of another body or disable itself from exercising a discretion in each individual case. In the purported exercise of its discretion it must not do what it has been forbidden to do nor must it do what it has not been authorised to do. It must act in good faith, must have regard to all relevant considerations and must not be swayed by irrelevant considerations, must not seek to promote purposes alien to the letter or to the spirit of the legislation that gives it power to act, and must not act arbitrarily or capriciously. Nor where a judgement must be made that certain facts exist can a discretion be validly exercised on the basis of an erroneous assumption about those facts.[192]

It has been emphasized, however that 'there is no universal rule as to the principles on which the exercise of a discretion may be reviewed: each statute or type of statute must be individually looked at'.[193] The scope for review in any given case will depend upon

> the wording of the discretionary power, the subject-matter to which it is related, the character of the authority to which it is entrusted, the purpose for which it is conferred, the particular circumstances in which it has in fact been exercised, the materials

> available to the court and, in the last analysis, whether a court is of the opinion that judicial intervention would be in the public interest.[194]

In times of emergency the courts have taken a cautious approach; in cases arising out of the two world wars the judicial attitude was 'very much one of deference to the executive',[195] and despite the development of a more interventionist approach generally in recent years, the courts still exercise self-restraint where national security is shown to be at stake or speedy action is required.[196] The courts have also been more reluctant to intervene where a power is given to a government minister who is directly answerable to Parliament for the way it is used on the basis that Parliament will restrain any excesses.[197] The requirement for the regulations to come before Parliament about once a month for renewal would probably reinforce judicial caution in this area.[198]

In the light of these considerations, the scope for judicial review of the existence of an emergency under the Emergency Powers Act, which is couched in terms of executive opinion, seems very limited. The courts may simply hold that the question of whether the conditions for issuing a proclamation have been satisfied is non-justiciable, either because this is a political decision or because it requires knowledge of confidential information.[199] Even if it were held to be technically justiciable, a plaintiff may find it hard to prove that a proclamation is *ultra vires* in practice because

> the policies followed and the steps taken by the responsible Government may be founded on information and apprehensions which are not known to, and cannot always be made known to, those who seek to impugn what has been done.[200]

Bad faith cannot be imputed to the Crown,[201] and it is unlikely that a proclamation, or other evidence, would demonstrate patently that the executive had not formed the opinion that the requisite state of affairs existed. Even if a court were to conclude that the decision that a state of emergency existed could not have been reached without an element of misdirection as to the law or facts, this may not be fatal in the context of an emergency.[202]

As far as the regulations are concerned, it has been suggested that the power to make them, which is based on executive opinion as to their necessity, 'is so widely drawn that it would be difficult to establish that any such regulation was ultra vires'.[203] The courts refused to examine the necessity for exercising a similarly-worded power in the Emergency Powers (Defence) Act 1939 on any ground,[204] and in *McEldowney* v.

Forde[205] the majority of the House of Lords held that even where a power was expressed in objective terms, if its exercise in a particular manner was capable of being related to the prescribed purposes, the expediency of exercising it would be presumed. A court may infer misdirection if there appear to be no grounds on which a reasonable authority could have considered a regulation necessary,[206] but in the absence of this improbable contingency it seems unlikely that a court would find a regulation *ultra vires* for not being in furtherance of the prescribed purposes. A regulation which conflicted with one of the three limitations on the regulation-making power, however, would almost certainly not be applied by the courts. (These forbid the imposition of compulsory military service or industrial conscription, making it an offence to strike or peacefully persuade others to do so, and altering existing criminal procedure or giving the right to punish without trial.)

It was in this connection that the single legal challenge to the validity of the regulations occurred. In a prosecution arising out of the 1926 dispute, the defendant was found to have distributed to colliery managers copies of a resolution stating that safety-men would be withdrawn from local mines if coal were raised for purposes other than safety. He was charged with distributing a document containing a statement whose publication was calculated to impede, delay or restrict the supply or distribution of fuel contrary to the 1926 regulations. The Divisional Court quashed his conviction by magistrates on the ground, *inter alia*, that the second proviso protected such action, which was 'naturally and ordinarily involved in taking part in a strike or peacefully persuading others to do so'.[207] It is less easy to predict the attitude of the courts towards regulations which infringe the spirit rather than the letter of a proviso, such as regulations which suspended the statutory immunities against civil liability for strikes or which made it an offence to take industrial action short of a strike. (As previously mentioned, a regulation appearing in various codes since 1949 which could have had the latter effect was redrafted in 1973 to make clear that it did not do so.)

It is not entirely clear whether internment could be ordered under the 1920 Act. In *R.* v. *Halliday*[208] the power under the Defence of the Realm (Consolidation) Act 1914 to issue regulations 'for securing public safety and the defence of the realm' was held to authorize internment. It can be argued that internment is capable of being related to the purposes for which regulations may be made under the Emergency Powers Act. If this is so, the proviso which prevents regulations altering criminal procedure or punishment without trial would probably not invalidate internment orders, which can be seen as preventative measures rather than punishment.[209] Internment would, however, offend against article 5 of the European Convention on Human Rights, and an individual victim who had exhausted domestic remedies, or another signatory State, could take a complaint to the European Commission. As was stated earlier, article 15 of the Convention permits states to derogate from certain obligations '[i]n time of war or other public emergency threatening the life of the nation' but only to 'the extent strictly required by the exigencies of the situation' and 'provided that such measures are not inconsistent with. . . [their] other obligations under international law'. Both the Commission and the European Court of Human Rights have held that they may make their own determination as to whether an emergency exists and whether derogations are 'strictly required', but they allow a 'margin of appreciation' to the national government.[210] The Court has defined an emergency under Article 15 as 'an exceptional situation of crisis or emergency which affects the whole population and constitutes a threat to the organized life of the community of which the state is composed'.[211] This definition is clearly narrower than that contained in the Emergency Powers Act, and the United Kingdom may therefore not be able to avail itself of article 15 in all states of emergency.

Finally, it seems unlikely that a Government's failure to comply with the procedural provisions of the Emergency Powers Act would in fact affect the legal validity of the powers taken. Given that the proclamation and regulations take immediate effect, such compliance can be at most a condition subsequent to validity. There is no authority on whether a requirement to communicate the occasion of a proclamation to Parliament is mandatory or directory,[212] but the cases favour the view that a requirement to lay regulations – on which the requirement to obtain parliamentary approval for their continuance depends – is merely directory.[213] Moreover, a requirement may be held directory explicitly on grounds of convenience,[214] and this argument may well apply here, given that the existence of regulations could scarcely escape Parliament's attention. Even if the procedural requirements were held to be mandatory, 'forthwith'and 'as soon as may be', which set the time limits on compliance, cannot be defined with precision. Political pressure, therefore, would probably be the only remedy available against a government which refused to follow the procedure prescribed by the Act.

THE ENERGY ACT 1976

The Energy Act 1976 replaced the Fuel and Electricity (Control) Act 1973, which was passed during the 1973 state of emergency declared under the 1920 Act and was kept in force until the Energy Act came into operation. Section 1 of the Energy Act gives the Secretary of State standing powers to control by Order the production, supply, acquisition and use of crude liquid petroleum, natural gas, petroleum products, any other substance used as fuel, and electricity, where he considers such measures desirable to conserve energy. These powers include powers to fix maximum prices for petroleum products and to give directions to maintain at specified levels petroleum stocks and fuel stocks at power stations (ss. 1(4), 6,7). In addition, the executive, by Order in Council, may modify or exclude any statutory obligation or restriction which affects the use of a substance covered by the Act (s.4(3)).

Section 2 of the Energy Act gives the Secretary of State more extensive powers of direction over individual producers, suppliers or users of substances covered by the Act when an Order in Council under section 3 is in force. Such an Order may be made in one of two situations. The first is where the United Kingdom's international obligations, which arise from membership of the European Communities and the International Energy Authority and from signature of the International Energy Agreement, require emergency measures to be taken to deal with a reduction or threatened reduction in fuel supplies. The second is where

> there exists or is imminent in the United Kingdom an actual or threatened emergency affecting fuel or electricity supplies which makes it necessary in Her Majesty's opinion that the Government should temporarily have at its disposal exceptional powers for controlling the sources and availability of energy.

The Order must be laid before Parliament and, if made for the second of these reasons, must be approved by both Houses within twenty-eight days of being made if it is to remain in force. It has effect for twelve months, but Parliament may renew it for a further twelve. Once such an Order is in force, the powers the Government may take include issuing directions to producers of substances covered by the Act which prohibit or restrict the use of materials used in production; issuing directions to suppliers which prohibit or restrict supply to specified persons or require supply to specified persons; and issuing directions to users which prohibit or restrict use for specified purposes or during specified periods (s.2(2)). The Secretary of State may authorize a supplier or user of any of the specified substances to disregard any statutory or contractual obligation relating to or involving the supply or use of that substance (s.4(1)). The existence of an Order in Council also extends the power to fix maximum prices to crude liquid petroleum and natural gas, and enables the Secretary of State to relax certain road traffic and transport restrictions so as to permit unlicensed vehicles to operate as public carriage vehicles and unlicensed persons to drive public service vehicles and to relax rules as to drivers' hours (ss. 1(4), 4(2), Sched. 1).

It is an offence to contravene any provision of the Energy Act, or any Order or direction issued under it, without reasonable excuse, or to wilfully obstruct any person exercising a power or duty deriving from the Act (s.18(2)). Schedule 2 gives powers to request information, call for documents, and enter premises for inspection and enforcement purposes. In the absence of an Order in Council under section 3, offences are punishable by a maximum fine of £2,000, although failing to comply with controls on prices can attract an unlimited fine (ss. 19(1),(2)). When an Order in Council under section 3 is in force, offences are punishable by up to two years' imprisonment, an unlimited fine, or both (ss. 19(3), (4)). The penalties for contravening the Energy Act during an emergency are therefore considerably higher than those permitted under the Emergency Powers Act, which lays down a maximum penalty of three months' imprisonment, a fine of £2,000, or both.[215]

The Energy Act 1976 has not yet been invoked in the context of an industrial dispute; indeed, there have been no section 3 Orders to date for any reason. As previously described, the Government was able to use similar powers contained in the Fuel and Electricity (Control) Act to deal with the 1973–4 emergency, and the Energy Act might well furnish sufficient powers for any future dispute involving energy supplies provided that powers such as requisitioning were not required. Using the 1976 Act would avoid the political repercussions of declaring a full-scale state of emergency. It would also give Parliament considerably less formal control over the executive's response to the situation. A section 3 Order in Council requires approval within twenty-eight days of being made and then continues in force for a year, and there is no requirement for directions or Orders to be given approval.[216] By contrast, regulations issued under the Emergency Powers Act must be approved within seven days of being laid and require renewal every month. Given the greater opportunity for parliamentary debate which it provides, it would seem preferable from the viewpoint of democratic accountability for the 1920 Act to be used where the threat to energy supplies has been caused by industrial action.

AD HOC EMERGENCY LEGISLATION

On three occasions in recent years *ac hoc* legislation has been introduced in response to crises outside the scope of the Emergency Powers Act 1920 or the Energy Act 1976. In 1979 industrial action by civil servants in furtherance of a national pay dispute seriously interfered with the operation of the Scottish courts. The Court of Session, the High Court of Justiciary and the sheriff courts dealt only with certain categories of urgent business, and procedural time limits laid down by the courts were suspended.[217] After four weeks of disruption, the Labour Government introduced the Administration of Justice (Emergency Provisions) (Scotland) Act 1979. The purpose of this Act was to 'preserve rights which would otherwise be irretrievably lost'[218] during the 'emergency period', which ran from February 23, one month before the legislation came into force, until a date prescribed by the Secretary of State for Scotland (s.1). Detention during the 'emergency period' did not count in computing the 110 days for which an accused person can be held in custody without trial in Scotland,[219] and time limits relating to civil and criminal proceedings which expired during the 'emergency period' were extended until one month after the end of that period (ss.3,2). Judges were authorized to do the work of any officer of the court and could also authorize other people to do such work provided the consent of the Secretary of State had been obtained (s.5). The requirement for such consent was designed to remove 'any suggestion that the judges. . . [had] . . . been given a "strike breakers" charter'.[220] The 'emergency period' ended on May 28, shortly after the dispute had been settled.

The Imprisonment (Temporary Provisions) Act 1980 was hurriedly enacted after three weeks of a campaign by prison officers to secure meal-break allowances. Their industrial action, which was on a scale unprecedented in the prison service, prevented essential maintenance work being carried out, closed some prison workshops, and led to a serious deterioration in conditions in many prisons. Most serious for the Government was the refusal of prison officers at many establishments to receive prisoners remanded in custody or sentenced by the courts. By the time the legislation was introduced, some 3,500 people who would otherwise have been in prison were being held in police cells.[221]

The Act permitted prisoners to be detained in 'any place' in England and Wales approved by the Home Secretary, and any person who was made responsible for their custody was given, like a prison officer, all the powers, authority, protection and privileges of a constable (s.1).[222] An unfinished dispersal prison, Frankland, and an army camp, Rollestone, were designated approved places. Both establishments were run by senior prison staff in conjunction with the armed forces and the police, and up to 955 prisoners were held there during the course of the dispute.[223] Specific authority was also given to keep prisoners in police cells where it was 'not practicable' to secure their admission to a prison or other institution (s.6), and the numbers detained in often very cramped and unhygenic conditions rose at one point to 4,028.[224]

Another provision, designed to deal with the problem of prison officers refusing to readmit prisoners, enabled prisoners remanded in custody to be further remanded in their absence unless the remanding magistrates specifically required their presence (s.2). To meet objections that prisoners' chances of being given bail would be prejudiced, the Home Secretary asked the courts to consider granting legal aid at the first remand hearing so they would have legal representation from an early stage.[225] The Home Secretary was also given powers to order the release of unconvicted or unsentenced prisoners and the early release of particular classes of prisoner to 'make the best use of the places available for detention', and to order magistrates' courts not to imprison for non-payment of money (ss.3,5,4). None of these powers was used. However, a Home Office Circular, despatched shortly before the Act came into force, asked courts to use fines or suspended sentences instead of prison whenever possible, and it was later estimated that 55 per cent of the 2,500 to 3,000 drop in the prison population during the dispute was due to magistrates and judges avoiding prison sentences for those in the under eighteen-month sentence group.[226]

The Imprisonment (Temporary Provisions) Act was given effect for twelve months, with a power for the Home Secretary to extend its operation by Order for a further twelve months provided that Parliament approved the extension within forty days of the Order being made (s.8). Most of the substantive provisions required monthly parliamentary approval to remain in force. In fact, despite its title, the Act has been renewed on an annual basis since its enactment, and the power to hold prisoners in police cells, which does not require monthly renewal, still remains in force. The Home Secretary could reactivate by Order the remainder of the powers provided that Parliament gave its approval to this. The power contained in the 1980 Act to order the early release of prisoners to make the best use of available places has now been placed on a permanent basis by section 32 of the Criminal Justice Act 1982.

For the sake of completeness, mention should also be made of regulations issued during a dispute involving registrars of births, marriages and deaths in 1982.[227] As part of their industrial action, this group was refusing to submit certain returns to the Registrar General. These regulations laid down time limits for the submission of this information and provided that registrars would be fined by the Registrar General if they failed to comply with these time limits.

THE INDUSTRIAL RELATIONS ACT 1971

The emergency procedures contained in the Industrial Relations Act

1971 ss. 138–45, which was repealed in 1974, allowed the executive, with judicial sanction, to interfere directly in the conduct of 'emergency' disputes by imposing a 'cooling-off' period or compulsory ballot of the work-force. They were intended to make states of emergency under the 1920 Act unnecessary. They were singularly unsuccessful in achieving that aim, and it is of value to consider the reasons why this was so.

Sections 138–45 were inspired by the American Taft-Hartley Act of 1947, ss. 206–10. Briefly, this Act enables the President of the United States to appoint a board of inquiry whenever in his opinion a work stoppage affecting an entire industry or a 'substantial part' will 'imperil the national health or safety'. The board reports to the President on the facts of the dispute, and this report is made public. The President may then direct the Attorney-General to petition a district court for an injunction to enjoin the stoppage, and provided the court finds that the conditions as to the extent and impact of the action are met, which it almost invariably does, it must grant the injunction. While the injunction is in force, the parties are under a duty to try to reach a settlement, and they are assisted in this by the Federal Mediation and Conciliation Service. If no settlement has been reached after sixty days, the original board of inquiry reports to the President on the current position of the parties, the efforts made towards a settlement, and the employer's last offer. The National Labor Relations Board then conducts a secret ballot within the next fifteen days of all employees involved in the dispute on whether they wish to accept that offer. At the end of eighty days, the injunction must be discharged and the parties are then free to resume the strike or lock-out. The President is supposed to submit a 'full and comprehensive report of the proceedings' to Congress, but this is rarely done.[228]

Much of the debate preceding the introduction of the Industrial Relations Act procedures centred on 'scant and misleading' reference to the American experience.[229] The Donovan Commission had concluded that the success rate of the Taft–Hartley provisions did not encourage emulation, and that the British Government's flexibility of response was to be preferred to the 'more rigid arrangements of the cooling-off period'.[230] Labour spokesmen echoed these arguments in opposing the provisions. The Conservatives, however, claimed that the American experience had been a success; that their own proposals, which were more flexible than those contained in the Taft-Hartley Act, cured any defects in that Act; and that the procedures, far from restricting the Government's freedom of choice, provided an 'additional weapon' in the 'armoury' which increased 'the room for manoeuvre'.[231]

Under the Industrial Relations Act, the Secretary of State for Employment could apply to the National Industrial Relations Court for a 'cooling-off' order of up to sixty days if he considered that there was an 'emergency situation' and delay or discontinuance of the industrial action causing the emergency would be conducive to a settlement by negotiation, conciliation or arbitration (s.138). The length of the cooling-off period was determined by the court. Alternatively or consecutively, he could apply for a ballot order if he thought first that there was reason to doubt whether workers wished to participate in the action and had been afforded an adequate opportunity of expressing their wishes, and secondly that the action either would lead to an 'emergency situation' or was likely to be seriously injurious to the livelihood of a substantial number of workers in the industry (s.141). Industrial action was then prohibited until the result of the ballot was known.

The definition of an 'emergency situation' was considerably broader than in the 1920 Act; it covered industrial action which caused or would cause

> an interruption in the supply of goods or in the provision of services of such a nature, or on such a scale, as to be likely (a) to be gravely injurious to the national economy, to imperil national security or to create a serious risk of public disorder, or (b) to endanger the lives of a substantial number of persons, or to expose a substantial number. . . to serious risk of disease or personal injury (s.138(2)).

The reference to the national economy seemed to allow intervention in most major disputes and disputes involving small groups of workers producing supplies for larger plants; indeed, as Sir Otto Kahn-Freund remarked at the time, 'one wonder[ed] how many strikes of any importance' would be outside the definition.[232] Theoretically, the court was required to be 'satisfied on the evidence' that there were 'sufficient grounds for believing' that an emergency situation existed, and the Government claimed that the court would thereby act as a 'watchdog' against abuse of the procedure.[223] It would have been a bold judge who overrode the Secretary of State's opinion, however, and Opposition criticism that the process merely enabled the minister to 'shelter behind the decision of a court and thus avoid answering for his actions' seemed justified.[234] Strangely, the court could exercise independent scrutiny only over the 'highly political question' of whether an emergency existed;[235] it was left to the Secretary of State to decide whether the remaning conditions were satisfied, and the courts could intervene only if he had misdirected himself, had taken into account extraneous considerations or had acted in bad faith.[236]

Another criticism of the procedures was the speed with which they forced the courts to act. In *Secretary of State for Employment* v. *A.S.L.E.F. (No. 2)*[237] the Court of Appeal took account of the exigencies of an emergency in declaring that the Secretary of State's error about the nature of the action which one of the unions was taking – which led him to conclude mistakenly that it was taking 'industrial action' as defined in the Act — was not fatal to his application for a ballot order. Lord Denning explained that the procedure had

> to be set in motion quickly, when there is no time for minute analysis of facts or of law. The whole process would be made of no effect if the Minister's decision was afterwards to be conned over word by word, letter by letter, to see if he has in any way misdirected himself.[238]

However, as Roskill L.J. stated in the same case, '[t]he judicial process cannot be conducted under the heat of the pressure of events or of the pressure of time',[239] and the role of the courts in these procedures was incongruous.

> In requiring the Industrial Relations Court to 'rubber-stamp' the Minister's view. . ., the Act went far towards making the Court an arm of Government, not part of the independent arm of the Judiciary.[240]

The emergency powers under the Industrial Relations Act were used only once, during a rail dispute over wages in 1972. Under pressure from the Government, which was attempting to de-escalate the level of wage settlements, the employers had met the unions' claim for a 16 per cent increase with a final offer of 11 per cent, and the unions began a work-to-rule and ban on overtime, rest-day and Sunday working. This immediately affected services, with reductions of over 50 per cent on some routes, and after two days of action the Secretary of State applied for a 21-day cooling-off order. The unions were not represented at the hearing, in accordance with T.U.C. policy. The Court accepted the affidavit evidence of two civil servants that the interruption to the supply of goods and commutor services was likely to cause grave injury to the national economy. Sir John Donaldson granted an order, but for only fourteen days, pointing out that it was 'a feature of industrial life that situations and attitudes. . . [could] change with great rapidity'[241] and that it was always possible for the Minister to apply for an extension. Much to ministers' relief, the unions complied with the order and instructed their members to resume normal working. As the Government was not prepared to allow British Rail to exceed its previous offer, however, further talks failed to advance a settlement. The General Secretary of the N.U.R. later complained that the cooling-off period had been 'the greatest period of inactivity we have had. Since. . . [it] began, we have had only four hours of negotiation with the board in fourteen days'.[242]

Once the cooling-off period had expired, the unions decided to reimpose their sanctions. On the evening before they were due to start, the Minister applied for a ballot order. This time the unions were represented, the T.U.C. having voted to change its policy on this issue. The hearing began at 8.30 on the evening of the application, despite protests by the unions that this left them insufficient time to prepare their case. At midnight it was adjourned until the following day. The appeal proceedings began the day after that, a Sunday. Both the National Industrial Relations Court and the Court of Appeal rejected the unions' argument that their members supported the action; that they did not was a view which 'a reasonable Minister might entertain'.[243] A postal ballot was ordered, and twenty-one days given for reporting the result to the court. 'Of those eligible 85 per cent voted, of those 84 per cent voted "yes" to the question of whether they were in favour of industrial action'.[224] Before industrial action could resume once more, the Government authorized British Rail to exceed its previous limit and fresh negotiations finally produced a settlement of over 13 per cent.

> Opinion on the use of the emergency procedures. . . generally held that from the Government's and British Rail's points of view it failed. While it had put off. . . industrial action, it did not noticeably promote a settlement. . . The ballot strengthened the union's negotiating position and it was only after the emergency procedures were exhausted that British Rail and the unions reached a settlement.[245]

To some extent they were never given a fair chance. The application for a cooling-off order was in the circumstances highly

> disingenous. . . [A provision] conceived to operate in a situation where industrial relations were unaffected by government policies on wages, was being used as a device for supporting what remained of the government wages policy. The time gained did not resolve the dilemma.[246]

In the end, invoking the procedures failed to support the policy, and 'their use for this purpose had discredited the Act'.[247] The Government tacitly acknowledged their failure by choosing not to invoke them in later disputes where it might have done so, preferring to declare a state of emergency in the cases of the 1972 dock strike and the 1973 campaigns by miners, electricity power engineers and railwaymen.

The Industrial Relations Act was repealed in 1974. It has sometimes been suggested that emergency procedures along the lines of those contained in that Act should be reintroduced, but the subsequent Conservative Government's Green Paper on Trade Union Immunities, published in 1981,[248] was singularly unenthusiastic about this idea. It took a much less rosy view of the American legislation than the Heath administration had done, observing that the compulsory ballots had nearly always endorsed the original decision to strike and that 'it may be counter-productive for the Government to become involved in trying to find a settlement'.[249] Pre-strike ballots are now becoming a regular feature of the British industrial relations scene — official industrial action which is taken without a ballot has no civil immunity[250] — but the Government is not involved in enforcing them; the remedy lies only with affected employers. It seems unlikely that a British Government would readily wish to risk repeating the experience of the 1972 rail strike.

CONCLUSION

The Emergency Powers Act 1920 enables the executive to assume extensive powers to deal with the consequences of industrial action in a wide range of industries and services. Its scope has been generously interpreted by governments both in terms of the population affected and the damage suffered. Where services falling outside the purview of the Act have been disrupted, both Labour and Conservative Governments have been prepared to introduce *ad hoc* measures to alleviate the situation.

From the outset, all Governments have denied that the Emergency Powers Act is designed to promote or protect any sectional interest. Nevertheless, emergency powers necessarily lessen the impact of industrial action and to that extent they reduce trade union power. Moreover, the rhetoric of 'neutrality' is belied by the fact that official spokesmen have generally condemned the stoppages which caused the emergency, and on six of the twelve occasions when the Act has been invoked, the Government of the day had an interest in the terms on which the dispute was settled, either directly or because the survival of an incomes policy was at stake. On those occasions it is hard to separate the protection of essential supplies from the protection of Government policies. Declaring a state of emergency can be a useful tactic in this context; in 1966, in particular, the proclamation had more to do with portraying the seamen as 'enemies of the State' than with the exigencies of the situation. Conversly, the decision not to impose voltage reductions or electricity supply restrictions during the miners' strike of 1984–5, which would have been a useful way of stretching out coal reserves, reflected the Government's determination to demonstrate the miners' impotence. The 'adversarial' nature of the Government's handling of many emergencies is a theme which is taken up again in the chapter which follows.

The influence which Parliament has exercised over the use of the Emergency Powers Act has been minimal. M.P.s generally have failed to subject the powers taken to any serious scrutiny, and politicians of all major parties have connived in the policy of issuing a full code of emergency regulations on each occasion regardless of the circumstances. This practice, which is in conflict with the principles of the European Convention on Human Rights, is extremely undesirable in a democratic society, which should adopt emergency powers only when strictly necessary. Accountability for the use of these powers is also crucial. For this reason, it would be preferable for the Emergency Powers Act, rather than the Energy Act 1976, to be invoked when energy supplies are threatened by industrial action.

The Emergency Powers Act 1920 has not now been invoked for over a decade. This is partly because governments are able to exercise the important power to deploy troops as substitute labour without declaring a state of emergency, and partly because recent governments have chosen to adopt alternative methods of handling disputes. This does not mean that the Act is a 'dead letter', merely that governments today have in view a wider range of options than those of earlier times, either because of political preference or because of practical considerations. The Emergency Powers Act is not ideal for every situation because it does not allow the Government to order a striking work-force back to work or otherwise to restrict the conduct of industrial action and its effectiveness is therefore limited where a work-force cannot easily be replaced and the commodity the work-force in dispute produces cannot be stored or the service it renders cannot be supplied to a sufficient extent by other organizations. Nevertheless, the availability of emergency powers is still crucial to contingency planners contemplating administrative preparations to deal with the disruption of many kinds of essential service.

NOTES

1. S.2(3), as amended by the Criminal Justice Act 1982, s.41. £2,000 represents the maximum fine for level 5 on the standard scale at the time of writing.

2. This point is developed further at the end of this section. For a more detailed discussion, see Gillian S. Morris, A Study of the Protection of Public and Essential Services in

Labour Disputes 1920–1976, unpublished Ph.D. dissertation, University of Cambridge, 1978.

3. Termination of the War (Definition) Act 1918, s.1.

4. WC 433, Cab 23/9, January 31, 1919.

5. Regulation 43C, S.R. & O. 1919, No. 132.

6. CP 6998, Cab 24/76. This measure was to have been known as the 'Coal Strikes Bill' when enacted.

7. See, further, Chapter 4.

8. TC 58, Cab 27/74; TC 78, Cab 27/74.

9. HAC 70, Cab 26/2.

10. HAC 69(3), Cab 26/2, July 12, 1920.

11. October 26, 1920.

12. Notes of a conversation at Downing Street between Government and Miners' Federation Representatives, Cab 23/35.

13. Viscount Milner, Secretary of State for the Colonies, H.L. Deb., Vol. 42, col. 103 (October 28, 1920).

14. H.C. Deb., Vol. 133, col. 1454 (October 25, 1920).

15. As note 14, above, col. 1426.

16. Sir Gordon Hewart, Attorney-General, H.C. Deb. Vol. 133, col. 1872 (October 27, 1920).

17. H.C. Deb., Vol. 689, col. 1412 (February 20, 1964).

18. The second and subsequent proclamations in 1973–4 referred also to the reduction in oil supplies reaching the country.

19. Mr Clement Attlee, Prime Minister, H.C. Deb., Vol. 452, col. 1839 (June 28, 1948); Mr Chuter Ede, Home Secretary, H.C. Deb., Vol. 466, col. 2593 (July 8, 1949).

20. Mr Harold Wilson, Prime Minister, H.C. Deb., Vol. 729, col. 37 (May 23, 1966).

21. Mr Quintin Hogg, H.C. Deb., Vol. 729, col. 752 (May 26, 1966).

22. H.C. Deb., Vol. 133, cols. 1663–4 (October 26, 1920).

23. Review of the British Docks Strikes 1949, Cmd. 7851 (1949), para. 66.

24. Mr Edward Shortt, Home Secretary, H.C. Debs, Vol. 140, col. 341 (April 5, 1921).

25. See, for example, Mr Roy Jenkins, Home Secretary, H.C. Debs, Vol. 729, col. 739 (May 26, 1966).

26. H.C. Deb., Vol. 842, col. 1592 (August 8, 1972).

27. I.L.O., *Official Bulletin* Special Supplement Vol. LXVII: Series B (1984), para 479; see also I.L.O. *Official Bulletin* Vol. LIV (1971), para 110.

28. Emergency Regulations 1926 (S.R. & O. 1926, No. 556), reg. 24.

29. See above, note 1.

30. For a more detailed account, see Morris, above, note 2, Ch. 4. This chapter also considers in greater detail the relationship of powers contained in emergency regulations with the ordinary law.

31. The Emergency Regulations 1966 (S.I. 1966 No. 600), regs. 22 and 23.

32. The first set of regulations.

33. Emergency Regulations 1921, *The Board of Trade Journal*, April 7, 1921, reg. 13; as above, note 28, reg. 3.

34. The Emergency Regulations 1955 (S.I. 1955, No. 791), reg. 12.

35. The Emergency Regulations 1972 (S.I. 1972, No. 157), reg. 22.

36. As above, note 27, reg. 3.

37. See The Emergency Regulations 1966, as above, note 30, reg. 18; The Emergency Regulations 1970 (S.I. 1970 No. 1042), reg. 19. There has been no provision for the enforcement of these restrictions under the regulations.

38. Emergency Regulations 1921, as above, note 32, reg. 14.

39. The Emergency Regulations 1966, as above, note 30, reg. 14. The 1973 regulations gave a power to restrict the supply, acquisition, abstraction, impounding and consumption of water: The Emergency Regulations 1973 (S.I. 1973 No. 1881), reg. 21.

40. The Emergency Regulations 1972, as above, note 35, regs. 17 and 18.

41. The Emergency Regulations 1966, as above, note 30, reg. 15.

42. Emergency Regulations 1921, as above, note 32, reg. 16.

43. The Emergency Regulations 1949 (S.I. 1949 No. 1300). reg. 9.

44. See ss. 9, 11 (1).

45. Emergency Regulations 1921, above, note 32, regs. 3, 5, 9, 10.
46. The Emergency Regulations 1955, as above, note 34, regs. 1–7.
47. The Emergency Regulations 1966, as above, note 30, reg. 20; The Emergency (No. 2) Regulations 1966 (S.I. 1966 No. 740), reg. 21.
48. The Emergency Regulations 1970, as above, note 37, reg. 22.
49. The Emergency Regulations 1972, as above, note 35, regs. 25 and 26.
50. Emergency Regulations 1921, as above, note 32, reg. 8.
51. The Emergency Regulations 1966, as above, note 30, reg. 1.
52. The Emergency Regulations 1949, as above, note 43, reg. 3.
53. The police have the power at common law to disperse gatherings which they reasonably apprehend will lead to a breach of the peace: *Duncan* v. *Jones* [1936] 1 K.B. 218.
54. Emergency Regulations 1921, as above, note 32, reg. 20.
55. The Emergency Regulations 1926, as above, note 27, reg. 22.
56. There is no requirement for the consent of the local authority if the ban is within the area of the Metropolitan Police Commissioner or Commissioner of the City of London Police.
57. Emergency Regulations 1921, as above, note 32, reg. 17.
58. *Ibid.*
59. Emergency Regulations 1921, as above, note 32, reg. 19. For a more detailed discussion of these offences and powers, see David Bonner, *Emergency Powers in Peacetime*, Sweet and Maxwell, London, 1985, pp. 238–42. As Bonner points out (p. 238), 'It is useful to contrast the modern with the older and wider offences and police powers so as to indicate the potentially very wide interferences with liberty which can be authorised under the Act'.
60. The Incitement to Mutiny Act 1797, s.2, and the Incitement to Disaffection Act 1934, s.1, discussed in Chapter 2, both require proof of guilty intention.
61. The Police Act 1919, s.3, now the Police Act 1964, s.53(1), discussed in Chapter 2, offered a direct alternative to proceeding under the regulation, with a maximum term of two years' imprisonment.
62. The common law offence of sedition is extremely vague, but it seems now to be necessary that 'the words used. . . amount to a direct incitement to violence or public disorder': David Williams, *Keeping the Peace*, Hutchinson, London, 1967, p. 198.
63. The Emergency Regulations 1926, as above, note 27, reg. 21(2).
64. Emergency Regulations 1921, as above, note 32, reg. 23.
65. The Emergency Regulations 1949, as above, note 43, regs 5 and 6; cf. the Army Act 1955, s.193; Police Act 1964, s.51(3).
66. Emergency Regulations 1921, as above, note 32, reg 18.
67. The Emergency Regulations 1949, as above, note 43, reg. 3. Codes issued since 1970 have specifically included hovercraft and aircraft in the offence.
68. As above, note 67, reg. 4.
69. The Emergency Regulations 1926, as above, note 27, reg. 33.
70. The earliest proclamations of emergency within each category are listed first.
71. Broadcast May 16, 1966. For the text, see *Keesing's Contemporary Archives 1965–1966*, p. 21547.
72. Mr. Harold Wilson, *The Labour Government 1964–1970*, Weidenfeld and Nicolson and Michael Joseph, London, 1971, p. 231.
73. Sir Elwyn Jones, H.C. Deb., Vol. 729, col. 848 (May 26, 1966).
74. Harold Wilson, H.C. Deb., Vol. 730, col. 1721 (June 28, 1966).
75. Mr Chuter Ede, Home Secretary, H.C. Deb., Vol. 467, cols. 2275, 2258 (July 26, 1949).
76. Keith Jeffery and Peter Hennessy, *States of Emergency*, Routledge and Kegan Paul, London 1983, p. 205.
77. Mr Ramsey MacDonald, Prime Minister, H.C. Deb., Vol. 171, col. 1882 (March 27, 1924).
78. C23/24, Cab 23/47, March 27, 1924.
79. Mr John Boyd-Carpenter, Minister of Transport and Civil Aviation, H.C. Deb., Vol. 542, col. 286 (June 13, 1955).
80. Major Gwilym Lloyd George, Home Secretary, as above, note 79, col. 280.
81. *Keesing's Contemporary Archives 1955–1956*, p. 14242.
82. Mr John Davies, Secretary of State for Trade and Industry, H.C. Deb., Vol. 808, col. 251 (December 8, 1970). See Chapters 4 and 5.
83. The Electricity (Advertising and Display) Order (S.I. 1970 No. 1866).

84. Sir Laming Worthington-Evans, Secretary of State for War, H.C. Deb., Vol. 144, col. 1074 (July 12, 1921).

85. Mr David Lloyd George, Prime Minister, H.C. Deb., Vol. 140, col. 693 (April 8, 1921).

86. Sir Laming Worthington-Evans, H.C. Deb., Vol. 140, col. 1558 (April 18, 1921).

87. The Coal (Emergency) Directions 1921, issued by the Board of Trade.

88. C30/21, Cab 23/25, April 28, 1921.

89. Home Office Order, April 7, 1921, TC 172, Cab 27/75, April 11, 1921.

90. Roger Geary, *Policing Industrial Disputes 1893 to 1985*, Cambridge University Press, Cambridge, 1985, p. 57.

91. Archibald Hurd, 'The Navy on "Active Service"', *Fortnightly Review*, July 1926 (Vol. 120 N.S.), p. 87.

92. The Coal (Emergency) Directions, S.R. & O., 1926 No. 452; The Local Authorities (Coal Emergency) Order, S.R. & O. 1926, No. 453.

93. G.A. Phillips, *The General Strike: The Politics of Industrial Conflict*, Weidenfield and Nicolson, London, 1976, p. 156. See, further, Chapter 4.

94. Milk Distribution (Emergency) Order S.R. & O. 1926 No. 530; Milk Distribution (Emergency) No. 2 Order S.R. & O. 1926, No. 531.

95. George Glasgow, *General Strikes and Road Transport*, Geoffrey Bles, London, 1927, p. 94.

96. Christopher Farman, *The General Strike*, Rupert Hart-Davis, London, 1972, p. 118.

97. Hurd, 'The Navy on "Active Service"', note 91, pp. 91–4.

98. H.C. Deb. Vol. 195, col. 71 (May 3, 1926).

99. Roger Geary, *Policing Industrial Disputes 1893 to 1985*, as above, note 90, p. 62.

100. The Emergency Regulations 1926, as above, note 27, reg. 13A.

101. Sir William Joynson-Hicks, Home Secretary, H.C. Deb., Vol. 196, col. 2467 (June 17, 1926).

102. Stephen Roskill, *Hankey: Man of Secrets Vol. II 1919–31*, Collins, London, 1972, p. 425.

103. *Ibid.*

104. Thomas Jones, *Whitehall Diary Vol. 2 1926–30*, ed. Keith Middlemas, Oxford University Press, London, 1969, pp. 45–7. The General Strike was followed by the Trade Disputes and Trade Unions Act 1927, described in Chapter 2.

105. Judicial Statistics for England and Wales 1926, Cmd. 3055 (1928); Sir William Joynson-Hicks, H.C. Deb., Vol. 206, col. 2001 (May 25, 1927). 361 people were convicted for offences against the Coal (Emergency) Directions: Joynson-Hicks, Vol. 204, col. 239 (April 7, 1927).

106. Sir William Joynson-Hicks, H.C. Deb., Vol. 196, col. 824 (June 2, 1926).

107. James Klugmann, *History of the Communist Party of Great Britain Vol 2: The General Strike 1925–1926*, Lawrence and Wishart, London 1969, p. 164; Phillips, *The General Strike*, as above, note 93, p. 204.

108. Geary, *Policing Industrial Disputes 1893 to 1985*, as above, note 90, p.66.

109. Sir William Joynson-Hicks, H.C. Deb., Vol. 196, cols. 747–8 (June 2, 1926); Vol. 198, col. 2509 (July 20, 1926); Vol. 199, col. 9 (August 30, 1926).

110. Sir William Joynson-Hicks H.C. Deb., Vol. 199, col. 411 (September 28, 1926).

111. *Ibid.* col. 456.

112. Sir William Joynson-Hicks, H.C. Deb., Vol. 199, col. 1847 (November 17, 1926).

113. Sir William Joynson-Hicks, H.C. Deb., Vol. 200, col. 715 (November 26, 1926).

114. Eric Wigham, *Strikes and the Government 1893–1981*, Macmillan, London, 1982, p. 169.

115. J.E. Trice, 'Methods of and Attitudes to Picketing', *Criminal Law Review*, 1975, p. 271.

116. Mr John Davies, Secretary of State for Trade and Industry, H.C. Deb., Vol. 831, cols. 155–7 (February 14, 1972).

117. The Electricity (Advertising, Display and Floodlighting) (Restriction) Order (S.I. 1972 No. 160).

118. The Electricity (Non-Domestic Heating) (Restriction) Order (S.I. 1972 No. 169) (as amended by S.I. 1972 No. 239).

119. Mr Reginald Maudling, Home Secretary, H.C. Deb., Vol. 831, col. 34 (February 14, 1972).

120. The 'three-day week' restrictions were removed on February 28.

121. H.C. Deb., Vol. 867, col. 8 (January 9, 1974).

122. Mr Peter Emery, Parliamentary Under-Secretary for Industry, H.C. Deb., Vol. 863, col.

37 (November 2, 1973), written answer.

123. Tom Boardman, Minister for Industry, H.C. Deb., Vol. 864, col. 29 (November 12, 1973).

124. The Electricity (Advertising, Display, etc.) (Restriction) Order (S.I. 1973 No. 1901).

125. The Electricity (Heating) Restriction Order (S.I. 1973 No. 1900), as amended by S.I. 1973 No. 1913.

126. Mr Robert Carr, Home Secretary, H.C. Deb. Vol. 864 col. 690 (November 15, 1973).

127. The Electricity (Industrial and Commercial Use) (Control) Order (S.I. 1973 No. 2120); The Electricity (Industrial and Commercial Use) (Control) (No. 2) Order (S.I. 1973 No. 2172).

128. *Keesing's Contemporary Archives 1974*, p. 26299.

129. Mr Tom Boardman, H.C. Deb., Vol. 864, col. 949 (November 19, 1973).

130. The Motor Fuel (Restriction of Supplies) Order (S.I. 1973 No. 1943).

131. Cf. the Emergency Powers Act 1920, ss.1(1), (2), 2(2).

132. S.6.

133. S.10.

134. Mr Tom Boardman, H.C. Deb., Vol. 865, col. 757 (November 29, 1973).

135. Restrictions imposed under the Fuel and Electricity (Control) Act were technically not subject to Parliamentary scrutiny, but in practice they were published and laid as Statutory Instruments.

136. Mr Robert Carr, H.C. Deb., Vol. 866, col. 1303 (December 18, 1973).

137. Mr Eric Varley, *Keesing's Contemporary Archives 1974*, p. 26426.

138. Richard Clutterbuck, *Britain in Agony*, Penguin, Harmondsworth, 1980, p. 112.

139. Mr David Lloyd George, Prime Minister, H.C. Deb., Vol. 140, col. 1608 (April 18, 1921).

140. G.D.H. Cole, *Labour in the Coalmining Industry (1914–1921)*, Clarendon Press, Oxford, 1923, p. 201.

141. *Ibid*, p. 234.

142. C40/25, Cab 23/50, July 28, 1925.

143. C42/25, Cab 23/50, July 30, 1925.

144. Report of the Royal Commission on the Coal Industry, Cmnd. 2600 (1926).

145. Text of a letter from Mr Stanley Baldwin to the T.U.C. negotiators quoted in Charles Loch Mowat, *Britain between the Wars 1918–1940*, Methuen, London, 1966, p. 307.

146. *Ibid*, p. 334.

147. See *Keesing's Contemporary Archives 1965–1966*, p. 21547.

148. Harold Wilson, *The Labour Government 1964–1970*, as above, note 72, p. 227.

149. As above, note 147.

150. Richard Crossman, *The Diaries of a Cabinet Minister Volume One. Minister of Housing 1964–66.* Hamish Hamilton and Jonathan Cape, London, 1975, p. 524.

151. First Report of the Court of Inquiry into certain matters concerning the shipping industry. Cmnd. 3025 (1966).

152. Harold Wilson, *The Labour Government 1964–1970*, above, note 72. p. 235.

153. H.C. Deb., Vol. 730, col. 42 (June 20, 1966).

154. H.C. Deb., Vol. 730, col. 1616 (June 28, 1966).

155. Eric Wigham, *Strikes and the Government 1893–1981*, as above, note 114, p. 138.

156. John Davies, H.C. Deb., Vol. 808, col. 252 (December 8, 1970); Vol. 831, col. 161 (February 14, 1972).

157. Report of a Court of Inquiry into a dispute between the National Coal Board and the National Union of Mineworkers under the chairmanship of the Rt. Hon. Lord Wilberforce C.M.G., C.B.E., Cmnd. 4903 (1972).

158. Campbell Balfour, *Unions and the Law*, Saxon House, Farnborough and Lexington, 1973, p. 82.

159. See, for example, Mr Robert Carr, H.C. Deb., Vol. 864, col. 259 (November 13, 1973).

160. *Keesing's Contemporary Archives 1948–1950*, p. 9365.

161. Mr George Isaacs, Minister of Labour, H.C. Deb., Vol. 466, col. 1789 (July 4, 1949).

162. Mr Chuter Ede. H.C. Deb., Vol. 466, col. 2593 (July 8, 1949).

163. Mr J.R. Clynes, Lord Privy Seal, H.C. Deb., Vol. 171, col. 1752 (March 16, 1924).

164. David Marquand, *Ramsey MacDonald*, Jonathan Cape, London, 1977, p. 319.

165. H.C. Deb., Vol. 169, col. 1753 (February 20, 1924).

166. Interim Report by a Court of Enquiry concerning the stoppage of the London Tramway and Omnibus Services, Cmd. 2087 (1924).

167. *The Times*, March 28, 1924.

168. Richard W. Lyman, *The First Labour Government 1924*, Chapman and Hall, London, 1957, p. 219,

169. Mr Ramsey MacDonald, H.C. Deb., Vol. 171, col. 1683 (March 27, 1924).

170. Mr Ramsey MacDonald, H.C. Deb., Vol. 171, col. 1440 (March 26, 1924).

171. H.C. Deb., Vol. 960, col. 1959 (January 18, 1979).

172. Mr. James Callaghan, Prime Minister, *ibid*, col. 1960.

173. Mr Merlyn Rees, Home Secretary, H.C. Deb., Vol. 960, col. 1318 (January 15, 1979). *The Guardian*, January 19, 1979, reported that troops could move at most 5 per cent of normal supplies.

174. Mr James Callaghan, as above, note 171, col. 1958.

175. Mr Alan Williams, Minister of State at the Department of Industry, H.C. Deb., Vol. 963, col. 3 (February 19, 1979).

176. Peter Jenkins, *The Guardian*, January 19, 1979.

177. Peter Wilsher, Donald Macintyre and Michael Jones, *Strike: Thatcher, Scargill and the Miners*, André Deutsch, London, 1985, p. 218.

178. *Ibid.*, p. 219.

179. Peter Wallington, 'Policing the Miners' Strike', *Industrial Law Journal* 14 (1985), 145 at 146.

180. The Energy Act 1976 could also be used where electricity supplies are under threat.

181. Wallington, 'Policing the Miners' Strike', as above, note 179, at p. 159.

182. Ronald Kidd, *British Library in Danger*, Lawrence and Wishart, London, 1940, pp. 48, 51.

183. Apart from the first motion.

184. Mr Michael Foot, H.C. Deb., Vol. 831, col. 153 (February 14, 1972). See also Lord Champion, H.L. Deb., Vol. 328, col. 26 (February 15, 1972).

185. Mrs Shirley Williams, H.C. Deb., Vol. 864, cols. 694–7 (November 15, 1972).

186. Although emergency regulations are numbered and printed as Statutory Instruments, which may not generally be amended by either House, it seems that technically they are not Statutory Instruments because the 1920 Act excluded the application of the Rules Publication Act 1893: Statutory Instruments Act 1946, s.1(2).

187. H.C. Deb., Vol. 866, col. 1282 (December 18, 1973).

188. See The Emergency Regulations 1974 (S.I. 1974 No. 33), reg, 32.

189. Where purely public law rights are at issue, using actions rather than an application for judicial review may constitute an abuse of process of the court, but ordinary actions may be used to to challenge exercises of power by public authorities which interfere with private rights; see Bonner, *Emergency Powers in Peacetime*, as above, note 59, p. 51. For a brief account of the *locus standi* required to pursue applications for judicial review see S.A. de Smith, *Constitutional and Administrative Law*, 5th edn., ed. Harry Street and Rodney Brazier, Penguin, Harmondsworth, 1985, Ch. 29.

190. Quoted in Jeffery and Hennessy, *States of Emergency*, as above, note 76, p. 141.

191. CP (49) 148, Cab 129/35.

192. J.M. Evans, *de Smith's Judicial Review of Administrative Action*, 4th edn., Stevens, London, 1980, p. 285.

193. Lord Wilberforce in *Secretary of State for Education and Science* v. *Tameside Metropolitan Borough Council* [1976] 3 W.L.R. 641 at 665. For a fuller discussion of the attitude of the courts to reviewing the exercise of emergency powers, see Bonner, *Emergency Powers in Peacetime*, above, note 59, pp. 50–71.

194. Evans, *de Smith's Judicial Review of Administrative Action*, as above, note 192, p. 281.

195. Bonner, *Emergency Powers in Peacetime*, as above, note 59, p. 55.

196. See, for example, *R.* v. *Home Secretary ex parte Hosenball* [1977] 1 W.L.R. 766; *Council of Civil Service Unions* v. *Minister for the Civil Service* [1984] 3 W.L.R. 1174; *Secretary of State for Employment* v. *A.S.L.E.F. (No. 2)* [1972] 2 Q.B. 455.

197. See *R.* v. *Halliday* [1917] A.C. 260; *Point of Ayr Collieries* v. *Lloyd George* [1943] 2 All E.R. 546; *R.* v. *Home Secretary ex parte Hosenball*, as above, note 196.

198. The fact that a case is before the courts on the validity of subordinate legislation, or that a prosecution has been brought under it, will not prevent debate upon renewal of the regulations: H.C. Deb., Vol. 835, col. 1915 (December 15, 1954); Vol. 734, col. 843 (October 25, 1966).

199. See *Liversidge* v. *Anderson* [1942] A.C. 206 and *R.* v. *Home Secretary ex parte Hosenball*, as above, note 196. Three Privy Council judgements on the justiciability of the decision that a state of emergency exists offer little guidance. In *Bhagat Singh* v. *King-Emperor* (1931) L.R. 58 I.A. 169 and *King-Emperor* v. *Benoari Lal Sarma* [1945] A.C. 14 the statutes under review did not define an emergency situation and the decision was held to be one for the executive alone. In *Ningkan* v. *Government of Malaysia* [1970] A.C. 379 an emergency was defined but was not required to be caused by any particular event and the matter was deliberately left open. It is possible that a court might be more willing to intervene in a case concerning the British legislation, which requires a definite state of facts to exist. See also *Dean* v. *Attorney-General of Queensland* [1971] Qd. R. 391 and *McLeod et al.* v. *Labour Relations Board of Saskatchewan, Bakers Electric Ltd et al.* [1971] 1 W.W.R. 363, 371.

200. *Ningkan* v. *Government of Malaysia*, as above, note 199, p. 390.

201. Evans, *de Smith's Judicial Review of Administrative Action*, as above, note 192, p. 287.

202. *Secretary of State for Employment* v. *A.S.L.E.F. (No. 2)*, as above, note 196.

203. de Smith, *Constitutional and Administrative Law*, as above, note 189, pp. 528–9. The Act provides that the regulations are to have effect 'as if enacted in this Act' (s.2(4)). There are conflicting House of Lords' dicta on the meaning of this phrase. In *Institute of Patent Agents* v. *Lockwood* [1894] A.C. 347, the majority of the court considered that it precluded the court from reviewing the validity of the regulations. In *Minister of Health* v. *R., ex parte Yaffe* [1931] A.C. 494, however, it was said that *Lockwood* applied only where the subordinate legislation was made in conformity with the parent Act. It is widely assumed that the interpretation in *Yaffe* would prevail (see, for example. The Committee on Ministers' Powers Cmd. 4060 (1932), para. 8), and this approach would accord with that taken in *Anisminic Ltd* v. *Foreign Compensation Commission* [1969] 2 A.C. 147.

204. *R.* v. *Comptroller General of Patents, ex parte Bayer Products Ltd* [1941] 2 K.B. 306; *Progressive Supply Co. Ltd* v. *Dalton* [1943] Ch. 54.

205. [1971] A.C. 632.

206. See, for example, *Ross-Clunis* v. *Papadopoullos* [1958] 2 All E.R. 23.

207. *Smith* v. *Wood* (1927) 43 T.L.R. 178, Lord Hewart C.J. at 108.

208. As above, note 197.

209. See Carlton Kemp Allen, *Law and Orders*, 3rd edn., Stevens, London, 1965, p. 507; cf. Evans, *de Smith's Judicial Review of Administrative Action*, as above, note 192, p. 603, where it is argued that in this context 'punishment' includes preventative administrative action. In *Re McElduff* [1972] N.I.L.R. 1, the distinction was made for the purposes of release on bail between 'preventative detention for the public good' under emergency regulations and custody after arrest for an offence.

210. *Lawless* v. *Ireland (No. 3)* [1961] 1 E.H.R.R. 15; *The Republic of Ireland* v. *United Kingdom* [1978] 2 E.H.R.R. 25. See further Bonner, *Emergency Powers in Peacetime*, as above, note 59, pp. 83–90.

211. *Lawless* v. *Ireland (No. 3)*, as above, note 210, para 28.

212. In 1955, Viscount Kilmuir L.C. considered that the communication of the occasion of a proclamation to Parliament was a mandatory requirement where there was a Parliament in existence: H.L. Deb., Vol. 193, col. 38 (June 13, 1955).

213. *Starey* v. *Graham* [1899] 1 Q.B. 404 at p. 412. In *Bailey* v. *Williamson* (1873) L.R. 8 Q.B. 118, a decision generally cited as authority for this view, the court did not consider the possibility of subsequent invalidity from a failure to lay. The dictum of Streatfield J. in *R.* v. *Sheer Metalcraft Ltd* [1954] 1 Q.B. 586 at p. 590 that the making of an instrument is complete after it has been laid before Parliament, is clearly inapplicable to the Emergency Powers Act, under which the regulations take immediate effect.

214. *Simpson* v. *Attorney-General* [1955] N.Z.L.R. 271.

215. See above, note 1.

216. Orders made under the Energy Act (not including section 3 Orders in Council) must be made by Statutory Instrument and are subject to annulment in pursuance of a resolution of either House of Parliament.

217. Mr Bruce Millan, Secretary of State for Scotland, H.C. Deb., Vol. 963, col. 902 (March 5, 1979).

218. Mr Ronald K. Murray, Lord Advocate, H.C. Deb., Vol. 964, col. 1380 (March 20, 1979).

219. The 110-day period is laid down in the Criminal Procedure (Scotland) Act 1975, s.101.
220. Mr Bruce Millan, H.C. Deb., Vol. 964, col. 1322 (March 20, 1979).
221. Mr William Whitelaw, Home Secretary, H.C. Deb., Vol. 991, col. 38 (October 27, 1980).
222. Prison officers have these attributes under the Prisons Act 1952, s.8.
223. National Association for the Care and Resettlement of Offenders. *Some effects of the Prison Officers' Dispute 6 October 1980–11 February 1981*, N.A.C.R.O., London, 1981, p.2.
224. *Ibid.*, p. 5.
225. Mr William Whitelaw, H.C. Deb., Vol. 991, col. 326 (October 28, 1980).
226. As above, note 223, p. 2. This Circular was seen by the chairman of the Magistrates' Association, the honorary secretary of the Justices' Clerks Society and others as an unwarranted interference by the executive with the work of the courts: Colin Munro, 'The Separation of Powers: Not Such a Myth', *Public Law* (1981) 19 at 23.
227. Registration of Births, Deaths and Marriages (Amendment) (No. 2) Regulations 1982 (S.I. 1982 No. 955).
228. Christopher J. Whelan, 'On Uses and Misuses of Comparative Labour Law: A Case Study', *Modern Law Review* 45 (1982), 285 at 288.
229. *Ibid.*, p. 290.
230. Royal Commission on Trade Unions and Employers' Associations 1965–1968, Cmnd. 3623 (1968), paras. 423–4.
231. Sir Geoffrey Howe, Solicitor-General, H.C. Deb., Vol. 812, col. 714 (February 24, 1971).
232. Otto Kahn-Freund, *Labour and the Law*, Stevens, London, 1972, p. 240.
233. Lord Drumalbyn, H.L. Deb., Vol. 320, col. 227 (June 9, 1971).
234. Mr Harold Walker, H.C. Deb., Vol. 812, col. 713 (February 24, 1971).
235. Brian Weekes, Michael Mellish, Linda Dickens and John Lloyd, *Industrial Relations and the Limits of Law: The Industrial Effects of the Industrial Relations Act, 1971*, Blackwell, Oxford, 1975. p. 214.
236. *Secretary of State for Employment* v. *A.S.L.E.F.* (No. 2), as above note 196.
237. *Ibid.*
238. *Ibid.*, p. 493.
239. *Ibid.*, p. 511.
240. Aubrey Jones, *The New Inflation*, Penguin, Harmondsworth, 1973, p. 140.
241. *Secretary of State for Employment* v. *A.S.L.E.F.* [1972] 2 Q.B. 443 at 452.
242. *The Times*, May 10, 1972.
243. *Secretary of State for Employment* v. *A.S.L.E.F. (No. 2)*, as above, note 196, Lord Denning M.R. at p. 494.
244. Whelan, 'On Uses and Misuses of Comparative Labour Law' as above, note 228, p. 295.
245. Weekes, Mellish, Dickens and Lloyd, *Industrial Relations and the Limits of Law*, as above, note 235, p. 216.
246. Denis Barnes and Eileen Reid, *Governments and Trade Unions: The British Experience 1964–79*, Heinemann, London, 1980, pp. 160–1.
247. *Ibid.*, p. 161.
248. Cmnd. 8128 (1981).
249. *Ibid.*, paras. 317–8.
250. Trade Union Act 1984, ss. 10, 11.

4

Substitute Labour Forces and Contingency Planning

The replacement of strikers by a substitute labour force is one course open to employers faced with industrial action. This has not been the general practice of employers in Britain since the First World War. When the action affects an industry or service which the Government wishes to protect against undue disruption, however, the Government itself has made alternative labour available to employers. The first section of this chapter discusses the sources of substitute labour which have been drawn upon or considered and any legal problems associated with their deployment on work left undone by strikers.

The most prominant and widely used source has been the armed forces. Troops have a number of advantages as a substitute labour force. They operate within a hierarchical, disciplined structure, they are readily available, and they are trained to respond quickly and flexibly to crisis situations. They possess a wide range of skills, and they are relatively isolated from other groups of workers and, in particular, from trade unionists. Although the military authorities have never been enthusiastic about deploying troops in disputes, on the ground that such deployment interferes with their military functions and is not the purpose for which soldiers enlist, this has rarely discouraged the Government from relying on them. Another possible source of substitute labour, the police, has not been tapped in the past, on the ground that using them to perform the work of strikers would compromise their law enforcement role. There has been a greater willingness to risk that conflict in recent years. Civilian volunteers constitute an ostensibly attractive third source of alternative labour. Plans to harnass their services have not been pursued in any thoroughgoing fashion since 1926, but the idea has not been abandoned entirely and volunteers have played a role in replacing health service workers during disputes.

Making available substitute labour has been a crucial element in the contingency plans which governments since the First World War have formulated to meet disruption to essential services. The second section of this chapter outlines the history of official contingency planning, not with the object of giving a comprehensive account of the details of these plans, which have been adequately documented elsewhere,[1] but in order to trace the development and consider the implications of the Government's role in constructing what is now a highly sophisticated administrative machine which is ready to spring into action whenever the continued operation of essential services is put at risk.

THE USE OF SUBSTITUTE LABOUR

The Armed Forces

The legal position

The use of troops to replace strikers goes back at least as far as the nineteenth century.[2] Despite this, it seems that only after the First World War was any serious attention paid to possible legal problems associated with ordering soldiers to perform civilian tasks. The deployment of service labour was central to the Lloyd George Government's plans to deal with industrial disruption, and troops were used in 1919 to protect mines in Yorkshire from flooding and to convey food during the rail strike. The military authorities opposed this policy on a number of grounds: many soldiers then were trade unionists awaiting demobilization, who had not enlisted with such employment in view; troops were brought into contact with political agitators; and it jeopardized commitments overseas.[3] They also argued that it was extremely doubtful whether soldiers employed on doing work left undone by strikers were subject to the statutory code of military discipline which obliges a soldier to obey the 'lawful commands' of his superior officer.[4] If they were not so subject they could disobey orders to act as substitute labour with impunity. (The Liberal Attorney-General, Sir Rufus Isaacs, had refused to give a direct answer as to whether troops could be compelled to act as 'blacklegs' when pressed on the point by Labour M.P.s in 1912).[5] In 1920 the Government Law Officers investigated this question and concurred with the opinion of the Judge Advocate General that military discipline would apply only if some military object were being furthered, such as the transport of military personnel or supplies, or if the safety of the Realm and the Government were so endangered that the Crown decided to entrust particular services to military administration or control.[6] The military authorities were adamant that troops should be used only when subject to military discipline, and the need to put the situation beyond challenge was a major spur to enacting the Emergency Powers Act 1920.

Against the wishes of armed forces chiefs, the use of troops as substitute labour remained intrinsic to the Government's contingency plans to meet industrial emergencies, and the 1921 and 1926 sets of emergency regulations expressly extended military discipline to work declared by a Secretary of State to be 'of vital importance to the community'.[7] In the event, little or no use was made of troops to replace strikers in 1921, but in 1926 naval ratings worked in power stations and the docks and naval vessels were used to carry mail across the Irish Sea and yeast from Scottish and Irish distilleries to the mainland.

A wartime regulation issued under the Emergency Powers (Defence) Act 1939 gave the Admiralty, Army Council and Air Council standing power to authorize officers and men of the forces under their control 'to be temporarily employed in agricultural work or such other work as may be approved in accordance with instructions issued by . . . [them] as being urgent work of national importance'.[8] This power was intended to be used primarily where there were civilian labour shortages, but it was also invoked on occasion during disputes.[9] After the war had ended it was kept in force by a succession of renewal provisions,[10] and ample use was made of it by the Attlee Government to deal with disruption caused by industrial action as well as by continuing labour shortages. Finally, in 1964, the power to use servicemen for non-military duties was placed on a permanent statutory basis by the Emergency Powers Act 1964. Section 2 of that Act allows the Defence Council (which replaced the Admiralty, Army and Air Councils)[11] to

> authorise officers and men of Her Majesty's naval, military or air forces . . . to be temporarily employed in agricultural work or such other work as may be approved in accordance with instructions issued by the Defence Council as being urgent work of national importance, and thereupon it shall be the duty of every person subject to the . . . [discipline of the armed forces] . . . to obey any command given by his superior officer in relation to such employment, and every such command shall be deemed to be a lawful command within the meaning of the Naval Discipline Act, the Army Act, 1955, or the Air Force Act, 1955, as the case may be.

Parliamentary debate on this important measure was a low-key affair. Home Office ministers emphasized the 'invaluable services'[12] performed by the Armed Forces in areas other than industrial disputes, such as helping with harvesting, floods, heath fires and severe weather conditions, and pointed out that the Defence Regulation had been used to deal with industrial action only once since 1955 (during an unofficial seaman's strike in 1960). The Labour Opposition did not put forward any objection in principle to the power to use servicemen on non-military tasks having a permanent place on the statute book.

Section 2 of the Emergency Powers Act 1964 enables troops to be used as substitute labour without any sanction by Parliament.[13] All that is required is authorization by the Defence Council, which is composed of defence ministers, military commanders and senior civil servants.[14] This authorization can be given by any two members of the Council, who need not be politicians. However '[t]he Defence Council would not authorise such employment unless it was so requested by the civil authority'[15] In practice, '[t]he mobilization of troops . . . usually begins with a request from the strikers' employer . . . [This request] goes through the industry's sponsoring department . . . the government department with responsibility for their kind of work'.[16] In recent years, if the sponsoring department has acquiesced in the request, its next step is to go to the Civil Contingencies Unit, the body in charge of Government contingency planning for disputes.

> When a specific request for military assistance is being considered, ministers from the sponsoring department and the . . . [Ministry of Defence] (and the Welsh, Scottish and Northern Ireland Offices if they are affected) will be prominent in making the decision. The decision to use troops would not normally go to the Cabinet . . . unless a state of emergency is going to be declared.[17]

The cost of mobilizing troops, apart from their basic pay, is passed on to the sponsoring department, which usually sends the bill to the employer. The charge is not passed on if troops are not, in the event, deployed.[18] Employers may come under strong pressure from the Government to 'ask' for service labour; the Home Office informed one researcher that at the outset of the 1977–8 firemen's strike '[W]e invited local authorities to request the use of troops'.[19]

A state of emergency under the 1920 Act would only be required if the executive considered that it needed further powers, such as authority to regulate supplies or to requisition property or equipment; the possibility of requisitioning port facilities was given as a reason for issuing proclamations in 1948 and 1966. Where the Services rely on their own equipment, such as ambulances, or other equipment in the Government's possession (such as the 'Green Goddess' fire engines used during the firemen's strike), no additional emergency powers may be necessary. The practice in recent years has been to avoid declaring a state of emergency whenever possible. In some situations where troops have been employed, such as the health service workers' and prison officers' disputes, a state of emergency could not have been proclaimed under the 1920 Act because there was no interference with the 'supply and distribution of food, water, fuel, or light, or with the means of locomotion' as required by section 1(1) of that Act.

The most striking feature of the present power to use troops as substitute labour is the complete lack of any legal or political accountability for using that power. Unlike the 1920 Act, the Emergency Powers Act 1964 contains no requirement to consult, or even to inform, Parliament about the decision to use troops, nor is the Defence Council, or anybody else, under any obligation to explain why a particular task involves 'urgent work of national importance'. Clearly, however, 'what work is of national importance or necessary to the survival of the community is a matter on which a wide range of political judgement is possible'.[20] The authorities have certainly been disposed to take a broad view of these concepts in the past; perhaps the most unlikely candidate for inclusion was the task of keeping the boilers stoked at Buckingham Palace during a strike by Ministry of Works employees in 1948. There have also been many other occasions when the work performed by troops has affected only a small geographical area, such as the Scottish Isles, Glasgow or part of London. The 'national importance' of some of these tasks is hard to discern. The 1920 Act could not have been invoked for these purposes because of the requirement that a 'substantial portion' of the community must be deprived of essential supplies (s.1(1)).

The use of troops

Table 3 sets out the occasions since 1945, over thirty in all, when troops have been deployed to replace striking workers. All these instances involved reliance upon the 1964 Act or its predecessor apart from the work performed at military establishments during the 1978, 1979 and 1981 civil service disputes and at West Drayton Air Traffic Control Centre in 1977. In these cases the Ministry of Defence considered that the work was 'military' and that troops could therefore be ordered to carry it out in the ordinary course of their duties. This argument was disputed by the air traffic controllers, who claimed that the work performed by troops affected civil aviation as well as a military flight monitoring system housed at the Control Centre.[21]

The Attlee Labour Government used troops on fourteen occasions between 1945 and 1951, reaching a stage at which calling in the military became 'an automatic response to serious disputes'.[22] All fourteen disputes were unofficial, and a number were alleged to have been initiated or prolonged by 'subversive' Communist sympathizers.[23]

Most affected the supply or distribution of foodstuffs, of which there were still considerable shortages in the post-war years. The Minister of Labour, Mr George Isaacs, consistently affirmed that troops would be employed only for the purposes of 'safeguarding vital supplies' and not for 'strike-breaking',[24] yet in the 1945, 1948, 1949 and 1950 dock strikes the Government made clear that troops would handle all cargoes, and not just food supplies, with the aim of ensuring that traffic was fully maintained. Most union leaders acquiesced in the policy of using troops, but on six occasions (the 1949 and 1950 dock strikes, the three meat-handlers' disputes and the 1949 electricity strike) the arrival of troops caused the dispute to spread.

Between October 1951 and the end of 1969, troops were brought in to only four disputes. The first official dispute in which they intervened following the war was the 1955 railway strike, called by the footplatemen's union, A.S.L.E.F. Service aircraft and lorries carried essential mail, but no troops were used anywhere on the railways. The (Conservative) Government thus avoided alienating the other rail union, the N.U.R., whose members continued to run a skeleton service. In the second official dispute, the seamen's strike of 1966, the Labour Government also confined troops to a narrow role – that of maintaining supplies to the Scottish islands. The union warned that if the Government went beyond this and used troops to ease congestion in the ports, any goods from ships manned by troops would be 'blacked' and it could lead to a General Strike and 'the downfall of the Labour Government'.[25] The dispute ended before further plans to use Royal Air Force transport planes to deliver important exports and post to and from Northern Ireland could be put into effect.

Between 1970 and the middle of 1985, troops intervened in fourteen disputes, nearly all of them official, the exceptions being the Glasgow strikes. In some cases intervention was on a very small scale: in the 1982 railwaymen's strike it was limited to laying wire netting in London parks in preparation for additional car-parking, and in the health service dispute of that year only one army ambulance was actually used, although many more were standing by. By contrast, in the 1977–8 firemen's strike, 20, 750 troops, assisted by fire officers and part-time firemen, replaced an entire labour force of some 32,000 for nine weeks. (The details of this dispute are described in chapter 5.) The length of intervention has also varied considerably, ranging from a single day to seventeen weeks in the prison officers' dispute, when 1,000 troops helped senior prison staff and police officers to run two 'emergency' prisons housing prisoners whom prison officers had refused to admit.

In addition to those occasions when the military have acted as substitute labour, there have been many times in recent years when troops have been on stand-by, ready to intervene within seventy-two hours should the need arise. These include industrial action or threatened industrial action

TABLE 3. *The use of troops in industrial disputes in Great Britain since 1945*

Year	*Workers in dispute*	*Locality troops used*
1945	Dockworkers	Glasgow, Humberside, Swansea, Cardiff, London.
	Dockworkers	Merseyside, London, Humberside, Avonmouth
1946	Meat-handlers	Smithfield Market, London
	Dockworkers	Southampton
1947	Meat-handlers	Smithfield Market, London
	Dockworkers	Glasgow
	Corporation workers	Tower Bridge London (operating bridge)
1948	Ministry of Works employees	Buckingham Palace, London
	*Dockworkers	London, Merseyside
1949	*Dockworkers	Avonmouth, Liverpool, London
	Electricity manual workers	Four London power stations
1950	Dockworkers	London
	Meat-handlers	Smithfield Market, London
	Gas maintenance workers	Three London gasworks
1953	Oil-tanker drivers	London area
1955	*Railwaymen	National (aircraft and lorries for essential mail)
1960	Seamen	Scottish Western Isles (supplies from mainland)
1966	*Seamen	Scottish islands (food supplies and mail)
1970	Local authority manual workers	Tower Hamlets, London (clearing refuse)
1972	*Dockworkers	Scottish islands (food and fuel supplies)
1973	Firemen	Glasgow

Year	*Workers in dispute*	*Locality troops used*
1975	Refuse collectors	Glasgow
1977	Air traffic control assistants	West Drayton, London
1977–8	Firemen	National
1978	Industrial civil servants	Faslane submarine base
1979	Ambulance drivers	London and Manchester
	Civil servants	Devonport naval dockyard
1980–1	Prison Officers	Frankland Prison, Rollestone Army Camp
1981	Civil servants	Coulport submarine base
	Ambulance drivers	South Wales
1982	Railwaymen	London (laying wire netting in parks for cars)
	Ambulance drivers	London

Note: *indicates that a state of emergency under the 1920 Act was declared.

involving dockworkers (1970), petrol-tanker drivers (1978 and 1979), nuclear power workers (1977), waterworkers (1979, 1981 and 1983), local authority manual workers (1979) and firemen (1980). The use of troops was also on the agenda during the 1984 dock strike. During the official waterworkers' strike of 1983, military intervention would have been very much a last resort; it would have led to the workers in dispute withdrawing emergency cover and N.A.L.G.O., which represents most managerial and supervisory staff in the industry, indicated that its members would refuse to give any assistance, without which troops could not intervene effectively. Sometimes governments have pursued a strategy of co-operation with the unions, making clear that troops would be called in only if voluntary arrangements broke down. Military intervention was averted when the unions agreed to a request by the Heath Government to move perishable foodstuffs during the 1970 dock strike, and the Government agreed with the unions involved in the local authority manual workers' dispute of that year not to use troops to deal with threats to public health until the unions had consulted their members about doing the work themselves. During the 1979 road haulage dispute, discussed in Chapter 3, the Labour Government relied in the first instance on the operation of a code of practice listing essential supplies which the T.G.W.U. recommended to its members, maintaining that this was 'the quickest and most efficient way of minimising disruption'.[26]

The ability of troops to replace a striking workforce is subject to two major limitations: skill and numbers. 'The Armed Forces are almost a complete society of their own',[27] and although troops receive 'no specific training to undertake civilian jobs in the event of industrial disputes . . . the nature of Service training is such as to provide a number of Service men with useful skills of more general application'.[28] These skills include:

> Royal Navy engine specialists, earmarked for running power stations; thousands of HGV licence holders (mainly army), able to drive civilian lorries; army Royal Engineers who can operate water and sewage pumping stations; oil (including petrol) handling training through the army petroleum depot in Dorset; warders for military prisons, used during the 1980 prison officials dispute; fire-fighting training via the RAF and RN specialist establishments . . .; railway and docks operation through the Royal Corps of Transport; plus all the other military personnel working in the armed forces: postal services, catering, medicine, computors, electronics, etc.[29]

In addition:

> Once ministers have authorised the use of Service men in a specific emergency then they may also approve the provision of further training if it is felt it would help those concerned to carry out more effectively the particular duties they are required to perform.[30]

This was done, for example, before the firemen's strike of 1977–8. Despite the wide range of skills available, however, increasing specialization and technological sophistication in many industrial sectors means that troops are not equipped, or at least not equipped in sufficient numbers, to take over strikers' jobs without the co-operation of managerial and supervisory staff. This has been true of the electricity supply industry for many years, and it also applies to the water industry and probably to the fire service.

Even where the work left undone by strikers is relatively unskilled, troops are restricted by numbers.

> The Ministry of Defence can only supply a labour force of just over 20,000 at any one time without endangering its purely military commitments, which may be enough to take over a national,

> non-labour intensive industry (such as the fire service) or a localised labour intensive one . . . but is inadequate for a national, labour intensive service such as the coal miners.[31]

It was estimated during the 1979 road haulage strike that troops could move only about 5 per cent of normal supplies,[32] and this was the main reason given by the Government for relying upon arrangements with the unions.

Despite these restrictions on the capacity of the armed forces, the power to use them as substitute labour still remains important in many contexts. As in the case of the 1920 Act, governments have presented the decision to invoke this power as a disinterested measure, designed only to protect the 'community'. Mr Winston Churchill told the House of Commons in 1919:

> To use soldiers or sailors kept up at the general expense of the taxpayer to take sides with the employer in an ordinary trade dispute . . . would be a monstrous invasion of the liberty of the subject . . . [and] be a very unfair, if not an illegal order to give to the soldier. But the case is different where vital services affecting the health, life or safety of large cities or great concentrations of people are concerned . . . [T]his intervention of the state is not in the interest of private profit or private employers but solely in the interests of the general public who must be supplied with these vital necessities[33]

This claim that using troops does not further 'the interests of . . . employers' does not survive close examination. As in the case of declaring a state of emergency under the 1920 Act, military intervention, or the threat of it, inevitably affects the bargaining power of the parties to a dispute. Moreover, on many occasions the Government itself has been among the parties, either as an employer, as in the civil service disputes, or as defender of an incomes policy, as in the firemen's strike. It is also hard to argue that the role of troops has been confined to supplying 'vital necessities'; apart from the notorious example of Buckingham Palace, the Attlee and Wilson Governments certainly went beyond this in using, or contemplating using, troops to handle cargoes for economic purposes during disputes in the docks and shipping industry.

Whether or not to call in troops on any particular occasion is essentially a political decision. The factors to be looked at, quite apart from the capacity of soldiers to do the job, include whether the work is sufficiently vital to constitute 'urgent work of national importance' and whether the presence of troops will inflame the situation, either by provoking the workers in dispute to take further measures or by extending the action to other groups. Given its political nature it is quite extraordinary that this decision can be taken without any form of debate or scrutiny which is exposed to public view. Merely to argue that the Secretary of State for Defence, the Chairman of the Defence Council, is answerable to Parliament is not enough, particularly in view of the limited opportunities which are afforded for questioning ministers.[34] It would seem excessive to require a state of emergency under the 1920 Act to be declared whenever troops are used, especially in the light of the undesirable practice of introducing a full code of regulations regardless of the situation, but there is a strong case for amending the 1964 Act to subject the power to deploy troops to formal and direct parliamentary control.

The police

Traditionally the role of the police in industrial disputes has been confined to preserving the peace and upholding the law. Until recently, any suggestions that they should act as substitute labour were firmly rejected on the ground that this would tarnish their impartial reputation. Even during the 1926 General Strike, which all the resources of the State were mobilized to defeat, Sir John Anderson, Permanent Under-Secretary to the Home Office, successfully resisted plans to use police vans to carry medical supplies to London hospitals, arguing that this would contravene 'the principle that in a dispute the police do not help either side'.[35] In 1975 it was proposed in the House of Lords that specialized sections of the Special Constabulary, the police reserve force, should be formed to maintain gas, water and electricity supplies and to man docks and sewage plants, should these be disrupted by industrial action.[36] Lord Harris of Greenwich, a junior Home Office minister in the then Labour Government, remarked that this 'would be certain to undermine the almost unanimous acceptance of the police in this country as an impartial law enforcement agency' and would 'embitter relations between . . . [them] and the community as a whole'. The specials would then be 'represented and believed by a substantial number of their fellow citizens to be a corps of licensed strike-breakers', and this would damage recruitment to the force.[37]

In early 1979 the practice of safeguarding the impartial status of the force was departed from when the police used their own ambulances to maintain an emergency service during the ambulancemen's dispute when ambulancemen themselves refused to provide emergency cover. This was the first occasion on which the police had undertaken jobs normally performed by workers in dispute; during the 1977–8 firemen's strike police visited the scenes of reported fires to assess their seriousness before troops were called in, but they did not carry out any fire-fighting duties. The police took on the same role as in 1979 during the 1981 and 1982 ambulancemen's disputes, and they are now the first source of alternative labour to be called upon by the ambulancemen's employers if emergency cover is put at risk. They were also relied upon to help when social workers took industrial action in 1979.

The deployment of troops as substitute labour raises substantial legal problems.[38] One fundamental issue is whether policemen could refuse with impunity to perform such tasks. The Police Discipline Code requires constables to obey 'lawful' orders,[39] and if the analogy with military discipline is followed,[40] 'lawful' in this context means 'pertaining to a policeman's duties'. The range of police duties is ill-defined, however; they clearly include preserving the peace, preventing crime and protecting life and property,[41] but beyond that their precise scope is uncertain. The Police Federation took the view that carrying patients to hospital was part of the obligation to protect life, and '[t]he fact that ambulance workers are employed to do this job in no way relieves the police' of this obligation.[42] This was also the opinion of the Home Office.[43] However, it should not be the nature of the work which is crucial in assessing whether it falls within the scope of police duties — servicemen are often required to perform tasks which correspond to civilian jobs as part of their regular military duties — but whether performance of such tasks in a particular context is appropriate to the broader function of the force in question. The possibility that an individual constable may seek to challenge the lawfulness of an order to act as substitute labour should not be discounted.[44]

Another objection to using the police to replace strikers is that it puts a question-mark over their independence. The police are not subject to operational control by either central or local government, and 'it may be plausible to suppose that . . . their perceived independence of political institutions is an asset worth preserving'.[45] During the 1979 ambulancemen's dispute, according to the Home Office, police assistance was furnished at the discretion of the Chief Officer of Police. To this extent the constitutional theory of 'independence' was maintained. However, as Whelan points out, this development 'represents a major undermining of the traditional responsibility [of government] for industrial dispute policy, particularly as it can be argued that the police were used *instead* of service personnel'.[46] Police involvement as substitute labour risks falling between the Scylla of governmental control and the Charybdis of unaccountability. By contrast:

> [t]he armed forces . . . are undoubtedly employees of the Crown, and in general, subject to the orders of Ministers. They have,

> therefore, no such impartial and independent reputation to dissipate; and their use to take the place of strikers is to that extent less objectionable.[47]

There are strong arguments, both legal and political, against the continued use of the police in this role.

Reserve forces and civilian volunteers

Each of the armed services, the Army, Navy and Air Force, has a reserve force which can be called out on permanent service by Royal Proclamation in times of imminent national danger or great emergency.[48] Its members can then be ordered to perform any tasks on which the regular forces can be employed, including acting as substitute labour. This has never been done. The Reserves have been called out only once during an industrial dispute, at the outset of the 1921 coal stoppage, when the railwaymen and transport workers threatened sympathetic action. For nearly two months, 58,000 men, including many trade unionists, were mobilized, but their activities were restricted to patrol duties.[49] The military authorities subsequently protested that calling on these forces to deal with civil unrest, as opposed to threats from overseas, could damage recruitment, and the Baldwin Government decided against using them during the General Strike, in line with its policy of relying on the police rather than the military to maintain order.

Another force which could be seen as a source of substitute labour is the Territorial Army, now over 76,000 strong, which may be mobilized once a proclamation has been issued calling out the Army Reserve. (The Government has recently announced that it intends to increase its numbers to 86,000 by 1990.)[50] Again this force has never been used to replace strikers, although the idea was considered by the Thatcher Conservative Government in 1980 in the context of a general discussion about civilian volunteers. The then Foreign Secretary, Mr Francis Pym, apparently persuaded the Prime Minister that taking this course could jeopardize the military functions of the force, particularly as many of its members belong to trade unions in civilian life.[51] The Government was given the opportunity to clarify its position officially in February 1981. In a parliamentary written answer, a junior Defence minister, Mr Philip Goodhart, denied that the Government was contemplating inviting Territorials to indicate their willingness or otherwise to serve alongside the regular forces during disputes and confirmed that there were 'no plans' to use Territorial Army Centres to muster civilian volunteers. Nevertheless, individual members of the force may still have a role to play. Mr Goodhart confirmed that it would still be open to them as private citizens 'to volunteer assistance to the appropriate civil authorities during an emergency, just like any member of the general public'.[52]

There is no general corps of civilian volunteers ready to act as substitute labour, although the idea of forming such a force has been considered on several occasions both by governments and by unofficial organizations. Governments have always been wary of the provocative effect such a move could have, however, and with the exception of the period 1925–6, have not welcomed outside bodies assuming this role because of their potential for independent action. Members of the first of these bodies, a 'Volunteer Police Force' formed to maintain services and preserve the peace in the wake of the 1911 railway strike, were urged by the Home Secretary to contact 'responsible police authorities' rather than join an organization whose 'methods inevitably become open to suspicion'.[53]

The recruitment of skilled civilian volunteers on a large scale first became an important element in Government contingency planning for disputes after the First World War. Enthusiasm for this idea was due partly to the reluctance of the military authorities to release servicemen for civilian tasks, particularly as demobilization progressed, and partly because it provided useful propaganda in demonstrating public opposition to strikes. Volunteers replaced the regular workforce during the strikes in the Yorkshire mines and on the railways in 1919, and various learned and technical societies compiled registers of members willing to work in power stations should the need arise. In February 1920 the Cabinet approved plans to establish eighty-eight 'Volunteer Service Committees' throughout the country, chaired by prominent local people, to recruit volunteers for food distribution, transport and shipping, leaving local authorities to organize the maintenance of gas, electricity and water. Appeals to the public to pump mines and provide transport services at the outset of the 1921 coal dispute suggests that enrolment had not progressed very far at that time. General official recruiting was halted after this stoppage and was not resumed until the General Strike of 1926.

The General Strike was the last occasion on which civilian volunteers were used in large numbers to replace workers in dispute. The Baldwin Government waited until the strike began before issuing any general call for help to the public, mainly for administrative reasons.[54] However, it lent its support to a private organization, the Organization for the Maintenance of Supplies (O.M.S.), which was established in 1925 as

> an association of loyal citizens organised in the public interest to provide the Government in times of emergency with classified lists of those who will assist in maintaining essential public services.

It claimed to be 'non-political and non-party in character' with no 'aggressive and provocative aims' and open to citizens 'of all classes'.[55] The O.M.S. Governing Council, headed by Lord Hardinge, a former Viceroy of India, included several eminent public figures, and there is some evidence that ministers had a hand in its inauguration.[56] Its existence certainly deflected attention from the Government's own preparations for the General Strike.

The relationship between the O.M.S. and the Government's emergency machine was initially left undefined, and Home Office officials feared that it might prove problematic. At a meeting in December 1925 officials insisted that once an emergency arose, control of the organization must pass to the Government. In the event, the practical value of the O.M.S. proved to be negligible. Despite its illustrious founders, the organization failed to secure the financial support for which it had hoped, and the necessity to train its members in secret to avoid allegations of provocation also created problems. Of the 100,000 names handed over to the Government at the start of the strike, only 5 per cent had a skill of any kind and only a tiny proportion of the persons listed were actually called upon to help.[57] Of far greater use were the volunteers recruited by the Government. A broadcast appeal on the eve of the strike brought forward 488,155 civilians, and although again these were largely unskilled, 62,629 were allotted some task.[58] Particularly successful were the preparations to maintain power stations, especially in London, where suitable civilian volunteers had been earmarked for service in advance.[59]

Post-war Governments have fought shy of recruiting volunteer labour on a formal basis, although approval has sometimes been given to utilizing existing sources of assistance. The contingency planners in the Attlee Government gave prolonged consideration to the establishment of special recruiting machinery, but this was vigorously opposed by the Minister of Labour, Mr George Isaacs, and it was decided that volunteers would be recruited if necessary to deal with specific emergencies. Some employers maintained their own lists of suitable substitutes during this period, however; the Electricity Authority supplied volunteers loaned from plant installation contractors to work alongside service labour during the London electricity strike of 1949, and the Railway Executive also collected details of persons with 'particular skill or experience'.[60]

No serious official consideration was given to recruiting a volunteer corps between 1948 and 1980. In the mid-1970s, however, two private organizations under the leadership of retired military commanders were established. Both General Sir Walter Walker and Colonel David Stirling, who founded 'Unison' and 'Great Britain 75' ('GB 75'), respectively, contended that the Government lacked the available manpower to deal with a General Strike or near General Strike and that neither major party contemplated acquiring it for fear of being accused of 'strikebreaking' or 'union bashing'. Confidential documents about 'GB 75', published by the pacifist newspaper *Peace News*,[61] indicated that the organization intended drawing on contributions from 'Industry, Commerce and the City' and would recruit and train volunteers to maintain essential services and broadcasting and to preserve law and order. Both men denied any sinister political motives and Stirling specifically declared he would have 'no truck with the extreme right and neo-fascists'. Assurances that they would act only at governmental request were later modified, however. Arguing that the Labour 'left-wing captivated' administration would not issue a request for help until it was too late, Walker said he would answer the call of a chief constable or 'any other legitimate local body'.[62] Stirling talked of 'rounding-up' workers who 'sat-in' at essential plants.[63]

The Labour Government gave an understandably unenthusiastic reception to the formation of these organizations. The Secretary of State for Defence, Mr Roy Mason, denounced 'GB 75' as a 'near-fascist groundswell', and the Home Secretary, Mr Roy Jenkins, said that Walker's ideas were 'at best misconceived and ill-considered and at the worst dangerous'.[64] The amount of support these organizations attracted is unclear. Walker claimed at one time a force of half-a-million but this figure has not been independently verified; it was later reported that GB 75 had decided to concentrate its resources on electricity supply,[65] suggesting that it may have attracted a rather limited response.

Section 2 of the Public Order Act 1936 makes it an offence to take part in the 'control or management' of any association organized, trained or equipped for the purpose of enabling its members to be employed 'in usurping the functions of the police or of the armed forces of the Crown' or for 'the use or display of physical force in promoting any political object or in such a manner as to arouse reasonable apprehension that they are organised and either trained or equipped for that purpose'. Prosecution requires the consent of the Attorney-General. Walker and Stirling denied that they were contemplating private armies, and Lord Hailsham, Lord Chancellor at the time of writing, was of the opinion that they were doing nothing illegal, but had these organizations started to intervene in disputes without the consent of the Government their legality could have been open to question.

In mid-1980 the Thatcher Government gave fresh consideration to organizing an official volunteer labour force. That this was happening first came to light when *The Times* published a confidential Department of the Environment document on emergency planning which specified the use of volunteers in disputes as one of its objectives, in pursuit of which talks were to be held with local authority associations.[66] Although 'the 10 Downing Street press office took great pains to pour cold water over the notion',[67] Mrs Thatcher indicated in replies to Parliamentary Questions that she would not wish to discourage this development. On the day the story appeared, a Conservative backbencher asked the Prime Minister whether she recognized the desire of unemployed youth to serve the community by 'keeping essential services, such as hospitals, running in the event of strike action by those who have jobs'. Her reply was as follows:

> I very much agree that large numbers of school leavers are anxious to give service to the community, including voluntary work. They expect to see essential services kept going. If a time were to come when those services were not kept going, young people would be the first to lend a hand.[68]

A few days later the Prime Minister was asked directly whether there were proposals to encourage the use of volunteers to replace strikers in public services. She replied that she recognized

> the value of the work of established voluntary organisations in helping to maintain essential public services in an emergency, and . . . [she had] no doubt about the willingness of private individuals volunteering to help in such situations, where they can usefully do so.[69]

However, the Minister for Local Government denied that any discussions had been held with local authorities on the matter at that stage.[70]

The issue was debated by ministers for some months. Contingency planners apparently advised against volunteers on the ground that they would generally be more trouble than they were worth: they would be unable to help a great deal in most industries and would probably exacerbate any dispute in which they became involved.[71] By the autumn it had been decided not to deploy the Territorial Army to replace strikers and, although no resolution of the broader question of using civilian volunteers was reached, any such proposals seem to have been dropped for the time being. Government policy now appears to be that '[i]t is for employers to take whatever steps they may consider appropriate to arrange for volunteers to assist [during disputes]'.[72]

One particular area where volunteers have played a significant role in recent years is the N.H.S. Ever since 1973 it has been common practice to call for volunteers during disputes involving ambulancemen, and the St. John's Ambulance Brigade and the Red Cross are now the second source of alternative labour for striking ambulancemen after the police. As far as replacing hospital workers is concerned, one convenient source of substitute labour for less-skilled workers would be the pool of volunteers who permanently work alongside paid staff. Aware of the difficulties which this might cause, the Volunteer Centre has issued guidelines, drawn up by representatives of unions, management and voluntary organizations, designed to prevent any conflicts during disputes which might jeopardize the co-operation which the unions generally afford to such people. These guidelines state that volunteers should do no more work during disputes than they would do normally unless management and staff representatives agree otherwise, and they should not attempt to cross hostile picket lines.[73] As described in Chapter 6, at the beginning of the ancillary workers' campaign in 1979 the D.H.S.S. reminded health authorities of these provisions but finally allowed volunteers to be used when the action intensified. In contrast, the Conservative Government's Circular 'If Industrial Relations Break Down', issued later in 1979, encourages health service employers to make 'such use of volunteers as they think fit' during disputes[74] and makes no reference to the Volunteer Centre's guidelines beyond warning that the position of regular volunteers may require special consideration. During the extensive 1982 health service dispute, external volunteers were called for in only one Region, although there was widespread use of volunteers drawn from existing staff, mainly managers and nurses. The survey of health service administrators, reported in Chapter 6, indicates that local administrators would wish to bring in external volunteers only as a desperate last resort.

The evidence suggests that in general the main value of calling on civilian volunteers to replace strikers would be the 'public relations' aspect identified by the Lloyd George administration; it would provide a concrete demonstration of opposition to a dispute. In most cases, a 'demonstration' is all there would probably be, however. Good intentions could not compensate for lack of the skill necessary to do the job, and unlike soldiers, civilians are unused to obeying orders. Short of creating literally alternative labour forces, fully trained in performing particular kinds of work, civilian volunteers are unlikely to provide much real assistance in maintaining supplies, and in many services, such as the public utilities, fire service and areas of the health service, they could cause additional hazards both to themselves and others. Moreover, their presence, being voluntary, would almost certainly provoke much greater hostility on the part of strikers than that of the military. For all these reasons it is to be hoped that the idea of organizing civilians to replace strikers will be laid to rest in the 'rejected' file of contingency planners.

GOVERNMENT CONTINGENCY PLANNING FOR DISPUTES

The development of contingency planning

The idea that the Government should maintain standing administrative machinery ready to meet the disruption which industrial action in essential services can bring dates back to the period of industrial unrest which followed the First World War. (The nature of this unrest is described briefly in Chapter 3.) During the war, for the first time

> central government assumed wide powers of supervision over many, if not most, areas of national life . . . . Through the creation of a central apparatus to secure the supply of essential goods and services in wartime a precedent was established for the provision of a similar function in peacetime, albeit in a less highly developed form.[75]

The initial step came early in 1919 when the Government established an Industrial Unrest Committee, under the chairmanship of the Home Secretary, to formulate plans to counter major industrial disputes; this committee in turn appointed sub-committees to deal with particular areas. The Government machine worked efficiently during the week-long railway strike in 1919, and the Government decided to continue the development of centralized contingency planning. The Industrial Unrest Committee was replaced by the more neutrally titled Supply and Transport Committee (S.T.C.), this time chaired by the Minister of Transport, and work began on drafting legislation to enable the Committee's plans to be put into operation in times of crisis. The end-product of these drafts was the Emergency Powers Act 1920. In addition, eleven Civil Commissioners for England and Wales were appointed to co-ordinate the military, the police and the provision of essential services at a local level. Hand in hand with the development of centralized administrative machinery went a centralization of intelligence gathering, a process which had also started during the First World War. From May 1919 all intelligence-collecting activities which were conducted by the police, the military and agents of various government departments were co-ordinated by the Police Special Branch.[76]

The S.T.C. took limited measures at the start of the miners' strike in October 1920 and again in March 1921, when it resolved that a state of emergency should be declared, that troops should be put on alert and that coal exports should be halted. The Committee was fully prepared for the strike to be extended to the railway and transport workers, and according to Tom Jones, a member of the Cabinet Secretariat, was most disappointed when the threat receded. He recorded in his diary:

> The strike committee very sick[sic]. They had been waiting for two years to press the button. They had pressed it. The Strike Books had been issued from the secret banks where they had been concealed, the milk cans were rolling down to Devon and could not be stopped, the troops were steaming in ship and train from Ireland, from Malta, from Silesia to defend us from the men of Fife . . . . But John Thomas [the railwaymen's leader] upset it all and despoiled Sir Hindenburg Geddes [the Minister of Transport] of the fruits of victory.[77]

After the Triple Alliance's failure to act on that occasion, the prospect of transport and food supplies being disrupted seemed more remote, and, against a background of cuts in Government expenditure, it was decided towards the end of 1921 to disband the organization in its existing form and retain only a small nucleus under the supervision of the Home Secretary. This was done partly to save money (emergency services for the years ending March 31, 1921 had cost over £776,000)[78] and partly out of a desire to force local authorities and private trade bodies to make their own arrangements. The President of the Board of Trade argued that

> Traders and consumers alike have become so accustomed during the last two years to regard the maintenance of food and other essential services as a normal function of government that private enterprise can hardly be expected to reassert itself adequately unless the necessity is made absolutely clear.[79]

A circular issued to local authorities in May 1922 confirmed that henceforth they themselves must prepare to deal with the disruption of local services, and the Government resolved to intervene only where local authorities and/or trade associations were unable to cope.[80]

The arrival of a Conservative Government late in 1922 brought another change of direction. A committee under the chairmanship of a senior civil servant, Sir John Anderson, recommended that 'if only as a preventative measure' the Government should prepare plans to deal with emergencies of the kind specified in the Emergency Powers Act 1920.[81] The committee proposed that each government department should be responsible for emergency preparations within its sphere of influence, under the supervision of an *ad hoc* Cabinet Committee composed of the ministers principally concerned. It also recommended resuscitating administrative machinery at local level.

The Government accepted this report and Mr J.C. Davidson, Chancellor of the Duchy of Lancaster, was given the task of rebuilding the contingency planning machine. In January 1924, however, the Conservatives were forced to resign and the first Labour Government took office. Davidson feared that his work would then be undone, but these fears proved ungrounded. Faced with a threatened dock strike, Labour established its own S.T.C. and adopted the Anderson report in full. There was one departure from previous practice, however: the Government attempted to seek union co-operation in transporting essential foodstuffs and fuel during the strike rather than declaring a state of emergency.[82] The dispute ended before the union could give its reply to this request.

On the Conservatives' return to office late in 1924, a new S.T.C. was rapidly activated, and in July 1925 the Home Secretary informed the Cabinet that the Committee had aimed to construct a nucleus organization which could then be expanded to meet the exigencies of any situation.[83] The nine months between then and the start of the General Strike saw a filling-out of these plans, with preparations being made to meet a complete stoppage in all vital industries and services in anticipation of the time when the Government's subsidy to the mining industry, which had postponed a stoppage in 1925, expired. By February 1926 the Home Secretary was proclaiming publically that the Government was ready to meet any crisis which might occur.[84]

The Government's organization involved an extensive bureaucracy at local level. England and Wales were divided into ten regions, each headed by a Civil Commissioner, which were then further divided into areas. Each area had its own Food Officer, Road Officer, Coal Emergency Officer, Haulage Committee, and representatives for other essential services. A Circular issued to local authorities in November 1925 stressed that it was

> not intended that the Government should substitute new machinery for that ordinarily existing to meet the needs of the community. . . . [The organisation was designed] to supplement and to assist . . . the normal methods of communication, supply

and distribution and to give to all those who can help an opportunity of doing so in the manner most required.[85]

In line with this policy, the Government planned that food should be distributed on a normal commercial basis, with hauliers and traders using their own resources (and any additional drivers they might require) in co-operation with Government representatives. This was also cheaper for the Government and ensured that contractors continued to supervise their own vehicles. (During the railway strike of 1919, volunteer drivers had absconded with requisitioned vehicles to distant destinations and sometimes took the goods as well.)[86] However, the division of responsibility and density of Government supervision ensured that little was left to the political whims or administrative laxity of local bodies; only the maintenance of local public utility services was left solely in the hands of the local authorities.

In general, the Government machine coped well with its long-awaited adversary, the nine-day General Strike. A state of emergency was declared on the eve of the miners' stoppage and broad powers to requisition and direct supplies, described more fully in Chapter 3, appeared in the emergency regulations. However, the successful working of the voluntary arrangements and the T.U.C.'s desire to maintain essential food supplies made it largely unnecessary for Government officials to rely on compulsory powers to regulate the supply and distribution of essential commodities other than coal. Orders for the transport of priority supplies[87] were enforced in only two regions, and the only foodstuff of which the Government took direct charge was milk.[88] It seems that there were few significant shortages: indeed, on May 12, the day the strike was ended, *The Guardian* claimed that

> [t]he ordinary householder would have no reason to imagine that a General Strike had been proclaimed, and to a large extent enforced, over a week ago. It is reflected neither in the price nor in the quantity of food supplies in the shops.

George Glasgow, in a eulogistic account of the road transport system published the following year, stated that

> [i]t was the view of the authorities in the North-Western division – a view shared generally in every Division in the country – that after the first week's experience of the emergency organisation, the food supplies of the people could have been secured for an indefinite period.[89]

The S.T.C., too, was largely satisfied with the organisation's performance; a report compiled in 1929 concluded that experience in 1926 indicated that it required 'little or no overhauling'.[90]

Not all officials at local level were so sanguine, however. Colonel Strange, the South-Western Divisional Food Officer, believed that '[h]ad the General Strike lasted another fortnight or even another week a very different story would have had to be recorded'.[91]

Once the General Strike was over, the emergency organization was rapidly wound down and the S.T.C. played little part in dealing with the continuing stoppage in the mines. Contingency planning for disputes then remained at a fairly low level until after the Second World War. Only minor adjustments were made in the years up to 1929, and the S.T.C. went into abeyance entirely during the 1929–31 Labour administration. There was rather more activity after 1932: following a memorandum from Sir John Anderson, each government department accepted responsibility for emergency planning within its sphere, and an S.T.C. sub-committee met occasionally to review the organization as a whole. In general, however, '[e]mergency planning during the 1930s concentrated on civil defence in response to external military aggression rather than on establishing a strikebreaking organisation'.[92]

Whether or not to re-establish a standing organization to deal with the dislocation of essential supplies was a matter of heated debate within the post-war Labour Government. Senior civil servants and the Home Secretary, Mr Chuter Ede, were convinced that this was imperative, but initially there was trenchant opposition from two prominent left-wingers, Mr Aneurin Bevan, the Minister of Health, and Sir Stafford Cripps, President of the Board of Trade. Bevan argued that such an organization would be difficult to defend politically and that it was impossible to prepare in advance 'plans for meeting a purely hypothetical situation'; rather the Government 'should rely on improvizing arrangements at the last moment to meet the particular kind of situation with which they were faced'.[93] These objections were overruled by the Prime Minister and other ministers, however, and early in 1946 it was decided that civil servants from the various government departments should begin to prepare detailed emergency schemes. Further impetus to these preparations was provided in January 1947 by a road haulage dispute which interrupted food and other essential supplies and threatened to spread to the whole transport industry.

> [B]ecause post-war emergency planning had so far been limited to the secret preparation of paper plans at a high official level, the government had no organisation immediately available.

> Instead they had hurriedly to improvise arrangements . . . . The resulting action was inefficient, unco-ordinated and in sharp contrast to the apparently smooth running of the pre-war organisation.[94]

The Home Secretary was determined that this situation should not recur. A Cabinet Committee which had been formed to deal with the road haulage dispute was reconstituted without debate after the crisis had passed in order to supervise the formulation of plans to provide and maintain in any emergency supplies and services essential to the life of the community. From then on there has always been a standing Cabinet Committee charged with this function. Another policy adopted at that time which has also continued is that of involving management representatives from the relevant industries in the planning process.

The Attlee Government's Emergency Committee met on several occasions to deal with disputes in the docks, transport and electricity industries and

> [b]y the time the . . . administration left office in 1951, a fully fledged . . . Committee, with a Civil Service shadow, had drawn up immensely detailed plans to cope with the consequences of disputes in a whole list of fuel and power, transport and food industries.[95]

The concept of a standing emergencies organization was accepted without question by the incoming Conservative administration, and the contingency planning machine continued along much the same lines as before. For almost two decades it received few serious challenges: an oil-tanker drivers' strike in 1953, a railway strike in 1955 and a seamen's strike in 1966. This lack of use seems to have sent the organization into a near-moribund state; in the early 1970s it rapidly became obvious that the planners had failed to take sufficient account of the implications of more sophisticated technology and increase in trade union power. This was first made manifest by industrial action in the electricity supply industry in 1970, the immediate impact of which apparently took the Heath Government by surprise. Mr Douglas Hurd, then political secretary to the Prime Minister, recorded that it was 'clear that all the weeks of planning in the Civil Service ha[d] totally failed to cope with what . . . [was] happening'.[96] It took the 1972 miners' strike, however, to provoke the Government into pursuing any major reform. The lack of preparedness to deal with this dispute, which, as Chapter 3 describes, forced drastic reductions in electricity supply, led the Prime Minister to commission a review of the entire contingency planning procedure. This review resulted in the transfer of responsibility for contingency planning from the Home Office to the Cabinet Office and the replacement of the old Emergencies Committee by the Civil Contingencies Unit (C.C.U.). The C.C.U. has remained in charge of contingency planning ever since.

Both civil servants, who meet alone to deal with the routine aspects of planning, and ministers are involved in the work of the C.C.U., which, when ministers sit, is chaired by the Home Secretary. Individual government departments prepare plans to counter disruption within their respective spheres of responsibility[97] but

> [t]he C.C.U. is the focus of Whitehall emergency planning, employing the most experienced planners, who give advice to their colleagues in the government departments, and it is the place where all the threads of state contingency planning are pulled together.[98]

It has close links with the police and the military. In times of actual emergency full meetings, with both ministers and officials present, may take place daily.[99] During the 1978–9 'winter of discontent' the Prime Minister also set up a secret *ad hoc* ministerial committee to take decisions on political strategy.[100] This pattern was repeated in 1984 when an *ad hoc* Cabinet Committee was established to receive reports from the Secretary of State for Energy on the impact of the miners' strike.

> The Committee consisted also of representatives from interested departments (Trade and Industry, Employment, Transport, the Home Office and the Scottish Office) with the services of the Attorney-General and representatives of armed forces' interests. The docks strike in July widened the group to take in the Prime Minister's Deputy . . . and the Chancellor.[101]

The C.C.U.'s work is not confined to strikes in essential services; it also encompasses other types of civil emergencies ranging from natural disasters to terrorist threats.[102] Its organization includes a network of Regional Emergency Committees composed of senior officials from various Government departments under the chairmanship of regional directors of the Environment or Transport Ministries. These committees, which can be activated whenever circumstances require, were used to monitor the supply situation during the 1979 road haulage strike and on that occasion also included representatives of local authorities, the police and the military.[103] The home civil defence structure, which contains plans for establishing regional seats of government, can also be relied upon should the need arise.

One of the first tasks undertaken by the secretary of the C.C.U. after its foundation was to draw up a list of the essential industries and services most vulnerable to disruption, together with an assessment of the capacity of the military to act as substitute labour in maintaining them. Electricity has always remained at the top of this list, on which sixteen industries appear.

> Others have moved up and down as amendments have been made in the light of experience. After the 1979 winter, the haulage industry is somewhat higher than the sixteenth place it occupied in 1972. Water, always in the top ten, moved up to join docks, coal, rail and oil in the group just beneath power, when the docility of its labour force could no longer be taken for granted.[104]

Since 1972, detailed plans have been made and refined by both Conservative and Labour Governments to deal with specific levels of disruption in each of these industries. These plans may involve taking precautionary measures well in advance of actual disputes; as indicated in Chapter 3, the electricity authorities were under pressure from the Thatcher Government to build up coal stocks and keep expensive oil-burning stations in working order in anticipation of a stoppage in the coalmining industry, and coal stocks at pitheads were also built up. These policies, combined with continued production in the Nottinghamshire coalfield and extensive police operations to prevent mass secondary picketing, meant that when the 1984–5 miners' strike took place, the Government was able to achieve its aim of denying the miners 'the satisfaction of seeing a single 60-watt bulb go out'.[105]

Contingency planning to meet disruption of essential services is now highly sophisticated. As the recent miners' strike has shown, it now includes a very significant role for the police. Another by-product of the 1972 miners' strike, along with the formation of the C.C.U., was the establishment of the National Reporting Centre, which co-ordinates mutual aid between police forces. It works under the operational command of the President of the Association of Chief Police Officers. Police Special Branches, whose functions include assisting the Security Services in defending the Realm from the actions of persons and organizations which may be judged to be 'subversive' to the State, are also part of the machine. Home Office guidelines define 'subversive activities' as 'those which threaten the safety or well being of the State, and which are intended to undermine or overthrow parliamentary democracy by political, industrial or violent means'. National disputes in essential services are unlikely not to be regarded as falling within this definition. The strategies adopted to deal with disputes may vary between Governments, but there is little doubt that the maintenance of a standing organization to meet industrial 'emergencies' is accepted by most politicians as a legitimate and necessary function of government.

Characteristics of contingency planning

The dominant characteristic of British contingency planning is the emphasis which has been placed on keeping the nature of the plans, and sometimes their very existence, as confidential as possible. From the inception of the emergencies organization in 1919, ministers and officials feared accusations that they were preparing machinery for 'strikebreaking', a view which could provoke the very action it was designed to counter. Initially, expenditure by the S.T.C. was disguised in Home Office allocations[106] and the resuscitation of the organization in 1923 was a closely guarded secret. The involvement of local authorities and trade representatives necessitated some publicity for preparations to meet the General Strike, but the Government used this to good psychological advantage in assuring the public of victory over any challenges which the unions might present. In 1945 Home Office officials identified the 'main problem' of the pre-war planners as having been 'how to maintain the nucleus of an organization which would be ready to function at reasonable notice of large-scale industrial troubles without giving the organization undesirable publicity'.[107] Contemporary Government spokesmen have made no secret of the fact that contingency plans for disputes exist and are kept under regular review, but they have refused to disclose any further details. Such information which is available is generally the product of 'leaks' to the press.

Occasionally, attempts have been made to lift the veil of secrecy. Josiah Wedgwood, Chancellor of the Duchy of Lancaster and Chief Civil Commissioner in the 1924 Labour administration, argued that a Labour Government could and should take the public into its confidence on the ground that it had nothing of which to be ashamed. In the past there had been 'an almost melodramatic air of secrecy about the whole business as though a revolution were being contemplated, rather than a straight-forward effort being made to keep the essential services going'; this had fostered 'suspicion' and a 'Fascist atmosphere'. What was needed was an 'open statement of what the Government require[d] and what it mean[t] to secure in case of emergency'.[108] The Labour Government did not remain in office for long enough for this proposal to be translated into action. Aneurin Bevan and Sir Stafford Cripps pleaded for greater openness by the post-war Labour

Government, but their arguments fell on deaf ears. A recent, rather surprising advocate of a more open approach is Lord Jellicoe, ministerial head of the C.C.U. in 1972–3. In 1979 he put forward the view that

> the Government should come clean about civil contingency planning. It is an important area about which the public ought to be reassured. I do not consider it strike-breaking. It is a matter of sensible precautions, which any government should be thinking about, to mitigate the consequences of industrial action for the benefit of society as a whole. The generalities should not be concealed. Specific contingencies are another matter.[109]

The present Government shows no signs of taking up this suggestion. Indeed, details of plans to use servicemen to replace ambulancemen and ancillary health service workers which were sent by the D.H.S.S. to regional health authorities in 1980 included a covering letter which emphasized that disclosure would be 'extremely damaging to the Government's industrial relations policy'.[110]

The emphasis on secrecy reflects another characteristic of contingency planning; its adversarial nature. Although Governments claim that they are not taking sides as between employers and workers in preparing to safeguard essential supplies, the effect is clearly to lessen the impact of industrial action aimed at their disruption, thereby reducing union power. Moreover, management representatives from essential service operators are closely involved in the preliminary stages of the planning process; union representatives are not. Efforts by Aneurin Bevan to secure trade unions a place at the planning table were given short shrift. In addition, as Chapter 3 and earlier sections of this chapter have indicated, Governments of all persuasions have frequently used their powers to meet emergencies to counter disputes where their own economic policy is at stake. Machinery which in theory is designed only to protect the 'community' may therefore be employed in bolstering up the broader strategy of the Government of the day.

As well as preparing for disputes, contingency planning may also extend to making decisions that industrial action in particular sectors should be avoided if at all possible. In 1978 the Conservative M.P. Mr Nicholas Ridley drafted a report on the strategies which a future Conservative Government should adopt to deal with the nationalized industries.[111] This report classified these industries into three groups according to the degree of difficulty which their disruption would present. Sewage, water, gas, electricity and the health service were seen as the most problematic, followed in the next category by the railways, docks, coal industry and refuse collection, and lastly by eduction, ports, telephones, steel, air transport and buses. Ridley concluded that where industries had 'the nation by the jugular vein' the only feasible option was to 'pay up'. It may have been with an eye to this advice that industrial action in the water industry in 1980 and 1981, and in the electricity industry in 1982, was narrowly averted by last-minute improvements in pay offers, although efforts to settle the conflict in the water industry in 1983 did not avoid a strike. The post-1979 Conservative Governments have not adopted a formal incomes policy, but their *de facto* pay policy for the public sector implemented by setting cash limits and 'pay norms' has been able, as Sir Leo Pliatzky argued in 1982, to take account of 'industrial muscle' as 'grounds for special treatment'.[112]

CONCLUSION

The Government now has at its disposal an elaborate administrative machine, which involves ministers, civil servants, the military and the police, ready to spring into action whenever the disruption of essential services is threatened. There are standing contingency plans, often formulated in co-operation with employers, which are designed to minimize disruption and which may include taking measures well in advance of particular disputes. The doubts which beset governments of earlier times as to the legitimacy and political wisdom of maintaining such an organization have now evaporated.

The use of troops as substitute labour has always been a crucial aspect of Government contingency plans. Where strikes occur in technologically complex areas, or if they involve a large labour force, the capacity of troops to act as replacement labour may now be limited. Nevertheless, the power to deploy them on civilian work still remains important. In a political system which is based on the principle of democratic accountability, it is inexcusable that such a power can be exercised without reference to Parliament. A more recent development has been the employment of police on work left undone by strikers. Such employment is incompatible with the force's law enforcement role and should not be repeated. It is also open to question whether policemen are legally obliged to carry out such tasks.

Governments of all complexions have consistently denied that they are furthering sectional interests by making plans to mitigate the impact of disputes and invoking them on particular occasions. It is impossible to argue that the contingency planning process is not designed to diminish workers' industrial strength, however, and the distinction between protecting essential services and strikebreaking can only be one of degree, depending upon the level of activity it is sought to maintain. The idea that the Government is remaining 'neutral' when it puts its plans into operation is pure rhetoric. As James Klugmann wrote, '[i]f that impossible phenomenon, a neutral Government, could exist, it would bring in the troops on Monday to scab on the dockers, and on Tuesday despatch them to swell the picket line'.[113]

The mask of 'neutrality' is also belied by the secrecy which has traditionally surrounded the contingency planning process and the refusal of governments to make trade unions privy at any level to their arrangements. This 'adversarial' approach has led to the development of more sophisticated tactics on the union side, described in greater detail in chapters 5 and 6. Industrial action planned by electricity supply workers in 1982 was designed to increase the costs of electricity generation and prevent revenue collection whilst safeguarding supplies to consumers. Future campaigns may follow the strategy advocated by health service workers in 1982 of pulling out key workers whose wages can be maintained by those who continue at work; this causes maximum disruption at minimum cost to the unions and to those on strike. In 1980 the firemen planned one-day strikes without warning, with the specific aim of threatening local authorities with the expense of maintaining troops on permanent standby as well as the payment of firemen's wages for the days on which they worked. The cost of implementing contingency plans to counter industrial action is one of the factors to be borne in mind when evaluating the merits of the various approaches to disputes in essential services discussed in the concluding chapter.

NOTES

1. Keith Jeffery and Peter Hennessy, *States of Emergency*, Routledge and Kegan Paul, London, 1983.
2. K.G.J.C. Knowles, *Strikes: A Study in Industrial Conflict*, Blackwell, Oxford, 1952, p.133.
3. Cab 24/84, GT 7881 and 7884.
4. See now the Army Act 1955, s.34; the Air Force Act 1955, s.34; the Naval Discipline Act 1957, s.12.
5. H.C. Deb., Vol. 36, col. 1305 (April 10, 1912).
6. See TC 54, Cab 27/74. The issue turns on the scope of the concept of a 'lawful' command. In *Warden* v. *Bailey* (1811) 4 Taunt. 67, an action for false imprisonment by a sergeant against his colonel, Mansfield C.J. stated (at 89) that an order to attend a school to read and write was 'not a part of military discipline', although clearly to carry it out would not be unlawful. The Manual of Military Law defines a 'lawful' command as one which is not only not contrary to the civil law or international law, but which is also 'justified by military law' in relating to some 'military duty or usage' (Part 1, para. 34, note 3a). The Judge Advocate General identified the duties of the soldier as being to defend the Crown 'against all enemies foreign and domestic, to train and prepare himself for that purpose and do all acts and things connected therewith or incidental thereto, and in connection with such service to obey the orders of His Majesty or any superior officer'.
7. The Emergency Regulations 1926, S.R. & O. 1926 No. 556, reg. 24.
8. The Defence (Armed Forces) Regulations 1939 S.R. & O. 1939 No. 1304, reg. 6.
9. Jeffery and Hennessy, *States of Emergency*, as above, note 1, p.144.

10. By the Emergency Laws (Transitional Provisions) Act 1946, the Emergency Laws (Miscellaneous Provisions) Act 1947, various Continuance Orders under section 7 of the 1947 Act, and the Emergency Laws (Repeal) Act 1959.

11. The Defence (Transfer of Functions) Act 1964.

12. Mr Henry Brooke, H.C. Debs, Vol. 689, col. 1413 (February 20, 1964).

13. In *Troops in Strikes*, The Cobden Trust, London, 1984, Steve Peak argues that the common law may give only magistrates, and not the Government, the power to mobilize troops within the Realm (pp. 53–62). Given the view of the Ministry of Defence that the only effect of section 2 is to extend military discipline to these tasks, Peak argues that section 2 is inadequate to give the Government the authority to deploy troops on civilian work. It seems extremely unlikely that the executive's power under the Royal Prerogative to dispose of the armed forces is restricted in this way, however; see Stephen C. Greer, 'Military Intervention in Civil Disturbances: The Legal Basis Reconsidered', *Public Law* (1983), 573; Geoffrey Marshall, *Constitutional Conventions*, Clarendon Press, Oxford, 1984, Ch. 9. The important and complex question of where responsibility lies for military intervention in suppressing civil disorder is beyond the scope of this book.

14. The Defence Council consists of the Secretary of State for Defence, the Ministers and Parliamentary Under-Secretaries of State for the Armed Forces and for Defence Procurement, the chiefs of the Defence, Naval, General and Air Staffs, the First Sea Lord, the Vice Chief of the Defence Staff, the Chief of Defence Procurement for the Ministry of Defence, the Chief Scientific Adviser of the Ministry of Defence and the Permanent Under-Secretary of State of the Ministry of Defence.

15. Mr Francis Pym, Secretary of State for Defence, H.C. Deb., Vol. 978, col. 761 (February 14, 1980).

16. Peak, *Troops in Strikes*, as above, note 13, p.68.

17. *Ibid.*, p.69.

18. *Ibid.*, p.77.

19. *Ibid.*, p.133.

20. Marshall, *Constitutional Conventions*, as above, note 13, p.163.

21. Peak, *Troops in Strikes*, as above, note 13, pp.65, 129–30.

22. Jeffery and Hennessy, *States of Emergency*, as above, note 1.

23. See Review of the British Docks Strikes 1949, Cmd. 7851 (1949); Report of a Court of Inquiry into Unofficial Strikes in the London Docks, Cmd. 8236 (1951).

24. See, for example, H.C. Deb., Vol. 416, col. 1525 (November 28, 1945) (written answer).

25. Harold Wilson, *The Labour Government 1964–1970*. Weidenfeld and Nicolson and Michael Joseph, London, 1971, p. 231.

26. The Attorney-General, Mr Sam Silkin, H.C Deb., Vol. 961, col. 719 (January 25, 1979).

27. Peak, *Troops in Strikes*, as above, note 13, p.72

28. Dr John Gilbert, Minister of State, Ministry of Defence, H.C. Deb., Vol. 940, col. 1099 (December 6, 1977).

29. Peak, *Troops in Strikes*, as above, note 13, p.73.

30. Mr Barney Hayhoe, Under-Secretary of State for Defence for the Army, H.C. Deb., Vol. 990, col. 324 (August 7, 1980) (written answer).

31. Peak, *Troops in Strikes*, as above, note 13, p.73.

32. *The Guardian*, January 19, 1979.

33. H.C. Deb., Vol. 116, col. 1511 (May 29, 1919).

34. See E.C.S. Wade and A.W. Bradley, *Constitutional and Administrative Law*, 10th edn., Longmans, London, 1985, pp.204–6.

35. John W. Wheeler-Bennett, *John Anderson, Viscount Waverley*, Macmillan, London, 1962, p.158.

36. Lord Bourne, H.L. Deb., Vol. 358, col. 695 (March 18, 1975).

37. *Ibid.*, cols. 729–33.

38. See Gillian S. Morris, 'The Police and Industrial Emergencies', *Industrial Law Journal* 9 (1980), 1.

39. The Police (Discipline) Regulations 1985, S.I. 1985 No. 518.

40. See above, note 6.

41. Police Act 1964, Sched. 2.

42. Letter to the author from Mr Tony Judge, Secretary of the Police Federation, April 18, 1979.

43. Letter to the author, June 26, 1979.

44. It may be difficult for a constable who is disciplined for failing to obey an order to act as substitute labour to obtain a court order quashing the disciplinary penalty, however; see Morris, 'The Police and Industrial Emergencies', as above, note 38, pp. 8–10.

45. Marshall, *Constitutional Conventions*, as above, note 13, p.159.

46. Christopher J. Whelan, 'Armed Forces, Industrial Disputes and the Law in Great Britain' in *Military Intervention in Democratic Societies*, ed. Peter J. Rowe and Christopher J. Whelan, Croom Helm, Beckenham, 1985, p.126.

47. Marshall, *Constitutional Conventions*, as above, note 13, p.159.

48. Reserve Forces Act 1966,. s.5.

49. G.D.H. Cole, *Labour in the Coal-Mining Industry*, Clarendon Press, Oxford, 1923, pp. 203, 303.

50. *The Financial Times*, September 24, 1985.

51. Jeffery and Hennessy, *States of Emergency*, as above, note 1, p.259.

52. H.C. Deb., Vol. 998, cols. 312–3 (February 10, 1981) (written answer).

53. Mr Reginald McKenna, H.C. Deb., Vol. 32, col. 1009 (December 4, 1911).

54. ST (24), Cab 27/260.

55. *The Times*, September 25, 1925.

56. Patrick Renshaw, *The General Strike*, Eyre Methuen, London, 1975, p. 132; Christopher Farman, *The General Strike*, Rupert Hart-Davis, London, 1972, p. 41.

57. A. Mason, 'The Government and the General Strike', *International Review of Social History* XIV, 1 (1969), 1.

58. Sir William Joynson-Hicks, Home Secretary, H.C. Deb., Vol. 197, col. 2179 (July 7, 1926).

59. Jeffery and Hennessy, *States of Emergency*, as above, note 1, pp. 113–4.

60. *Ibid.*, p. 202.

61. *Special Issue*, August 23, 1974.

62. *The Times*, December 11, 1974.

63. *Ibid.*, August 24, 1974.

64. *Ibid.*, August 24, 1974; October 4, 1974.

65. *Ibid.*, March 19, 1975.

66. *Ibid.*, July 17, 1980.

67. Jeffery and Hennessy, *States of Emergency*, as above, note 1, p. 257.

68. H.C. Deb., Vol. 988, col. 1750 (July 17, 1980).

69. H.C. Deb., Vol. 989, col. 13 (July 21, 1980) (written answer).

70. Mr Tom King, H.C. Deb., Vol. 989, col. 375 (July 24, 1980).

71. Jeffery and Hennessy, *States of Emergency*, as above, note 1, p.258.

72. Mr Philip Goodhart, Under-Secretary of State of Defence for the Army, H.C. Deb., Vol. 998, col. 312 (February 10, 1981) (written answer).

73. 'Guidelines for Relationships between Volunteers and Paid Non-Professional Workers', The Volunteer Centre, Berkhamsted, 1977.

74. HC 79(20), para. 9.

75. Jeffery and Hennessy, *States of Emergency*, as above, note 1, p.3.

76. Roger Geary, *Policing Industrial Disputes 1893 to 1985*, Cambridge University Press, Cambridge, 1985, pp. 58–61.

77. Thomas Jones, *Whitehall Diary Vol. 1*, ed. Keith Middlemas, Oxford University Press, London, 1969, p.153.

78. Appropriation Account of the Home Office for Emergency Services, Civil Services and Revenue Report 1922 for 1920–1, Accounts and Reports 5.

79. CP 3433, Cab 24/129, September 21, 1921.

80. CP 3800, Cab 24/133, March 3, 1922.

81. Report to Cabinet, CP 314 (25), Cab 27/259, July 5, 1923.

82. See Chapter 6 for further discussion of this policy.

83. CP 356 (25), Cab 24/174, July 14, 1925.

84. *The Times*, February 9, 1926.

85. Circular 636, Ministry of Health, November 20, 1925

86. Wilfred Harris Crook, *The General Strike*, University of North Carolina Press, Chapel Hill, 1931, p.309.

87. The Road Transport Regulation (Ministry of Transport) Order; the Road Transport

Requisition Order and the Regulation of Priorities Order, quoted in George Glasgow, *General Strikes and Road Transport*, Geoffrey Bles, London, 1927, pp.124–34.

88. Milk Distribution (Emergency) Order, S.R. & O. 1926 No. 530; Milk Distribution (Emergency) No.2 Order, S.R. & O. 1926, No. 531.

89. Glasgow, *General Strikes and Road Transport*, as above, note 87, p.80.

90. Quoted in Jeffery and Hennessy, *States of Emergency*, as above, note 1, p.135.

91. *Ibid.*, pp.125–6.

92. Geary, *Policing Industrial Disputes 1893 to 1985*, as above, note 76, p.58.

93. Quoted in Jeffery and Hennessy, *States of Emergency*, as above, note 1, p.166.

94. *Ibid.*, p.172.

95. Peter Hennessy, 'Whitehall Contingency Planning for Industrial Disputes', in *Military Intervention in Democratic Societies* ed. Peter J. Rowe and Christopher J. Whelan, Croom Helm, Beckenham, 1985, p.98.

96. Quoted in *ibid.*

97. Mrs Margaret Thatcher, H.C. Deb., Vol. 31, col. 55 (November 8, 1982) (written answer).

98. Peak, *Troops in Strikes*, as above, note 13, p.67.

99. William Rodgers, 'Government Under Stress: Britain's Winter of Discontent 1979', *Political Quarterly* 55 (1984) 171.

100. Hennessy, 'Whitehall Contingency Planning for Industrial Disputes', as above, note 95, p. 103.

101. David Bonner, *Emergency Powers in Peacetime*, Sweet and Maxwell, London, 1985, p. 33.

102. Jeffery and Hennessy, *States of Emergency*, as above, note 1, p. 238.

103. As above, note 102, p. 244.

104. Peter Hennessy, 'Whitehall Contingency Planning for Industrial Disputes, as above, note 95, p. 101.

105. Peter Wilsher, Donald Macintyre and Michael Jones. *Strike; Thatcher, Scargill and the Miners*, André Deutsch, London, 1985, p. 219.

106. Civil Service and Revenue Departments 1920 Accounts and Papers 5; Civil Service and Revenue Departments 1921 Accounts and Papers 4.

107. Quoted in Jeffery and Hennessy, *States of Emergency*, as above, note 1, p.148.

108. Memorandum, February 15, 1924, App. to Cab 24/259; see also Memorandum, March 21, 1924, Cab 24/259.

109. *The Times* November 23, 1979.

110. *The Financial Times*, January 1, 1981.

111. This report was published in *The Economist*, May 27, 1978.

112. Sir Leo Pliatzky, 'Cash Limits and Pay Policy', *Political Quarterly* 53 (1982), 16 at 20.

113. James Klugmann, *History of the Communist Party Volume 1*, Lawrence and Wishart, London, 1968, p. 258.

5

The Conduct of Disputes in Essential Services: The Fire Service and the Electricity, Gas and Water Industries

The next two chapters examine the conduct of disputes in five sectors which are 'essential' even on a restrictive definition of that term, in that they furnish services whose disruption can put at risk the health or safety of a substantial proportion of the population. These five sectors are the fire service, the electricity, gas and water industries, and the National Health Service. The aim is not to analyse the causes and incidence of disputes, but rather to investigate the policies which workers' organizations in these sectors have adopted towards taking industrial action, the sanctions which workers have imposed and the responses which industrial action has drawn from employers and, in some cases, the Government. In particular, the discussion focuses upon the kinds of disruptive action chosen and the impact which this has produced on the service in question.

Traditionally, trade unions with members in essential services have been concerned to ensure that public health and safety are not jeopardized during disputes. Limiting the scope of industrial action to safeguard basic services may be seen as serving three major purposes. First, it avoids inflicting hardship to a degree which could dissipate public sympathy whilst at the same time emphasizing the essential nature of the service the workers provide. Secondly, assurances that essential services will be maintained may be required in order to persuade some workers to participate in disruptive action; this was probably true of early campaigns in the health service. Thirdly, it protects the interests of workers themselves, and their family and friends, who clearly are not immune from the consequences of disputes. As the T.U.C. recognized when planning the General Strike '[o]n the one hand it would be the function of the unions to make the stoppage as complete as possible. . . [but] if this was carried to an effective conclusion, would mean that commodities would be withheld from even our own members'.[1]

During the public sector stoppages of the 1970s it became common practice for unions to issue codes of conduct laying down broad guidelines on the services which members should seek to protect. In February 1979, when the 'winter of discontent' disputes in the road haulage industry, health service and local government were in full swing, the T.U.C. formalized this approach in its Guide to Affiliated Unions on the Conduct of Industrial Disputes, which was issued at the same time as the 'Social Concordat' between the T.U.C. and the last Labour Government.[2] The Guide advises unions to 'make arrangements in advance and with due notice, in consultation and preferably by agreement with the employer, for the maintenance by their members of supplies and services essential to the health or safety of the community or otherwise required to avoid causing exceptional hardship or serious pollution'. This principle was later adapted to disputes in the N.H.S. in a code of practice proposed by T.U.C.-affiliated unions with members in that area.[3]

Adherence to a code of conduct clearly limits the impact of disruptive action and may thereby reduce the bargaining strength of the work-force in dispute. As a *quid pro quo*, observance of a code of conduct has generally been made conditional on employers exercising reciprocal self-restraint by not seeking to undermine the action in ways which are considered unacceptable by the unions. This may involve management agreeing to pay workers who maintain emergency cover their normal wages, even though they are failing to perform their full range of contractual duties, or agreeing, expressly or by implication, that certain services should not be provided during the dispute. If managers transgress these limits by, for example, sending workers home or cutting pay, or calling for volunteers or outside contractors to perform strikers' jobs, this may lead to withdrawal of emergency cover by the unions. The operation and implications of this mutual self-restraint, or 'Queensberry Rules', approach to disputes is an important aspect of the discussion which follows. Further material for consideration of this approach is provided by a survey of the attitudes taken towards it by a sample of local-level managers in the N.H.S., based partly on their experiences in responding to a national dispute in 1982. This survey appears in the latter part of Chapter 6. The concluding section of Chapter 6 assesses the extent to which the 'Queensberry Rules' approach to disputes has operated in the sectors under discussion and looks at the attitudes which successive governments have taken towards co-operating with trade unions during disputes to minimize the dislocation of essential services and supplies during periods of industrial action.

THE FIRE SERVICE

Since 1938 all areas of Great Britain have been protected by a public fire brigade which furnishes fire-fighting services free of charge. Responsibility for maintaining a brigade rests with local authorities, although the Home Secretary (and Secretary of State for Scotland) have overall responsibility for the service and ensure that brigades maintain their operational efficiency.[4] Firemen perform in practice a wide range of duties other than fire-fighting, from assisting people locked out of houses to coping with major disasters, and they can be seen as providing a general 'civil emergency service'.[5] Since 1948 firemen's terms and conditions of employment have been determined on a national basis by the National Joint Council for Local Authorities' Fire Brigades, with power to deal with fire officers being delegated to a separate committee.

The risks to life and property if firemen withdraw their labour completely are obvious. Prior to a national strike in 1977, industrial action in the fire service was largely confined to banning routine duties, such as fire prevention, training, drills and equipment testing; answering only 'emergency' calls; refusing to ride on appliances which did not conform to Home Office specifications; and banning stand-by duties. There were official national campaigns involving sanctions of this nature in 1951, 1970 and 1975, and local campaigns in 1954 (in Glamorgan) and 1970 (in London and Essex). There was also unofficial action in London in 1968 and in Glasgow in 1973. All these disputes were concerned with pay apart from the 1954 campaign, which centred around a new duty system.

Until 1977 the F.B.U., which has both firemen and fire officers in membership, was firmly opposed to strikes in the fire service and was always keen to stress its concern for public safety during disputes. When Glasgow firemen began a week-long strike in 1973 the F.B.U. condemned them for jeopardizing a national claim and did not oppose assistance from neighbouring brigades or the deployment of troops, 500 of whom provided emergency cover. The only official action before 1977 to put safety at risk was in 1975, when fire cover in London reached a dangerously low level after three months of a national work-to-rule. The dispute was settled before any emergency measures became necessary. The other union with firemen in membership, N.A.F.O., has never organized industrial action, although it has threatened it on both a national and a local level. Membership of N.A.F.O. was until 1981 restricted to fire officers, but it is now open to all grades within the service. N.A.F.O. is recognized by the employers but it has been refused admission to the T.U.C., which takes the view that the F.B.U. has sole organizing rights in this sector.

The national strike of 1977–8 was called against the advice of the F.B.U. Executive Committee. The union had submitted a claim for an increase of 30 per cent, which was designed to bring firemen's wages up to the average weekly earnings of adult males plus 10 per cent to take account of the skill and danger involved in their job. The employers responded by offering 10 per cent, the maximum permissible under the Labour Government's pay guidelines which were then in operation, together with continued discussions on reduction of the working week and determination of the appropriate position of firemen in the national pay league. The F.B.U. Executive recommended negotiating within this framework and was clearly nervous about the prospect of a strike; the General Secretary, Mr Terence Parry, emotively asked firemen to consider whether they wished to allow old people's homes and city centres to burn to further their claim. Despite this appeal for restraint, a union delegate conference voted by a two-to-one majority for an all-out strike with no emergency cover. The union gave one week's notice of the strike, which began on November 14.

The Government responded to the crisis by bringing hurriedly into use some thousand old-fashioned 'Green Goddess' fire engines, which had been kept in store for purposes of civil defence. These were issued to fire authorities on the basis of one for every two regular appliances used to cover urban areas.[6] It also took rapid steps to train some troops to man them. This was the first occasion on which troops had been used to replace an entire work-force (of about 32,000) on a national scale and over 20,000 men were deployed, including sixty-six R.A.F. and 43 Navy fire-fighting teams. The remaining troops received only rudimentary training; the Government was advised that attempting to teach them to use breathing apparatus and other sophisticated equipment in a short period would only inspire a false sense of security and could be 'extremely dangerous'.[7] In order to avoid equipment being 'blacked' by the F.B.U. after the dispute was over, no attempt was made to use appliances from fire stations.

N.A.F.O. was not a party to this dispute but it advised its members at the outset not to exceed their normal duties or work with non-brigade appliances or personnel and not to cross official picket lines. This advice was later modified to allow officers to cross picket lines on a fireground to advise on the safety of military and fire services personnel engaged in fighting fires, and it seems clear that many fire officers did co-operate in the supervision of troops; they were said by the Prime Minister to have been 'the salvation of the service'.[8] Many thousands of part-time firemen also assisted in providing cover, and there were occasions when F.B.U. members left picket lines to help to deal with emergencies. The Home Office established a fire service operations room which maintained contact by telex with each brigade and

> 999 emergency fire telephone calls were diverted by the Post Office to the police where a military liaison officer was on duty. Co-ordination between the military and the police (including the checking of alarm calls by police and the accompanying of the Army to fires) meant that out of 255 calls in London in the first week of the strike, the Army attended only 36.[9]

Although the strike had serious financial consequences (insurance figures subsequently published showed that the cost of fire damage to property during the strike was roughly £117 million as compared with £52 million in the corresponding period the previous year)[10] no tragedies involving life or health were attributed to it. The action was finally called off after nine weeks when it became clear that under no circumstances would the employers exceed the 10 per cent limit. The firemen obtained a very valuable agreement for the future, however; an undertaking to bring their pay up to the upper quartile of manual workers' earnings by November 1979 and to maintain it at that level thereafter.

The formula agreed to end the 1977–8 strike has been applied to firemen's pay (and also, *pro rata*, to that of fire officers) up to the time of writing. It came under threat in 1980, however, when the Tory-dominated employers' side of the National Joint Council offered a 6 per cent increase to comply with the Conservative Government's guidelines for the public sector rather than the 18.8 per cent demanded by the formula. The F.B.U. and N.A.F.O. both gave notice of a one-day strike, to be followed by a series of one-day stoppages without any prior warning. This tactic was designed to ensure that troops would have to be kept on permanent stand-by at the expense of local authorities, which would also be liable to pay wages for the days when firemen worked. N.A.F.O. made clear that on this occasion its members would refuse to co-operate with troops in any way; in the words of its General Secretary, Mr Roy McGregor, there was to be 'a total closedown of the emergency service'.[11] The firemen's case attracted much public sympathy and the Government was embarrassed by revelations of pledges made by ministers whilst in Opposition to honour the 1978 agreement.[12] The employers finally conceded an 18.8 per cent rise, although in two installments, and the strike was called off hours before it was due to start. Following this dispute the employers gave notice to end the pay formula, but in May 1981 Labour acquired control of the employers' side of the National Joint Council and the formula was reinstated.

The operation of the pay formula has protected the fire service against industrial action over wages. One-day strikes were threatened by the F.B.U. Executive over an increase in pension contributions in 1983, but delegates decided against this course when the Government agreed to implement the increase in two stages. At present, redundancy seems the most likely issue to provoke a crisis; it is F.B.U. policy to recall its delegate conference with a firm recommendation for a national strike if any full-time fireman is made redundant. In the event of another strike, a greater number of troops would probably be better prepared than in 1977, but they would still be reliant on Green Goddesses unless the Government took the risk of requisitioning regular fire service equipment. The F.B.U. would probably picket army camps and take a tougher line against rendering assistance in emergencies. N.A.F.O.'s preparedness to co-operate with troops would depend on the circumstances and, in particular, whether it was itself in dispute: in the absence of supervision by fire officers the dangers to life and property would be greatly increased. Avoidance of any major tragedies during the 1977–8 strike does not mean that a future firemen's strike would be similarly controlled.

The relationship between industrial action and the statutory Discipline Code which governs the fire service[13] has proved problematic in the past. Offences such as disobeying lawful orders, insubordination, neglect of duty and lateness or absence are inevitably going to be committed when firemen take industrial action. Under the Code a chief fire officer can impose penalties ranging from a caution, reprimand or stoppage of pay to demotions or dismissal. During the 1951 dispute, disciplinary charges were preferred in many brigades and a wide variety of penalties were imposed, including demotion. This practice was vigorously opposed by the F.B.U., with T.U.C. support, and in most brigades charges were withdrawn and penalties rescinded once the dispute had ended, although it seems that they may have stood in some Scottish brigades.[14] In 1954 the Glamorgan Fire Authority also imposed penalties but these were quashed on appeal. The Discipline Code has not been invoked in disputes since then, and it is clearly inappropriate that it should be used in this context, although in local disputes, particularly unofficial ones (of which there were a growing number in the 1970s), the line between industrial action and insubordination may be hard to draw. At ground level, the problem may rest with a station officer. In an attempt to avoid its members being placed in an invidious position, N.A.F.O. issued guidelines in 1971 which were designed to ensure that decisions on how to react to disputes rested firmly with the Fire Authority. These guidelines were based on the premise that by accepting a 'demonstration' an authority tacitly agreed that certain duties would not be performed during it, and officers should not, therefore, order firemen to perform them. If industrial action exceeded the limits notified, officers should simply report the matter to the authority; they should not try to deal with the situation themselves. This approach helps to maintain the neutrality of officers during disputes and can prevent firemen engaging in disruptive action from committing breaches of the Discipline Code.

As well as invoking the Discipline Code, a few authorities in 1951 also suspended men who were refusing to work normally; on one particular day, out of 8,276 firemen outside London who were taking action, 348 had been suspended.[15] Firemen were also suspended in Essex during the 1970 dispute. Clearly, suspending men who are working restrictively carries the risk that the action will escalate into a total stoppage; in 1951 the F.B.U. alleged that the Home Office had advised authorities to implement suspensions only if relatively few men were involved in the protest.[16]

In 1977 A.C.A.S. recommended the application of a 'Queensberry Rules' approach to industrial action by firemen. This proposal was made in a report on industrial relations in the London Fire Service, where according to the employers, industrial action had become an 'almost normal feature' of Brigade life.[17] A.C.A.S. recommended that unions and employers should adopt a special set of rules for disputes which would allow firemen to demonstrate their grievances without losing pay but would also ensure that emergency services were maintained. This procedure should lay down a minimum notice period for industrial action and specify exactly which duties would, and which would not, be performed and any limitations on the employers' right to deploy men and appliances. The Discipline Code would not apply to conduct within the ambit of the demonstration but should continue to apply to attendance on emergency calls. The report included a specimen procedure in which, for example, it was stated that if a stand-by engine were moved to a station to replace a defective one, it should remain there until the dispute was over. If a station were forced to close because of the restrictions imposed, the firemen there would be deemed to be on strike. Although this proposal has not been formally adopted in the fire service, it is of considerable interest to observe that an independent body has accepted the implications of the 'Queensberry Rules' approach.

THE ELECTRICITY, GAS AND WATER INDUSTRIES

The electricity, gas and water industries are treated as a single category in Department of Employment strike statistics, and in the past their work-forces were covered by identical restrictions on taking industrial action. As essential public utilities they are subject to tight statutory regulation. Electricity and gas have been nationalized industries since shortly after the Second World War. The respective nationalizing statutes placed on the employers a duty to establish, by agreement with 'appropriate' organizations, negotiating machinery for settling the terms and conditions of employment of their workers,[18] and National Joint Councils were constituted to deal with manual and other grades in each industry. Before 1974 water supplies were furnished by a variety of statutory undertakers, including water companies, local authorities and joint water boards; since then, the bulk of supplies in England and Wales has come from ten regional water authorities, with private companies supplying the rest. The 1974 Water Act established a National Water Council with a statutory duty to operate negotiating machinery for the industry,[19] but since the abolition of the Council in 1983[20] arrangements for national negotiations now rest on voluntary agreement between employers and unions. At the time of writing, legislation is before Parliament which will return the gas industry to private ownership, whilst retaining British Gas' monopoly position. The Conservative Government is also considering the privatization of the electricity and water industries.

At one time workers in all three industries were subject to closed-shop agreements. Union membership became compulsory for electricity manual workers in 1969 and for clerical and administrative staff in 1977, and a closed shop has applied to gas manual workers since 1975 and to staffs and senior officers since 1976. Closed shops for manual workers and craft grades in the water industry were introduced in 1976 and 1977, respectively, but these agreements ended when the National Water Council was abolished, and its successor, the Water Authorities' Association, has refused to countenance a similar arrangement. Although the union membership agreements in the electricity and gas industries still remain in force, British Gas has stated that it will not in future dismiss employees for refusing to join a specified union.[21]

The impact of industrial action in any of these industries is potentially extremely severe, although disruption of electricity supplies would probably have the most drastic repercussions: '[i]n no other sector are the consequences of breakdown so swift, widespread or devastating in their effects on manufacturing industry, sewage or water pumping stations, and households'.[22] It is difficult to assess the impact which section 4 of the Conspiracy and Protection of Property Act 1875, discussed in detail in Chapter 2, may have had in restraining industrial action before its repeal by the Industrial Relations Act 1971. Strike notices in these industries were often given in the form of notice to terminate employment in response to the section,[23] but despite the fact that there must have been occasions when it was breached, only one charge (in the gas industry) was brought under it. It is illuminating to note that in giving evidence to the Donovan Commission, both the Gas and Electricity Councils, although wanting to retain section 4 as a reminder of the importance of their industries to public safety, felt that their workers' sense of responsibility was a more influential brake on lightning industrial action than the legislation.[24]

The electricity industry

There are two major groups of workers involved in the generation and distribution of electricity, manual workers and engineers. A total stoppage by either group would disrupt supply, although in the case of a strike by manual workers, the engineers could probably maintain a limited supply should they be willing to do this. In the event of supplies being reduced, the engineers are able to direct available supplies and organize rota cuts. In practice, with the exception of a one-day strike by engineers in 1972 which had no effect on supplies, all national official campaigns have involved industrial action short of a strike.

The manual workers' unions (the E.E.T.P.U., G.M.B.A.T.U., T.G.W.U. and A.U.E.W.) have organized two major campaigns, in March 1964 and December 1970. On both occasions the industrial action took the form of a work-to-rule and an overtime ban. The unions emphasized their concern to maintain essential services and in 1964 set up a special committee to co-ordinate action and safeguard supplies to hospitals and other places where cuts could endanger health and safety. The action had no discernable effect on supplies. In 1970 the action had much more impact; there were immediate voltage reductions and disconnections, and the employers alleged that in many areas there was not a 'work-to-rule' but a 'breach of rule', particularly in relation to refusals to honour flexibility agreements.[25] The Government ordered the Electricity Council to give preference in allocating supplies to essential public services and key sectors of industry, particularly exporters and continuous-process users, and remaining supplies were spread as evenly as possible. Arrangements again made by the unions to safeguard vital users were not always implemented in practice, and the unions accused the authorities of failing to make adequate contingency plans to do this. The Government responded by arguing that the employers' capacity to direct supplies selectively became 'progressively less effective' the more severe the cuts.[26] The Government declared a state of emergency on the sixth day of the strike and an order was issued prohibiting the consumption of electricity for advertising, floodlighting and display purposes,[27] but the dispute ended the day this restriction came into force.

Both the 1964 and 1970 disputes were over pay, and on each occasion the unions alleged that the Government had put pressure on the employers to limit their offers and refused to accept arbitration on the ground that arbitrators would be influenced by Government pronouncements as to the desirable level of settlement. Both times the Government was forced to set up a Court of Inquiry to end the dispute. The 1970 Court of Inquiry endorsed the employers' claim that workers had breached agreements in taking industrial action and criticized the unions for failing to give their members 'adequate guidance' on implementing the policy of non-cooperation at local level.[28] It agreed with the Electricity Council's view that bringing a prosecution under section 4 of the 1875 Act would not have helped the situation.[29]

In addition to participating in official campaigns, electricity manual workers have also taken unofficial action on a significant scale. Power cuts resulted from a work-to-rule and overtime ban in London and the South-East in January 1963, and similar action on a national scale in October 1977 brought immediate voltage reductions and power cuts throughout the country.[30] In 1977, as in 1970, the employers alleged that the men were breaking their contracts, and in the second week of the action warned that workers who refused to work normally would not be paid.[31] This provoked complete walkouts in ten power stations, four of which were then reopened by engineers, with the backing of their union, to ensure no further reduction in supplies. The shop stewards' committee which was organizing the action responded to this by calling for a national strike, but the appeal fell on stony ground and the action ended shortly afterwards. The then chairman of the C.E.G.B., Mr Glyn England, attributed the return to normal working to the firm line which was taken by the management.[32]

Although there has been no large-scale official industrial action since 1970, the industry came to the brink of being disrupted in 1982 by action which was designed to increase the costs of generating electricity whilst safeguarding consumers against any major interruptions in supply. The first stage was to be a ban on overtime and a reduction in the output of high-merit coal-fired power stations. The unions undertook to authorize overtime if necessary 'to prevent danger to life or limb', but it was emphasized that abuse of this arrangement could lead to 'more rigorous action'. This was to be followed a fortnight later by a rolling programme of strikes directed at the larger and more efficient power stations in order to force the employers to meet demand from older, more expensive stations. Nuclear power stations were not exempt from this programme, but they were placed towards the end of the list to allow the maximum time for the reactors to be closed down safely. The unions also intended to call out staff employed to read meters and collect revenue at this second stage. An improved pay offer brought a settlement shortly before these plans were due to be put into operation. Clearly, the strategy mapped out on that occasion was more sophisticated than that employed in earlier campaigns; future campaigns may also include as an initial step the calling-out of key workers whose earnings can be maintained in full by the union.

The engineers' association, the E.P.E.A.,[35] has also been conscious of the necessity to maintain essential supplies and took account of this in both the sustained campaigns it organized. A week-long overtime ban in November 1964 was specifically designed not to affect consumers and the E.P.E.A.'s General Secretary promised that the ban would be breached if necessary to restore disrupted supplies. At the outset of a two-month ban on stand-by duties in November–December 1973 in furtherance of a pay claim which challenged the Government's incomes policy, the Association again undertook not to endanger consumers or equipment. Although the effect of the ban itself was limited to a series of local power cuts, it took place against a background of risk to 'energy [supplies] as a whole',[34] and it was cited as a ground for declaring a state of emergency on its thirteenth day, alongside an overtime ban by miners. Restrictions aimed at saving 5 per cent of normal electricity consumption were put into immediate effect.[35] The dispute ended with a settlement technically within the Government's pay policy.

The E.P.E.A. has handled the weapon of industrial action with care, and it has a policy of not taking action in furtherance of disputes outside the electricity industry. It has not, so far, being willing to coutenance surrendering this weapon, however; at its 1982 conference delegates voted overwhelmingly against entering any agreement with the employers which restricted the freedom to strike. The engineers have enormous industrial muscle as it has been clear for many years that they are indispensable to the supply system and cannot be replaced. Even in 1926, when naval ratings and civilian volunteers took over when manual workers withdrew their labour, the assistance of the engineers, who were not then affiliated to the T.U.C., was acknowledged by the Government to have been crucial.[36] On the last occasion when troops were called into power stations, an unofficial strike in four London stations in 1949, naval technicians and volunteers supplied by the Electricity Authority performed poorly owing to unfamiliarity with the equipment. The Secretary of State for Trade and Industry, Mr John Davies, said that it would not be 'practical' to use troops to run power stations during the 1970 dispute,[37] and in 1977 the House of Lords was informed that the technology of individual power stations was now so specialized that they could be run only by the accumulated experience of resident staff. Drafting in unskilled people 'would produce catastrophic damage to the grid supply'.[38]

Although troops could help to maintain supplies under the supervision of engineers, it is most unlikely that the E.P.E.A. would agree to co-operate with them. The authorities believe that the engineers alone could produce 50 per cent of normal output for a substantial period, and experience during the 1977 manual workers' dispute was a small-scale demonstration of their ability to do this. However, the industrial action taken then was unofficial, and it is E.P.E.A. policy not to undertake work normally done by members of other unions who are engaged in an official dispute, or to do anything else to undermine their campaign, other than in circumstances in which there could be a risk to life or plant. Accordingly, in anticipation of industrial action by manual workers in 1982, the Association instructed its members not to exceed their normal duties unless a danger to life arose, and manual workers refused to deal with the problem. It also liaised with the manual workers' unions over their plan to reduce output at certain power stations, taking the view that if management refused to acquiesce in this plan, responsibility for any subsequent escalation of the action would lie with the employers.

The electricity authorities have informal arrangements with the unions to preserve safety in the event of industrial action, and it is most unlikely that the unions would initiate sanctions which would endanger the public or cause serious damage to equipment. As far as the maintenance of supply is concerned, many hospitals and other institutions acquired emergency generating equipment in the aftermath of the 1972 miners' strike, and in 1982 15 per cent of industry's electricity requirements came from private generators.[39] The Energy Act 1983 removed the previous statutory restriction on persons other than Electricity Boards supplying electricity as a main business activity, and this may increase the extent of private generation. Even if electricity workers were to walk out completely, the C.E.G.B. has contingency plans to use jet engines designed for Concorde and the Vulcan bomber to avoid a total blackout.[40] Nevertheless, it remains the case that workers in the electricity supply industry have the capacity to disrupt fundamentally the domestic and working life of virtually the entire population.

The gas industry

Industrial action in the gas industry which affected supplies would have far-reaching repercussions: British Gas has nearly 16 million domestic and 582,000 industrial and commercial customers. It would also present serious safety hazards, with the risk of explosions when supplies resumed if appliances had been left on while supplies were severed or if any leak had been left unattended. In the past strikes in the gas industry could directly jeopardize supplies. Now, however, a highly computerized grid system distributing gas from the North Sea means that supplies are highly unlikely to be interrupted for reasons other than safety. Gas staffs have the functions of monitoring gas pressures and interrupting supply if pressure reaches an abnormal level. Some senior managers have the technical expertise to take over if this group were to take industrial action. Most manual workers in the industry are employed on installation and maintenance tasks. In dispute conditions they would be likely to turn off supplies where there is a leak rather than carrying out repairs. Staff supervisors are generally able to do this job on a limited basis if manual workers are not available.

The gas industry has traditionally not been subject to a high incidence of industrial action, and the first national official campaign came only in 1973. There were instances of unofficial industrial action on a significant scale before that date, however. A series of strikes in 1945 and 1946 disrupted supplies in London, and after the first ten days of a strike lasting three weeks in 1950, parts of north London had virtually no gas whatsoever. This last dispute saw the only attempt to invoke section 4 of the Conspiracy and Protection of Property Act 1875 during its history. The Labour Attorney-General, Sir Hartley Shawcross, brought charges under the section against ten of the strike's organizers, but these were dropped after the men pleaded guilty to contravening a wartime order, continued in force, which required twenty-one days' notice to be given to the Minister of Labour before industrial action was taken, with compulsory arbitration in default of a negotiated settlement.[41] Although there had been numerous breaches of this Order in the past which had not attracted prosecution, the court refused to take this factor into account and the men were sentenced to one month's imprisonment, varied on appeal to a fine of £50.[42] The Attorney-General later explained that he had decided to prosecute in this case because the public were being caused 'inconvenience and hardship' and 'the Communists were keen to see the strike continue', and claimed that the prosecution had had 'a salutary effect'.[43] The dispute ended after the Government agreed to withdraw troops who had been sent in to two of the gasworks which were affected.

The 1973 dispute, which lasted for over five weeks, arose when the unions sought increases beyond the scope of the Government's counter-inflation policy. The G.M.W.U. (now the G.M.B.A.T.U.), to which most manual workers in the industry belong,[44] initially opposed strike action, and plans were made which limited sanctions to withdrawing co-operation and banning overtime. These limitations were conditional on the employers refraining from taking steps which would reduce the effectiveness of the action by, for example, bringing in outside contractors. Eventually, however, the campaign programme also included selective strikes. The G.M.W.U. emphasized its concern to maintain safety during the dispute, and it set up sub-committees in each region to vet detailed plans and participated in discussions with management on how to minimize possible dangers. Government forecasts that the industrial action could not be both safe and effective proved to be misguided. An estimated 3,500 industrial and commercial premises had their supplies disconnected and about 1,600 schools in various parts of the country were forced to close. Supplies in some parts of London and the West Midlands were cut off altogether after three weeks. There were no reports of any explosions, however, and the union later claimed that safety precautions had been observed to the letter. The dispute was settled on terms within the Government's pay policy following a ballot of the membership.

The next extensive campaign of industrial action came in July 1981 when manual workers and staff took part in a 24-hour strike in protest at the Government's plans to sell off British Gas showrooms, a move which the unions claimed could cost between 30,000 and 42,000 jobs. On this occasion emergency cover was not universally maintained. Although the union said that cover had been offered in all cases, in some areas local union officials and management failed to agree on the level of cover which should be provided. As this was such a short stoppage, which did not affect supplies, senior managers were able to cope, and there were no reports of the public having been put at risk. Threats of an indefinite strike to force the closure of the gas supply system were withdrawn when the Government decided not to go ahead with its proposals.

The principle that safety cover must be ensured at all times is enshrined in the National Agreement on General Obligations and Duties for manual workers, which states that '[e]mergency procedures shall be applied including acceptance of standby/callout and emergency working whenever required'. Discussions are held at a regional level on the appropriate number of workers required to furnish emergency cover when a dispute arises. A more detailed provision appears in the union membership agreement for gas staffs and senior officers, most of whom belong to N.A.L.G.O. Paragraphs 10 and 11 of this agreement read as follows:

> 10. The Trade Unions party to this Agreement recognise that British Gas have a special duty and statutory obligation to protect the safety of the public and to maintain a safe system of gas

> supplies; and that therefore, at all times, it is the responsibility of British Gas to determine the necessary cover and arrangements to ensure safety or to deal with emergencies. Nevertheless, it is agreed that in the event of industrial action being taken, the Trade Unions and Employers will have prior discussions about the necessary cover and arrangements to ensure safety or to deal with emergencies and will reach agreement, whenever possible, on the identity of those employees who are required to provide such cover. It is therefore agreed that the Trade Unions will grant special dispensation to any members so identified. The Trade Unions will also grant special dispensation to members who exercise their professional judgement in unforeseen emergency situations for which cover has not been provided.
> 11. Both parties also recognise the special position of certain categories of employee who, because of the nature of their job, will be required to continue to work during periods of industrial action. When there have been prior discussions and such employees have been jointly identified, the Trade Unions will grant special dispensation to them.

Clearly, it is possible that the union and management sides will fail to reach agreement on the appropriate level of cover; this seems to have happened in some places in July 1981, and again in November of that year when technical staff took strike action in a dispute over shift-work allowances. The provision of emergency cover varied between and within regions, and in some areas senior managers took over when the cover offered by the unions was deemed to be insufficient. The application of paragraph 10 in the absence of agreement being reached was examined by the Scottish Court of Session in 1980.[45] In furtherance of a dispute with Scottish Gas, all members of N.A.L.G.O.'s Edinburgh branch were called out on strike in 1978. After talks between the union and management failed to produce an agreement on safety arrangements, the employers wrote to Mr Partington, an engineer, ordering him to report for work to furnish emergency cover. Mr Partington complied with this instruction and was later expelled from the union on the ground that he had defied an official instruction to strike without having received dispensation. He claimed that his expulsion was outside the rules of the union and was, therefore, void. The court held that paragraph 10 left the overriding responsibility to ensure safety with Scottish Gas, and management was therefore entitled to call in employees required to maintain the necessary cover even though no agreement had been reached on this with the union. As it was agreed that the union membership agreement was a term of the employees' employment,[46] Mr Partington was contractually bound to provide safety cover under the terms of paragraph 10 when instructed to do so. The union could not frustrate paragraph 10 by disciplining a member who failed to obtain a specific dispensation from strike action under these circumstances, and Mr Partington's expulsion was therefore unlawful and invalid. Expulsion for failing to take industrial action in the gas industry would now almost certainly be held to be unreasonable under section 4 of the Employment Act 1980 (discussed in Chapter 2).

The terms of these agreements covering workers in the gas industry demonstrate the desire of the unions to avoid taking disruptive action which could jeopardize safety. If management were to take measures which undermined the impact of the sanctions which were imposed, however, this commitment to ensure safety could be put at risk. Up to now this does not appear to have happened.

The water industry

The greatest danger from a withdrawal of labour by water workers lies in the threat to public health. Water supplies can quickly become contaminated, and rivers become polluted, by sewage and industrial waste, and lack of appropriate chemical treatment brings the risk of water-borne illnesses. Electricity supplies would also be jeopardized as power stations require large quantities of pure water to drive turbines. If non-craft manual workers went on strike, experience suggests that managers and supervisors would probably be able to maintain clean supplies if the action were local, but their ability to cope with a national strike without emergency cover is much less certain. A study by Government contingency planners in 1979 concluded that troops could only prevent health hazards arising from a water strike with the assistance of supervisory staff.[47] The need to avoid industrial action which would put the public at risk was acknowledged in the union membership agreement which applied to manual workers between 1976 and the demise of the National Water Council in September 1983. This agreement stated that 'every effort' should be made

> to avoid any industrial action which would prejudice public health and public safety and. . . in the event of industrial action every effort should be made to avoid harm to the health of the consumers.

The first campaign of official industrial action on a national scale in the water industry came in 1983 (preceded by a one-day strike in October 1982 to protest at lack of progress in pay negotiations.) Before that, the only action to threaten supplies was an unofficial strike by manual workers in the Pennine Division of the North-West Water

Authority in January 1979. Troops were on stand-by at a local barracks ready to step in if needed, but the employers were reluctant to call for military assistance and, due to operations undertaken by managerial staff, were able to avoid doing so. Managers went into treatment plants at night to do essential tasks such as washing filters and applying chlorine to destroy bacteria, and by these and other expedients supplies were preserved for most of the population. Of a total 350,000 households in the area affected, only 2,000 suffered any disruption. Official strikes of manual workers were threatened in 1980 and 1981 but these were averted by last-minute improvements in the respective pay offers, although in 1981 there was limited unofficial action which had no widespread effect on supplies.

In 1983 the manual workers' unions (the G.M.B.A.T.U., N.U.P.E. and T.G.W.U.) were demanding an increase of 15 per cent, to fulfil a long-standing aim of bringing earnings into line with those of gas and electricity workers, together with a pay formula for the future. The employers offered 4 per cent in response. The unions alleged that the employers would have offered 6 per cent but for pressure from the Government, and they refused to allow the dispute to go to arbitration, despite a unilateral arbitration clause in their collective agreement which the employers invoked, on the ground that the employers had failed to bargain in good faith. As January 23, when the strike was due to start, drew nearer, it became clear that the Government was anxious to avoid a confrontation, but an improved offer of 7.3 per cent over sixteen months, recommended by an A.C.A.S.-appointed mediator, was not sufficient to produce a settlement.

At the outset of the dispute the unions declared their intention of avoiding harm to the health of consumers whilst at the same time making the action effective in the shortest possible time; Mr Eddie Newall, secretary of the union side of the National Joint Industrial Council, said members preferred the idea of 'swift sharp action' to the kind of 'prolonged' campaign which health service workers had recently undertaken.[48] The unions issued an outline code of practice which laid down the broad guiding principles to be followed by officials organizing the action at local level. Regional officials were instructed to establish channels of communication with water and health authorities in their respective areas, and to discuss arrangements for ensuring that supplies to priority users were maintained. Hospitals, clinics, and nursing homes topped the list of priority users; strikers were also instructed to see that home dialysis patients, who regularly require fresh treated water, were not put at risk and that old people's homes were not deprived of supplies. Of the remainder, the code gave private consumers priority over industrial and commerical users. To supplement this code G.M.B.A.T.U. also set up a 24-hour emergency operations room at its headquarters, with access to expert technical advice on health and safety, to deal with queries about the application of the guiding principles to specific situations.

Despite the thoroughness of these preparations, a strike in the water industry was an unknown quantity for the unions. Mr Newall admitted that he did not 'know what would happen' if it were to go on for a long period of time.[49] The Secretary of State for the Environment, Mr Tom King, was equally in the dark. When answering questions about Government preparations to meet the strike he stated that 'no one' was 'quite clear what types of situation may arise, their [sic] scale and frequency, the workload and the problems that may be posed'.[50] The D.H.S.S. formulated plans to deal with any serious illnesses that might result and advised health authorities to prepare to run hospitals on an emergencies-only basis and to admit home-dialysis patients to hospital if their water supplies were interrupted. Advice was also sent out to farmers on how to cope with toxic waste and other problems. At the start of the strike up to 15,000 troops, including 3,000 engineers, were on notice of stand-by, but it was widely reported that they would be used only if the sewage and supply system reached the point of collapse. The unions in dispute warned that bringing in troops would mean the removal of all emergency cover, and N.A.L.G.O., to which most managerial and supervisory staff belong, indicated that its members would refuse to co-operate with members of the armed forces.

In the event, the worst fears of the contingency planners did not materialize.[51] Mild weather for the first fortnight of the strike kept down the number of burst pipes in the public supply system; during this period about 1,700 properties per day lost supplies and were forced to rely on standpipes or tanker deliveries. A cold spell brought a trebling of this rate, but by the end of the strike only 91,000 properties (about 0.5 per cent of the total in England and Wales) had been completely cut off, although some areas suffered temporary loss of piped supply. (Advice from Lord Denning, the former Master of the Rolls, that householders could call in private contractors to repair bursts or faults which water workers were refusing to fix was not widely followed and was condemned as dangerous by the water authorities.)[52] From the beginning of the strike consumers in the South-West were advised to boil water as a precautionary measure and early advice was also given to boil water in Manchester, Yorkshire and parts of Wales because the bypassing of filters which were liable to become clogged, and lack of chemical treatment meant that appropriate levels of chlorine could not be guaranteed. By the end of the dispute 8,200,000 people were being advised to boil water, but there were very few reported cases of contamination and no outbreaks of water-borne illnesses. High lead concentration was a problem in a few areas, and in districts near Manchester, pregnant women and mothers of young children were advised to use special standpipes rather than piped supplies. Although the quality of effluent from many sewage works deteriorated as the dispute wore on, high river flows and low river temperatures meant that there was little permanent damage to rivers or fish.

The impact of the strike on industry was equally minimal, with reported difficulties being confined largely to the food and drink sectors. A number of industrial concerns made contingency plans in case of supplies being severed, and many of those which were cut off obtained water from tankers or special temporary pipelines. Electricity supplies were not affected, although generating capacity was reduced at two power stations and threatened at others; at a few stations water was drawn from artesian wells or recirculated after use, and electricity industry sources were reported as saying that other 'secret measures' were taken to mitigate the effects of the stoppage.[53] Threats by the electricity unions to take action if the electricity authorities altered their water supply arrangements were not put into effect.

The limited impact of the water workers' strike was due partly to the unions' commitment to providing emergency cover and the moderate behaviour of picket lines, which did not completely block deliveries of chemical and other essential supplies to treatment plants. Another factor was the willingness of managerial and supervisory staff to do manual workers' jobs, despite an instruction from N.A.L.G.O. that they should not exceed their normal duties. (The action in 1979, being unofficial, had not presented any such dilemma.) The manual workers' unions reacted strongly to this 'strikebreaking', and in several areas workers withdrew from joint arrangements with management to maintain emergency cover. Some plants and pumping stations were 'occupied' by strikers in the hope of deterring white-collar staff from entering them; the water authorities responded by obtaining injunctions against such activities. Tempers were further inflamed by reports that some managers, for example those in the London area, were receiving large overtime payments for working long hours and standing by. Other threats to union–management co-operation came from disputes over the definition of 'emergencies', with the unions claiming that managers were trying to include routine jobs. Relations were also soured by allegations that in some areas, such as South Wales, industry was being given more favourable treatment than private consumers. A statement issued by G.M.B.A.T.U. a week into the strike blamed the breakdown of joint arrangements on 'irresponsible attitudes by management' and warned that a 'very dangerous' situation could result. Nevertheless, the union reaffirmed their commitment to protecting priority users and undertook that where arrangements with water authorities were no longer operating, members would still respond to direct appeals from health authorities to safeguard supplies to hospitals and dialysis patients. Hospitals suffered no major difficulties during the dispute. Although there were clear breaches of the code in some areas, Mr King was perhaps rather grudging in attributing the maintenance of services only to the 'exceptional efforts' of water authorities' 'staffs'.[54]

The unions stood firm in their opposition to arbitration on their claim, despite repeated exhortations by the Government, and the two sides finally agreed to put the issues before a committee of inquiry headed by Dr Tom Johnston, principal of Heriott Watt University. The other members of the committee were Mr Bill Keys of S.O.G.A.T. 1982 and Mr Michael Bett, the industrial relations board member of British Telecommunications. The committee found considerable difficulty in reaching any conclusion, and the final report was signed only by Dr Johnston. It recommended increases worth about 11 to 12 per cent over sixteen months and was hailed as a great victory by the unions, despite its rejection of their claim for parity of earnings with workers in the gas and electricity industries. Acceptance of these recommendations brought the dispute to an end after one month of strike action.

This first water strike was described by *The Times* as a 'remarkably gentlemanly and tame affair',[55] and ministers apparently were 'peeved at the National Water Council for its over-gloomy forecasts'.[56] Mr King said that the dispute had shown 'how well the system performed' and that one result would be 'greater automation and mechanisation, more modern plants and... some reduction in manpower costs'.[57] Nevertheless, a lower level of co-operation from manual workers would have brought more problems, and the water industry, like electricity, is clearly heavily dependent on the goodwill of its white-collar staff. These staff might well refuse to supervise troops during an official strike of manual workers. It would be foolish to conclude from experience in 1983 that industrial action in the water industry could never present any real danger to health and safety.

CONCLUSION

Trade unions operating in the electricity, gas and water industries have generally been concerned to safeguard public health and safety when planning campaigns of industrial action. In the case of the gas industry the principle that safety cover must be provided at all times is enshrined in collective agreements, although sometimes there have been disputes between unions and management over the manning levels required for this purpose. These disagreements occurred in the context of short stoppages, and managers were able to furnish adequate cover. In the past, disputes in the gas industry could directly jeopardize supplies; the provision of gas from the North Sea means that supplies are now unlikely to be interrupted unless this becomes necessary for reasons of safety.

In the electricity industry there are informal arrangements between management and unions to preserve safety in the event of industrial action. These do not mean that supplies could never be affected, however; merely that power stations and equipment would be closed down in accordance with specified safety procedures. Electricity supplies were disrupted by the action of manual workers during three disputes; an official work to rule in 1970 and unofficial action taken in 1963 and 1977. If supplies are reduced, electricity power engineers are able to organize rota cuts and to direct supplies to priority consumers. In addition, many essential users now possess emergency generating equipment. If manual workers stopped work altogether, engineers could probably maintain a limited supply, but it is the policy of the E.P.E.A. not to undermine official industrial action by other groups unless life or plant is at risk. The engineers have taken only limited industrial action themselves, but they have rejected the idea of entering any agreement which would limit their freedom to strike. Troops are unable to maintain electricity supplies without the assistance of engineers, which would almost certainly not be forthcoming during an official dispute. A campaign plan issued by the manual workers' unions in 1982 indicates that any future action might well be aimed in the first instance at increasing the employer's financial burden rather than at severing supplies.

Industrial action in the water industry was taken for the first time on a national scale in 1983 when the manual workers went on strike. On that occasion the unions issued a code of practice which was designed to ensure that supplies were maintained to priority users, and advice was continuously available from union headquarters on the application of the code to specific situations. Withdrawals from joint arrangements with management to preserve emergency cover occurred in some areas; these instances were attributed by the unions to 'provocative' management action. The strike did not have the catastrophic consequences for health and safety which contingency planners had feared, but this does not mean that the impact of any future campaign would be equally limited. It seems that troops could only prevent health hazards arising from a water strike with the assistance of supervisory staff, which, as in the case of the electricity industry, would probably not be made available.

Before 1977 official industrial action in the fire service also took account of the need to preserve emergency cover. In 1977, however the F.B.U. was forced by grass-roots pressure to support an all-out strike without emergency cover, and threats of disruptive action since that time, issued both by the F.B.U. and by N.A.F.O., have contemplated total strikes. In 1977 fire cover was furnished by troops, assisted by fire officers, part-time firemen and the police, and although the strike had serious financial consequences, no loss of life was attributed to it. The co-operation of fire officers on that occasion was probably a crucial factor; a strike which involved the service as a whole would present far greater risks. The operation of a pay formula for firemen which resulted from the 1977 dispute has protected the service from conflicts over wages in recent years; any moves to withdraw this formula, or to impose redundancies upon firemen, would probably provoke further disruption.

The inability of substitute labour to maintain a safe service within the sectors discussed in this chapter without the assistance of supervisory staff makes it all the more important that trade unions should seek to protect health and safety when organizing campaigns of industrial action. In recent disputes limitations on the scope of disruption have generally been made conditional, explicitly or implicitly, on management exercising reciprocal self-restraint. This *quid pro quo* approach was acknowledged by A.C.A.S. in its report on the London Fire Brigade in 1977 when it proposed that procedures should be devised which would allow firemen to take industrial action which preserved emergency cover without losing pay or being subject to disciplinary action. The implications of this approach to disputes are explored in greater detail in the concluding section of Chapter 6.

NOTES

1. Walter Citrine, *Men and Work: The Autobiography of Lord Citrine*, Hutchinson, London, 1964, p. 152.
2. Annex to the 'Social Concordat', *The Economy, the Government and Trade Union Responsibilities: Joint Statement by the T.U.C. and Government*, H.M.S.O., London, 1979.
3. Trades Union Congress, *Improving Industrial Relations in the National Health Service: A Report by the T.U.C. Health Services Committee*, T.U.C., London, 1981, pp. 163-4.
4. Fire Services Act 1947, ss. 1, 17(1), as amended by the Fire Services Act 1959, s.5.
5. Report of the Cunningham Inquiry into the Work of the Fire Service, Cmnd. 4754 (1971), para. 299.
6. See the Report of Her Majesty's Chief Inspector of Fire Services for 1977, Cmnd. 7311 (1977), para. 5, for a summary of measures taken to deal with the dispute.
7. Dr John Gilbert, Minister of State at the Ministry of Defence, H.C. Deb., Vol. 940, col. 1099 (December 6, 1977).
8. *The Times*, December 1, 1977.
9. Christopher J. Whelan, 'Military Intervention in Industrial Disputes', *Industrial Law Journal* 8 (1979), 222 at 231.
10. Geoffrey Marshall, *Constitutional Conventions*, Clarendon Press, Oxford, 1984, p. 162.

11. *The Guardian*, November 20, 1980.
12. See *The Guardian*, November 21, 1980.
13. The Fire Services (Discipline) Regulations 1948, S.I. 1948 No. 545.
14. Report of Her Majesty's Inspector of Fire Services for Scotland for 1951, Cmnd. 8524 (1952), para. 10.
15. Statement from the Home Office, issued November 20, 1951.
16. *The Firefighter*, January 1952.
17. Advisory, Conciliation and Arbitration Service, *Report of a Committee of Inquiry into Industrial Relations in the London Fire Service*, A.C.A.S. Report No. 8, A.C.A.S., London, 1977, paras. 339–42 and App. 10.
18. Electricity Act 1947, s.53; Gas Act 1948, s.57.
19. S.26(2).
20. Water Act 1983, s. 3.
21. Mr Peter Bottomley, Under-Secretary of State, Department of Employment, H.C. Deb., Vol. 70, col. 113 (December 18, 1984) (written answer).
22. Keith Jeffery and Peter Hennessy, *States of Emergency*, Routledge and Kegan Paul, London, 1983, p. 246.
23. K.W. Wedderburn 'Industrial action, the State and the public interest' in *Industrial Conflict: A Comparative Legal Survey* ed. B. Aaron and K.W. Wedderburn, Longman, London, 1972, pp. 319–83 at p. 360.
24. Royal Commission on Trade Unions and Employers' Associations 1965–1968, Minutes of Evidence Nos. 11 and 12.
25. Report of a Court of Inquiry into a Dispute between the Parties Represented on the National Joint Industrial Council for the Electricity Supply Industry, Cmnd. 4594 (1971), para. 11.9.
26. Mr John Davies, Secretary of State for Trade and Industry, H.C. Deb., Vol. 808, col. 251 (December 8, 1970).
27. The Electricity (Advertising and Display) Order 1970, S.I. 1970 No. 1866.
28. As above, note 25.
29. *Ibid.*, para. 11.2.
30. A member of the shop stewards' committee which organized the action estimated that over 50 per cent of manual workers in the industry were taking part at one time: *The Times*, October 29, 1977.
31. The lawfulness of this response was upheld by the Court of Appeal in *Henthorn and another* v. *Central Electricity Generating Board* [1981] I.R.L.R. 361.
32. Glyn England, *Facing the Challenge*, Central Electricity Generating Board, London, 1982, p. 21.
33. In 1976 the E.P.E.A. decided to extend its field of recruitment to engineers and managers in other occupations and industries, and since 1977 the E.P.E.A. has been one constituent group within the E.M.A.
34. Mr Robert Carr, Home Secretary, H.C. Deb., Vol. 864, col. 684 (November 15, 1973).
35. The Electricity (Advertising, Display etc.) (Restriction) Order, S.I. 1973 No. 1901; The Electricity (Heating) Restriction Order, S.I. 1973 No. 1900, as amended by S.I. 1973 No. 1913.
36. Jeffery and Hennessy, *States of Emergency*, as above, note 22, p. 113.
37. H.C. Deb., Vol. 808, col. 251 (December 8, 1970).
38. Viscount Brookeborough, H.L. Deb., Vol. 358, Col. 711, March 18, 1975.
39. Mr Nigel Lawson, Secretary of State for Energy, H.C. Deb., Vol. 32, col. 870 (November 24, 1982).
40. Jeffery and Hennessy, *States of Emergency*, as above, note 22, p. 249.
41. Conditions of Employment and National Arbitration Order S.R. & O. 1940 No. 1305. Under the Order, industrial action was legal only if the Minister of Labour failed during the twenty-one days' notice period to take any steps towards a settlement. The Order continued in force after the war with the agreement of both sides of industry.
42. For details of these proceedings, see *The Times*, October 6, 1950, and November 22, 1950.
43. H.C. Deb., Vol. 483, col. 685 (January 29, 1951).
44. The T.G.W.U. and the E.E.T.P.U. also have a small proportion of manual workers in membership.
45. *Partington* v. *N.A.L.G.O.* [1981] I.R.L.R. 537.

46. No consideration was given in this case to the question of whether para. 10 was appropriate for incorporation into individual contracts of employment. For a discussion of this question, see B.A. Hepple, *Hepple and O'Higgins: Employment Law*, 4th edn., Sweet and Maxwell, London, 1981, pp. 128–31. It is arguable that an obligation on an individual to furnish safety cover if required amounts to a 'no-strike' clause which should be made in compliance with the Trade Union and Labour Relations Act 1974, s.18(4).

47. Jeffery and Hennessy, *States of Emergency*, as above, note 22, p. 250.

48. *The Guardian*, January 8, 1983.

49. *The Sunday Times*, January 9, 1983.

50. H.C. Deb., Vol. 35, col. 252 (January 18, 1983).

51. See Roger White, 'Statistics of a Strike', *Water Bulletin*, May 6, 1983, pp. 5–6, on which some of the account which follows is based.

52. *The Guardian*, February 15, 1983. Lord Denning argued that if a water authority was not carrying out its statutory duty to provide a supply of wholesome water pursuant to paragraph 31 of the Third Schedule to the Water Act 1945, then it would be a defence to a charge of interfering with the authority's equipment under paragraph 67 of the Third Schedule to the Act that the action was 'reasonably necesary' for the common good. The National Water Council said that, regardless of the legal position, it would be 'highly inadvisable on the grounds of safety' to interfere with an authority's apparatus. The Severn-Trent Water Authority threatened legal action against consumers who repaired burst mains.

53. *The Times*, February 8, 1983.

54. H.C. Deb., Vol. 37, col. 937 (February 23, 1983).

55. February 23, 1983.

56. Peter Hennessy, 'Whitehall Contingency Planning for Industrial Disputes' in *Military Intervention in Democratic Societies*, ed. Peter J. Rowe and Christopher J. Whelan, Croom Helm, London, 1985, p. 108.

57. H.C. Deb., Vol. 37, col. 940 (February 23, 1983).

6

The Conduct of Disputes in Essential Services: The National Health Service

This chapter examines the conduct of disputes in the National Health Service from the perspective outlined at the beginning of Chapter 5. The N.H.S., which was founded in 1948, is the largest single employer in the United Kingdom and it embraces a wide range of occupations. The discussion focuses upon four groups whose disruptive action has had, or has the potential to have, the broadest impact upon the running of the service: ancillary workers, ambulancemen, nurses and doctors. This is followed by a survey of the attitudes of health service administrators towards the issues raised by industrial action and the various methods of responding to the threat of disruption. The final section assesses the extent to which the 'mutual self-restraint' approach has operated in the N.H.S. and in the sectors discussed in Chapter 5 and looks at the attitudes which successive governments have taken towards co-operating with unions during disputes in order to minimize the dislocation of essential supplies and services during campaigns of industrial action.

An overview

Collective bargaining machinery in the N.H.S. follows the Whitley model established for the civil service after the First World War;[1] there are ten functional councils to negotiate the pay and conditions of individual groups and a General Council to deal with procedural matters and conditions of service common to all N.H.S. staff. The staff sides of the councils consist of representatives of organizations recognized by the D.H.S.S.; the management side consists of representatives of health authorities and Central Government Health Departments.[2] Negotiations may also take place outside the Whitley structure; the terms and conditions of doctors and dentists have always been settled by direct negotiation between the staff sides and the Health

Departments, and in 1962 a standing Review Body was established to make recommendations on remuneration. The functions of the Nurses' and Midwives' Council, and one of the councils for professions allied to medicine, have recently been superceded by the establishment of a Review Body covering these groups. The final authority to fix terms and conditions of health service workers rests with the Secretary of State for Social Services,[3] and the Government reserves the right not to accept recommendations made by Review Bodies. Among certain groups, particularly nurses, midwives, radiographers, physiotherapists and scientists, there is fierce competition for members between professional associations and multi-occupational trade unions. The professional associations, which are not, in general, affiliated to the T.U.C., have expanded greatly their industrial relations activities in recent years.[4]

There was no industrial action on any significant scale within the N.H.S. until the 1970s. This was due partly to a low level of union membership[5] and partly because 'issues were fought through the constitutional representative and procedural mechanisms, and militancy in the hospital was discouraged in case it affected patients'.[6] In the 1970s the psychological barriers against taking industrial action were well and truly broken. Ambulancemen (until 1974 classed as local authority workers) took action in 1969, and there were two short stoppages by laboratory technicians in 1971, but the first major national action was taken by ancillary workers in 1972–3. This was followed by campaigns involving nurses, paramedical workers and doctors in 1974–5; works supervisors in 1978; ancillary workers and ambulancemen in 1979; paramedical staff in 1980 and ambulancemen in 1981. 1982 then brought the first dispute involving all major health service groups acting together (excluding doctors, dentists and some craftsmen). The growth in national disputes was also accompanied by an increase in action at local level, generally by ancillary workers.[7]

In the discussion which follows, matters common to all the groups under review – the operation of general codes of conduct and the progress of the 1982 campaign – are dealt with in the section which covers ancillary staff.

ANCILLARY WORKERS

Ancillary workers perform a wide range of non-medical tasks in hospitals, including cleaning, portering, laundering, catering and the preparation of sterile supplies. Interference with any of these functions has an immediate impact on the running of a hospital. This was brought home by the dispute of 1972–3, when widespread industrial action, which many had previously not believed could happen, was taken by ancillary workers in support of a claim outside the limits of the

Conservative Government's counter-inflation policy. A ballot following a one-day strike, during which cover for emergency operations was maintained, produced a majority in favour of an indefinite strike, but the unions concerned (N.U.P.E., C.O.H.S.E., the T.G.W.U. and G.M.B.A.T.U.) decided instead on a campaign of selective strikes, overtime bans, working-to-rule and withdrawing co-operation. The unions' aim was to disrupt and reduce services without directly endangering patients, and they undertook at the outset to maintain emergency services. The Government resolved that this undertaking should not be put at risk by the introduction of volunteers, and hospital authorities were told not to call for outside help unless emergency services were not being maintained and the unions refused to provide extra cover. There was a 'hot-line' in operation between the D.H.S.S. and the unions' headquarters throughout the dispute, but the details of what was required, and the terms on which cover should be provided, was left to local negotiation.

The novelty of the situation meant that in many places neither unions nor management had the experience and organization to conduct such negotiations. In a survey of the conduct of the dispute in the Leeds Area,[8] Roger Dyson found that in only a minority of hospitals were discussions held before industrial action started; some administrators apparently refused to countenance the possibility that their staff would join in the campaign. This delay resulted in managers having to negotiate against a background of dwindling resources. Often there was no pre-existing committee of shop stewards with which to negotiate, and establishing such a body took up further time. Dyson found that the lack of prior preparation generally helped the unions. 'The longer. . . negotiations dragged on the weaker management's position became, whilst the stewards grew more confident. It was in these circumstances that the stewards forced management to accept the most restrictive levels of emergency service', often on favourable terms for their members.[9] Difficulties at local level were compounded by poor communication between union headquarters and local officials and by varying opinions on the definition of an 'emergency' service. There was considerable resort to internal volunteers to do ancillary workers' jobs. These were generally drawn from managers and nurses.

After three weeks of disruptive action about 300 hospitals were affected by strikes (most limited but some indefinite), with many more subject to other forms of action, and 12 per cent of acute or nearly acute beds were out of use.[10] The Government remained unmoved by this, or by pressure from the T.U.C. and Labour Party to treat the ancillary workers as a 'special case', and after six weeks the unions reluctantly agreed to a settlement within the pay policy. (By this time, the campaign seemed to have run out of steam; a call to workers to shut all London hospitals, apart from emergency services, for a day brought a poor response.) Although the action failed to achieve its objective, however, it had a fundamental impact on health service industrial relations.

> The most obvious effect was that ancillary workers proved to themselves and to the rest of the service that they had power which, although it could not defeat the government, could, if used at a local level, gain a measure of control over the way the service ran. . . The strike. . . increased the power of ancillaries and. . . encouraged greater bargaining with the administrators.[11]

This was illustrated shortly after the national dispute when ancillary workers in some hospitals took action in support of a campaign against private practice within the N.H.S.

The 1979 ancillary workers' and ambulancemen's dispute arose when both groups sought increases well beyond the Labour Government's 5 per cent pay limit. A one-day strike on January 22 was followed by selective action and various forms of restrictive working. The action had a rapid impact; by January 30, between a third and half of all hospitals were admitting only emergency cases, and over most of the country ambulancemen were handling only emergency calls.[12] As in 1972–3, the Government started by pursuing a strategy of co-operation with the unions. From the outset the unions urged their members to maintain emergency services, and ten days later they issued more precise guidance on what this involved. The guidance stated that workers should not impede the delivery of drugs, oxygen and fuel, and should fully maintain at all times services relating to cardiac, dialysis, cancer, intensive care and accident and emergency patients and to children. Emergency services were defined as those which 'directly involve the life or death of a patient or those which, if withdrawn, would cause serious hardship to high-dependency patients'. A hot-line between the D.H.S.S. and unions took up cases where action had exceeded these limits or where local attempts to solve a problem had failed, and on February 5 the Secretary of State for Social Services stated that the guidance was being 'very widely observed'.[13] He encouraged health authorities to discuss arrangements for maintaining emergency services with local union representatives and to call in full-time union officials immediately action went beyond 'tolerable levels'.[14] In line with this strategy the D.H.S.S. asked health authorities to await departmental advice before suspending or withdrawing pay from staff taking action or laying off staff who were unable to work because of action by others. It also counselled caution in using volunteers and reminded authorities of guidelines published by the Volunteer Centre in 1977[15] which state that regular volunteers should undertake no more work during a dispute than they would undertake normally unless management and staff organizations involved in the dispute agree otherwise.

The Government's policy of controlling the management response from the centre was not maintained consistently throughout the dispute. Subsequent to its initial advice, the D.H.S.S. gave health authorities greater discretion to impose sanctions on those taking industrial action but then withdrew this permission before granting it again when the action intensified in mid-March.

> The several changes in granting local discretion to administrators were related to the critical periods when settlement was thought to be near. Whenever the immediate prospects of settlement faded local discretion was given unqualified approval.[16]

These oscillations meant that there was no coherent response to the action nationally but neither could administrators feel free to pursue their own strategies in the light of local circumstances. In many districts administrators 'played safe' and continued paying staff taking action throughout the dispute; in some cases they agreed to admit only emergencies and not to reduce pay provided that specified essential services were maintained.[17] Despite the efforts of the unions, their guidance was breached in certain places and some hospitals were kept going only by extensive use of internal volunteers.

The unions held a ballot of their members on a revised offer of 9 per cent, together with a comparability study, and this produced a majority in favour of acceptance in all the unions except N.U.P.E., which then decided to intensify sanctions. All-out strikes, sometimes without notice, began in some areas. At this point the Government abandoned the strategy of co-operation altogether, and the Secretary of State announced that authorities which were facing severe disruption should 'at their discretion and in the light of local circumstances. . . respond to it with appropriate management measures', including the introduction of volunteers. There could be 'no question of union members disregarding their own code. . . while, at the same time, exercising an effective veto on the use of volunteers'.[18] In the event, volunteers helped in hospitals in thirty-two districts in England.[19] A settlement was finally reached on March 26 on the terms approved in the ballot.

The 1982 dispute was governed by a more extensive code of conduct. In response to a recommendation by the Royal Commission on the

National Health Service,[20] the T.U.C. Health Services Committee, which includes representatives of all affiliated unions with members in the service, set up a working party on industrial relations to draw up a document on which discussions with the Government and others could be based. Its report, published in 1981, included a chapter on the protection of patients during disputes. This proposed a single general code of conduct to which all health service unions could subscribe in order to avoid members of different unions in a work-place acting on conflicting advice.[21] (Some individual unions already had standing guidance on the conduct of disputes but in each case this was phrased in slightly differing terms.)[22]

This code, which applies the principles laid down in the general guidance issued by the T.U.C. in 1979,[23] states that any action which restricts services to patients must be consistent with respect for 'human life, safety and dignity' and urges unions involved in disputes to arrange in advance with management to maintain supplies and services essential for emergency services and services to high-dependency patients. In particular, workers should not impede the delivery and distribution of drugs, food, oxygen and fuel. The code defines 'emergency services' as those which 'directly involve the life, limb or ultimate safety of a patient' and gives 999 calls, renal dialysis, terminal discharges, maternity and radiotherapy patients as examples. 'High dependency patients' are those whose 'life, limb or ultimate safety might be at serious risk without the maintenance of services', such as children, the elderly or the mentally handicapped.

The unions made clear that observance of this code was conditional on a 'sensible local management response' which did not inflame the situation by implementing measures such as suspending those who refused to work normally or refusing to negotiate on, or pay for, emergency cover.[24] In particular, the unions urged the withdrawal of a Circular entitled 'If Industrial Relations Break Down',[25] which had been issued by the D.H.S.S. (under the new Conservative administration) in December 1979 after Regional Personnel Officers had requested standing guidance on dealing with industrial action following the uncertainties left by the 1979 dispute. The Circular, which still remains in force, places responsibility for handling industrial action at local level firmly with the health authorities and states that henceforth ministers would hope not to intervene in their decisions. Its only instruction is that staff on strike should not be paid and staff should not receive bonuses or other allowances which have not been earned. 'Beyond that, it is for Authorities themselves to decide in the light of local circumstances the timing and precise nature of their response'.

Although the rest of the Circular merely indicates the range of options open to management, it advocates asserting the management prerogative in a way which had not been done consistently in the past. It asks authorities to bear in mind four, sometimes conflicting, considerations: the need to maintain services to patients; the possibility that sending staff home or stopping pay may bring an earlier return to normal working although initially perhaps, escalating the action; the need for staff to work together after the dispute is over; and the undesirability of paying staff for work which they have refused to perform. It emphasizes that the full maintenance of services should not be secured regardless of cost. It assures ministerial backing for bringing volunteers in during disputes (without mention of consultation with the unions, as the Volunteer Centre guidelines provide) and exhorts authorities to give high priority to contingency planning. The provisions of the Circular are discussed in greater detail in the survey of local administrators later in the chapter. Despite strong protestations from the unions that the circular was intimidatory, provocative and damaging to industrial relations, the Secretary of State refused to withdraw it.

In 1982, the majority of health service groups had the same settlement date (April 1) for the first time. This increased the scope for union co-ordination and the T.U.C. Health Services Committee agreed a common core claim of 12 per cent. The D.H.S.S. cash limits allowed for rises of only 4 per cent. The Government made available additional funds to allow an increase of 6.4 per cent to nurses, midwives and professions allied to medicine, but kept offers to ancillaries and administrative and clerical staff at 4 per cent. (Ambulancemen were offered 5 per cent as part of a restructuring settlement.) The Secretary of State justified the 2.4 per cent differential on the basis that members of the first groups were responsible for 'the direct treatment of patients';[26] the unions attributed it to the Government's desire to split off nurses, the group most likely to attract public sympathy, from other workers. In the event, all these workers remained in dispute until mid-December. (In June, the offer for nurses etc. was raised to 7.5 per cent, that for ambulancemen and hospital pharmacists to 6.5 per cent, and that for the remainder to 6 per cent.) The Government refused to allow the claim to go to arbitration, on the ground that this would involve subcontracting the decision as to the amount the nation could afford.

C.O.H.S.E. members began taking limited industrial action on April 26, and on April 29 the T.U.C. Health Services Committee gave ten days' notice of industrial action by all affiliated unions involved in the claim. There was a 24-hour strike on May 19, during which many hospitals admitted only accident and emergency cases, followed by sanctions designed to reduce all hospitals to an emergencies-only service. This set the general pattern of the campaign: designated Days of Action (June 4, 8 and 23; July 19–21; August 9–13; a general Day of Action on September 22; and regional Days of Action from October 4), combined with continuing sanctions of various kinds applied at local level. The unions issued only general guidance to their members on what action to take, leaving it to local branches to determine the sanctions which would be feasible and effective in particular hospitals. As well as seeking to reduce services in general, in some areas securing a ban on treating private patients for the duration of the dispute was also a target.

Action other than on designated days was mostly taken by ancillary workers. One tactic which the unions encouraged was to pull out small groups of key staff, such as laundry, central sterile supplies department (C.S.S.D.), and stores workers in order to achieve maximum disruption at minimum cost; those on strike could then have their wages made up by strike pay, donations and levies on other workers. St Thomas' Hospital, opposite the House of Commons, was a prominent target of this strategy. Twenty-five of the twenty-eight C.S.S.D. staff there went on strike for nine weeks from June 23, leaving a small number of staff volunteers to maintain emergency supplies, and by the first week in July, 300 fewer beds than normal were in use, and operations had decreased from 120 to 30 per day. A tactic favoured by many domestic and catering staff was to stop work for short periods, perhaps one or two hours. By mid-August a D.H.S.S. survey found that, of a total of 183 health districts in England, hospitals in eighteen of them were admitting only accident and emergency cases, and hospitals in a further eighty-seven were admitting only these categories together with urgent cases. Hospitals in eighty-two districts continued to admit non-urgent cases.

Days of Action in June attracted sympathetic action from other workers, mainly miners, civil servants and local authority staff, and T.U.C. leaders decided to make September 22 a day on which all trade unionists would be encouraged to stop work for an hour or more in support of the N.H.S. campaign. Their appeal brought a large response, most notably in the public sector; 80 per cent of pits and two-thirds of the docks were brought to a standstill and 31,000 civil servants stopped work, despite warnings that those who had participated in previous Days of Action would be disciplined if they did so again.[27] There were no national newspapers that day.[28] A rally in Hyde Park drew an estimated 60,000 to 120,000 people. After the euphoria had worn off, however, it became clear that the unions had no plans for what was to follow this climactic day. One-day strikes were staged in each health region on consecutive days from October 4, but these attracted little sympathetic action and had much less impact than the national stoppages. The unions were then faced with the choice of escalating the action or allowing the momentum built up by September 22 to slip away entirely. In mid-October the Health Services Committee recommended seeking a mandate from members for indefinite strike action within the code, although this was opposed by C.O.H.S.E., in line with the decision of its conference, which had advocated a series of 'heartbeat' strikes, with members working and striking on alternate weeks. (N.U.P.E.'s conference in May had supported an all-out strike to close all but accident and emergency services). While the unions were considering their next step, the level of action declined and by the first week in December most staff were working normally. In mid-December the Health Services Committee finally accepted a revised Government offer of a two-year settlement which gave nurses and professions allied to medicine a 12.3 per cent increase over nineteen months, with the promise of a Review Body from April 1984, and other workers 6 per cent in 1982–8 and 4.5 per cent the following year. The dispute cost the service the loss of 610,150 man-days, half of them in the Northern, Yorkshire, Mersey and North-Western regions.

In 1982 the health service unions won the moral argument in the eyes of the public but lost the dispute. Some trade unions attributed defeat to the code of conduct; the General Secretary of N.U.P.E., Mr Rodney Bickerstaffe, later stated '[t]he unions were not prepared to lift emergency cover and let people die. This meant we were fighting with one hand tied behind our back;.[29] It is difficult to assess how effective the code was in protecting patient care. There were certain well-publicized instances where it broke down; for example at St Thomas' Hospital, at Leeds General Infirmary, where ancillaries withdrew cover for eight days, at a general and mental hospital in Edinburgh and at a children's and maternity hospital in Liverpool. Ministers made much of the unions' failure to secure total compliance. In some hospitals, on days of action at least, emergency services were maintained only with the assistance of internal volunteers. These were generally managers and nurses, who volunteered despite instructions from N.A.L.G.O., and advice from the R.C.N., that their respective memberships should not take such a course. (The R.C.N. later modified its advice to assure support for any members undertaking tasks necessary for essential patient care.) It seems that only in the Mersey region was any call for help put out to the public. It was generally accepted that the classification of cases as emergencies was a matter for clinical judgement and workers did not challenge cases before treatment, although an incident in Mansfield, when a three-year-old child had an operation postponed because porters refused to wheel him into the theatre, attracted a great deal of media attention.

The unions usually attributed breaches of the code to management 'provocation', consisting generally of threats to implement the non-mandatory provisions of 'If Industrial Relations Break Down' or admission of non-urgent cases in defiance of agreements to admit only emergencies. The D.H.S.S. did not monitor the sanctions imposed by managers, but it did receive reports that docking pay or sending staff home for working restrictively had intensified the action in some places. In line with the policy underlying the Circular, the D.H.S.S. did not give any further advice to authorities on handling the action nor was there any 'hot-line' to union headquarters. The Department was officially opposed to managers making 'deals' with the unions to restrict admissions in return for guaranteed emergency cover on the ground that they could encourage further strike action, and clearly ministers could not have endorsed such arrangements for political reasons, but reports from the districts indicated that 'deals' had been arrived at in some places. Further discussion of these arrangements appears in the survey of health service administrators later in this chapter.

It was widely predicted that in any subsequent dispute the health service unions would wish to bring the issue to a head much more quickly than in 1982.[30] N.U.P.E. has facilitated this process by voting at its 1985 annual conference not to adhere to the code of practice in future campaigns. Although emergency cover will still be provided, the union policy is now to leave the level of cover to 'the discretion of the local district committee or joint shop stewards' committee so that they can take into consideration the use of non-union members, managers and strikebreakers'. This clearly gives union officials much more flexibility and may make it harder for managers to reach agreement on cover.

In any future campaign, ancillary workers are unlikely to have the active support of nurses; by establishing a Review Body for Nurses and Midwives, the implementation of whose recommendations would be put at risk by industrial action, the Government has removed these groups from the arena for the time being. Over the past couple of years ancillary workers have been involved in local disputes over the contracting-out to private companies of cleaning, catering and laundry services, a measure pressed on health authorities by the Government, and this seems the most likely trigger for industrial action by this group in the immediate future.

AMBULANCEMEN

Ambulancemen, of whom there are about 17,000 in Great Britain, have taken industrial action several times in recent years. In all disputes from

1979 onwards their claim has involved recognition as an emergency service, alongside the police and firemen. This claim has been rejected on the ground that ambulancemen spend a relatively small proportion of their time on emergency work, but at the time of writing there are proposals to replace the existing system of hourly payment by a salary structure. During many disputes ambulancemen have refused to maintain emergency cover, contrary to the advice of their unions (N.U.P.E., C.O.H.S.E. the G.M.B.A.T.U. and T.G.W.U.). When emergency cover is withdrawn, the current practice of the employers is to call initially on the police (first used in 1979),[31] then on voluntary organizations (the St John's Ambulance Brigade and the Red Cross) and finally, if these resources prove inadequate, on the armed forces.

The first dispute seriously to threaten services arose in 1969 from a demand for recognition by the F.A.P., formed in 1966 with the object of raising ambulancemen from manual to professional status. (Many of its members also belonged to T.U.C. unions.) A two-hour strike in London, called without notice, was followed by a two-week campaign of lightning strikes and restrictive working in various parts of the country. With co-operation from the recognized unions, which opposed the F.A.P.'s demand, services were maintained without outside help. The employers undertook to consider the strikers' claim, but recognition was ultimately rejected and the Federation became defunct. The first dispute to occasion the use of volunteers came in 1973, a five-day unofficial strike in Durham over a local issue. They were also called in later that year in some areas during a five-week national campaign in support of a new pay structure agreed with the employers but prohibited under Government pay policy. Despite appeals from the unions to preserve accident and emergency services, there were unofficial strikes. The dispute was settled within the terms of Government policy but was followed shortly afterwards by a five-day unofficial strike in Scotland, called with less than twenty-four hours' notice. The Scottish Home and Health Department put out a general call for volunteers, and over 2,500 responded, enabling an accident service to be fully maintained.[32]

The formulation of more detailed codes of conduct by the unions has not prevented some ambulancemen from withdrawing their labour completely. There were all-out strikes in various areas during the 1979 campaign during which police and voluntary organizations provided cover; in London and Manchester army ambulances were also brought in to maintain an emergency service. In a further national pay dispute in 1981 there was a series of 24-hour strikes, in London and Scotland without emergency cover. Again, police and voluntary organizations dealt with emergency calls; troops were on stand-by but were not required other than in certain parts of South Wales. The 1982 dispute brought isolated total stoppages with which police and voluntary organizations were generally able to cope. These seem to have occurred largely in response to managers docking pay for limited working. On the September Day of Action many areas, including most of London, had no emergency cover; troops were on stand-by but only one army ambulance was deployed.

Many ambulancemen have argued in the past that it is necessary for them to withdraw emergency cover for their industrial action to have any significant impact. It is conceivable, however, that ambulancemen's willingness to strike has been influenced by the knowledge that adequately-trained substitute labour is likely to be available. Subsequent disputes in the ambulance service may receive less wholehearted support; since 1981, 4,500 ambulancemen have joined A.P.A.P., an independent trade union whose rules require a 60 per cent majority before official industrial action can be called. (A.P.A.P. is recognized by some local health authorities but has so far been refused recognition at national level.) It is possible also that a new salary structure will lead to a reduction in militancy throughout the service.

NURSES

Nurses, who constitute the largest occupational group within the N.H.S.,[33] have not so far exercised to any significant degree their considerable industrial strength. The organization of nurses is split between the R.C.N., founded in 1916 as a professional body and since 1977 a certified independent trade union, and unions affiliated to the T.U.C., mainly C.O.H.S.E. and N.U.P.E.[34] In July 1985 membership of the R.C.N., which is open only to qualified nurses and nurses in training, stood at 246,000. C.O.H.S.E. had an estimated 120,000 nurse members, of whom about a quarter are psychiatric nurses, and N.U.P.E. had 80,000. There is probably some dual membership of the R.C.N. and another organization but the precise amount of overlap is unknown.

The R.C.N. has always been opposed to nurses taking industrial action. Its traditional policy was recently expressed as follows:

> Nurses are entitled to all the rights which are accorded to employees by employment legislation; this includes the right to withhold their labour. However, the R.C.N. believes that because of the commitment which nurses voluntarily accept in qualifying and practicing as members of the nursing profession, they should not exercise this right because such action is a violation of their commitment to those in their care.[35]

Rule 12 of the College rules forbids any withdrawal of service in furtherance of a dispute, and this rule can only be changed by a two-thirds majority at a general meeting. Alternatively, the College in General Meeting, by a two-thirds majority, may empower its Council to take a decision in respect of limited industrial action if circumstances should be such as to warrant such action. In response to pressure from some members to change this rule, the College put the issue to the membership three times between 1979 and 1982; on each occasion a clear majority voted to retain it.[36] Even if the proposal for change had been accepted, the College would probably have authorized only very limited forms of action; examples of possible sanctions put forward in 1978 included limiting administrative and clerical work, refusing to perform portering or messenger duties or to make private cars available for N.H.S. work, and insisting on overtime pay for working over thirty-five hours a week. The establishment of the Review Body for Nurses, Midwives and Professions Allied to Medicine, described below, has removed pressure for the abolition of rule 12 for the time being. The rules of the R.C.M., the professional organization and trade union for midwives, also forbid industrial action; the College takes the view that any form of action would inevitably put mothers and/or babies at risk. About 22,000 out of an estimated 25,000 practising midwives belong to the College; again there is some overlap of membership with N.U.P.E. and C.O.H.S.E.

In contrast, the T.U.C.-affiliated unions with nurse members believe that nurses should be free to take industrial action like any other group, within the confines of the code of conduct. They were highly critical of a statement published by the General Nursing Council for England and Wales in July 1979 warning nurses that industrial action could constitute professional misconduct if it put the health, safety or welfare of patients at risk. (Chapter 2 discusses this statement in greater detail.) In response to it, N.U.P.E. prepared a list of forms of action which nurses could still take without endangering patient care. This list included restricting admissions to emergency cases only, banning overtime, sticking strictly to clinical nursing duties and shifts, insisting that all wards are staffed only by trained nurses and refusing to attend meetings not pertaining directly to patient care.

Nurses first took industrial action on a national scale in 1974, although other groups of workers demonstrated support for a nurses' pay claim in 1962 by token stoppages and protest marches.[37] In 1974 nurses demanded an independent inquiry into their pay and conditions, which had failed to keep pace with inflation. The Government initially rejected this demand and the R.C.N. threatened that nurses would resign from the N.H.S. and offer their services on an agency basis unless the inquiry was granted within three weeks. C.O.H.S.E. rejected proposals from other organizations for a combined campaign and on May 21 gave five days' notice of disruptive action unless nurses were awarded an immediate pay increase. Despite the announcement on May 23 of an unfettered inquiry, and the opposition of the R.C.N. and other unions, C.O.H.S.E. decided to proceed with its plans. Psychiatric hospitals, where the union's support was concentrated, bore the brunt of the disruption, which included selective strikes, but general hospitals were also affected, and within a few days admissions throughout the country were restricted. C.O.H.S.E. planned to intensify the action by banning non-emergency admissions, refusing to admit patients committed to psychiatric hospitals by the courts, refusing to work with agency nurses or nurse private patients, and banning the transfer of staff between hospitals and participation in management functions. Sanctions were lifted, however, when the Secretary of State, Mrs Barbara Castle, promised to consider an interim award if publication of the inquiry's report was seriously delayed. The report[38] gave nurses an average increase of 30 per cent and was welcomed by all the organizations.

Membership of C.O.H.S.E. increased significantly in the years following the 1974 campaign.[39] Later years brought even greater growth for the R.C.N., however, whose membership leapt from 90,000 to about 200,000 between 1977 and 1982. This increase has been attributed partly to decentralization of the R.C.N.'s organization, involving the appointment of shop stewards and full-time regional officers,[40] and partly to gains from C.O.H.S.E. and N.U.P.E. in reaction to their tactics during the 1979 ancillary workers' dispute.

It is difficult to assess the extent of industrial action by nurses during the 1982 dispute, which, as the previous section indicated, involved nearly all health service groups. At the outset of the campaign there were reports of nurses refusing to perform overtime work or non-nursing duties or to cover for absent colleagues. In general, however, it seems that as the dispute wore on, action by nurses was confined to stoppages of one or two hours and picketing in off-duty hours. The R.C.N. advised its members not to undertake tasks normally performed by other workers in dispute to avoid antagonizing other unions and detracting from nursing duties, but it later assured support for any members undertaking tasks necessary for essential patient care.

The T.U.C.-affiliated unions took the view in 1982 that all health service workers should receive an equal percentage increase. The R.C.N., however, supported a higher increase for nurses on the basis that they had a 'special relationship' with patients which was not shared by other groups involved in the campaign. In establishing the

Review Body for Nurses, Midwives and Professions Allied to Medicine, and affording these groups more favourable immediate treatment, the Government endorsed the R.C.N.'s case. It also presented the Review Body as a reward for not engaging in industrial action and imposed a no-strike commitment through the back-door by reserving the right to exclude from the Review Body's recommendations any groups which did resort to disruptive action.[41] This does not mean that the Review Body's recommendations will automatically be implemented, however; the Government reserves the right not to implement them for 'compelling national reasons'.[42] So far the Government has accepted its awards, although in 1985 it decided to pay the 9 per cent increase recommended in two stages, with 5 per cent being payable immediately and the remainder in February 1986. Although the General Secretary of the R.C.N. said that nurses were 'very disappointed' that the increase had been staged,[43] it is unlikely that nurses will be provoked into further industrial action over pay while the Government continues broadly to honour the Review Body's recommendations.

DOCTORS

The majority of doctors in Great Britain work either in N.H.S. hospitals or as general practitioners within the service, and if these doctors were to withdraw their labour completely, there would be no adequate alternative source of health care. Both groups have shown themselves willing to impose limited sanctions in furtherance of disputes over pay and conditions and have on occasion threatened to resign from the N.H.S. en masse. The dominant doctors' organization, and the only one to be recognized for collective bargaining purposes, is the B.M.A., which was founded in 1832 as a professional association and is now a certified independent trade union. In August 1985 it had 69,000 doctors in membership: 23,500 general practitioners (about 75 per cent of the total number), 18,000 junior hospital doctors (about 70 per cent of the total number), and 11,360 consultants (nearly 70 per cent of the total number).[44] It is not affiliated to the T.U.C. There are also two smaller organizations which represent specifically the interests of consultants and junior hospital doctors; the T.U.C.-affiliated H.C.S.A., formed in 1948, and the H.D.A. (previously the J.H.D.A.), established in 1969. These two unions together form the B.H.D.F. In mid-1985, the H.C.S.A. had approximately 3,000 members, the H.D.A. about 1,100. In addition, about 3,400 doctors, both general practitioners and hospital doctors, belong to the M.P.U., which was founded in 1914 and is now part of A.S.T.M.S. The distinctive feature of the M.P.U. is its opposition to any form of private medicine. Some doctors belong both to the B.M.A. and to another union, but the precise amount of dual membership is unknown. All these organizations uphold the freedom of doctors to take industrial action.

The first campaign of industrial action by doctors took place in 1970, although on two previous occasions (in 1957 and 1965) general practitioners had threatened to withdraw from the N.H.S. and form an alternative fee-paying organization, with special provision for poorer patients, if their demands were not met. The 1970 dispute arose when the Labour Government refused to implement in full a pay award recommended by the Review Body for Doctors and Dentists which had been established in 1962, a decision which led the entire Review Body to resign in protest. The B.M.A. advised its members not to sign sickness notes, and 75 per cent of all general practitioners complied with this advice over an eighteen-day period. The Association also held a ballot on whether members would wish to resign from the N.H.S. if the Review Body were not re-established, and this produced a majority in favour of resignation. The dispute ended when a new Conservative administration re-established the Review Body and agreed to pay a greater proportion of the original award than had previously been offered.

Hospital doctors applied sanctions for the first time, and only time on any significant scale, in 1975 in separate disputes involving junior doctors (all grades up to senior registrar) and consultants. The consultants' action was a protest against the terms of a new contract which the Labour Government proposed to introduce when its plans to remove private beds from the N.H.S. came into operation. A questionnaire sent by the B.M.A. to members affected by the change, which produced nearly 10,000 replies, indicated that 77 per cent of respondents thought that sanctions by senior staff were justified, 60 per cent were willing to work to rule, and 42 per cent were willing to sign undated resignations, and in January 1975 the B.M.A. gave official backing to a work-to-rule. In addition, 6,800 consultants threatened to resign from the N.H.S. and registered with employment agencies. The impact of the work-to-rule is hard to assess, but the H.C.S.A. claimed that it resulted in 25 per cent of out-patients having their appointments postponed or cancelled in January. In mid-March the H.C.S.A. escalated the action by advising its members not to work in sub-standard casualty departments, wards or hospitals; a spokesman argued that any injuries caused to patients by this ban would be considerably less damaging than those caused by inadequate facilities. The campaign was called off in mid-April after negotiations with the Government over the new contract were reopened, but further action began later in the year over the provisions of the Health Services Bill, which was designed to implement the separation of private practice from the N.H.S. The Government's proposals were presented by the representative organizations as an attack on consultants' independence and freedom of choice which the profession had no choice but to oppose. The B.M.A.'s Central Committee for Hospital Medical Services resolved that from December 1 consultants should handle only emergency cases and made plans to collect resignations. The action lasted until mid-February, when a majority of consultants who voted in a B.M.A. ballot indicated that they were prepared to accept compromise proposals from the Government for phasing out private beds. With the advent of a Conservative Government in 1979, this policy was reversed and private beds remain available within N.H.S. hospitals. Consultants are permitted to derive up to 10 per cent of their earnings from private practice.

The second campaign involving consultants coincided with the later phase of the junior doctors' dispute. The causes of this latter dispute were 'numerous and varied',[45] but it too centred around the terms of a new contract which, as originally drafted, meant that some doctors would suffer a drop in salary, although more would probably gain. The money available to finance the new arrangements was restricted by the Government's pay policy. Initially, sanctions were applied without the support of the B.M.A., whose negotiators favoured continuing talks with the Government, although the J.H.D.A., which at that time claimed 5,500 members, and the M.P.U. took a more militant line. Industrial action began in Leicestershire on October 12 and emergencies-only working spread rapidly; by the end of October the B.M.A. estimated that 8,500 junior doctors were taking action, affecting 11 per cent of N.H.S. hospitals. In mid-November the B.M.A.'s Hospital Junior Staffs Committee (H.J.S.C.) was subject to a motion of 'no confidence' and a newly elected committee recommended industrial action 'in the form of a forty-hour week worked flexibly according to the local needs and dealing with emergencies only'. The B.M.A. Council endorsed this recommendation by a narrow majority, and official action began on November 27. All areas of the country were affected, and thousands of out-patient appointments and non-urgent admissions were cancelled. Some small hospitals were closed to concentrate resources.

The action received little overt public support; it was condemned by both Labour and Conservative M.P.s for putting patients at risk and got minimal discernible backing from other trade unions. Following fresh negotiations, most doctors had complied with H.J.S.C. advice to return to normal working by the end of December, and after an independent audit of the money available under the terms of the Government's offer, the B.M.A. Council recommended suspension of the action in early January. The new contract was introduced in February. This did not bring the conflict to an end, however, and the B.M.A. Annual Representative Meeting recommended restarting industrial action when the Government unilaterally inserted a disputed term on leave payments into doctors' conditions of service. Sanctions were imposed in a number of areas and the H.J.S.C. drew up plans for a 24-hour strike. Before these could be put into effect, the Government withdrew the disputed term and a compromise settlement was reached.

As with any industrial action in the health service, it is extremely difficult to measure the real effects of the action taken by consultants and junior doctors. No deaths were attributed to these campaigns, and it may well be that doctors restricted services only when they knew that colleagues could cover for them. Patients in hospital or awaiting urgent treatment do not appear to have been put at risk. Nevertheless, the disputes do seem to have had more than a cosmetic effect on services. The D.H.S.S. Annual Report for 1975 claimed that consequences included:

> fewer admissions, longer waiting lists, and a smaller number of out-patient consultations. The number of in-patients treated was the lowest since 1968 and decreased by over four per cent compared with 1974. The number of patients waiting for admission rose by over twelve per cent and was the highest since 1948.[46]

Out-patient attendances fell by 7 per cent. As Treloar points out, '[t]he effects [on patients] of prolonged delay of admission or medical treatment cannot be assessed'.[47] Apart from the discomfort and inconvenience which may be caused in even non-urgent cases, a routine condition may become an emergency if treatment is put off for too long and diagnosis of urgent cases may be retarded.

The doctors' action in 1975 attracted opposition from many quarters within the medical profession. The Royal Colleges (professional bodies covering specific branches of medicine) refused to support it, and it was condemned by *The Lancet* and by many B.M.A. members because of the risks it presented to patients and the damage it caused to doctors' public esteem. Debate on the ethics of taking industrial action continued in the pages of the *British Medical Journal* and elsewhere[48] and at the B.M.A.'s Annual Representative Meeting in 1979 a resolution was passed 'unequivocally' condemning 'the kind of industrial action which increases the sum of human suffering'. At that time the B.M.A.'s *Handbook of Medical Ethics* was rather unclear about the circumstances in which industrial action by doctors might be justified. This was subsequently amended to take account of the Resolution. The current edition still leaves to individual doctors the decision on what action to take, but it draws attention to the 1979 resolution and to doctors' 'basic ethical duties'.[49] Unlike the equivalent nurses' body, the General Medical Council, the disciplinary body for the medical profession, has issued no specific guidance on industrial action.

Despite the 1979 resolution, the B.M.A. has no immediate intention of surrendering doctors' freedom to apply sanctions; the 1982 Annual Representative Meeting resoundingly rejected a motion asking the Council to investigate the possibility of a 'no-strike' agreement in return for guarantees that the Review Body's recommendations would always be implemented in full and without delay, and the issue has not been publically discussed since that time. (In 1978 the H.J.S.C. offered to abandon the freedom to take industrial action if junior doctors were given the right to direct bargaining on pay backed by binding arbitration, but this was rejected by the Secretary of State for Social Services, Dr David Ennals.) It is hard to predict exactly what sanctions the B.M.A. would now be prepared to authorize. In 1974 it issued a 'sanctions plan' which, it was claimed, would affect 'administration rather than clinical care'.[50] As well as the last resort of mass resignations, this proposed, *inter alia*, that hospital doctors should work strictly according to their contracts and that any further services should be paid for by health authorities on an agency basis, with the B.M.A. acting as an employment agency for this purpose. It also recommended general practitioners to 'operate a plan. . . [which was] intended to cause the maximum discomfort to the administration with the minimum of inconvenience to the doctor', although the details of this plan were not revealed. This plan no longer represents B.M.A. policy, but no further proposals have since been published. It is known that the Association still has plans for implementing mass resignations from the N.H.S., but the procedure for doing this and other possible sanctions remain confidential. It is probably safe to say that doctors would not repeat the 1975 experience readily and that, in the case of consultants at least, industrial action is more likely to take place over what is perceived as an issue of principle, such as private practice, than over a purely pay issue.

SUMMARY

For many years industrial action in the N.H.S. was virtually unknown. The 1970s witnessed a radical change in the conduct of industrial relations as ancillary workers, followed by nurses, doctors, ambulancemen and other groups, embarked on major campaigns of disruptive action. In all official disputes the organizers were concerned to protect patients requiring urgent treatment and those in need of continuous care, but the advice of national leaders was not always followed at local level; ambulancemen, in particular, frequently withdrew their services entirely. In some cases departures from official guidelines were attributed by the unions to 'provocative' management action, in accordance with the policy that self-restraint should be reciprocal. During ancillary workers' disputes there has been extensive use of internal volunteers, mainly managers and nurses, and this practice is tacitly accepted by the unions. The deployment of external volunteers would almost certainly be regarded as provocative, however, and they have rarely been called upon to cover for absent workers. In contrast, ambulancemen have often been replaced by outside labour, which now includes the police as well as members of voluntary organizations and troops. There have been no attempts to replace nurses or doctors with substitute labour, and it is very difficult to imagine this being done.

There have been three major national disputes involving ancillary workers. During the first of these, in 1972–3, the unions issued only outline guidance to their members on maintaining emergency cover. The Conservative Government pursued a policy of co-operation with the unions at national level but lack of local organization and negotiating experience, combined with disputes over the definition of an 'emergency', led to a severely limited service in many areas. The 1979 campaign was governed by more precise guidelines. The Labour Government also adopted a strategy of co-operation with the unions, and health authorities were requested initially not to implement sanctions against workers taking action, although this advice was subsequently modified. Towards the end of the dispute N.U.P.E. gave permission for all-out strikes, and the Government, too, abandonded the policy of self-restraint.

The 1982 dispute, in which the vast majority of health service groups were involved, was conducted in accordance with a code of practice drafted the previous year by T.U.C.-affiliated unions with members in the N.H.S. This campaign consisted of designated 'days of action' combined with continuous sanctions of a kind determined by local union branches. In line with its Circular 'If Industrial Relations Break Down', the Conservative Government left health authorities to deal with the disruption themselves and evidence from the survey of administrators discussed below and elsewhere indicates that managers in some areas continued to pursue a reciprocal 'self-restraint' policy, despite the 'hawkish' tone of the Circular. Negotiations on emergency cover were probably facilitated by the existence of a more detailed code of practice. The workers' defeat in 1982 was attributed by some unions to the limitations imposed by the code, and N.U.P.E. now favours an approach which gives greater discretion to local branches. Future campaigns would probably be brought to a head much more quickly than that of 1982.

Ambulancemen have taken industrial action several times in recent years, often, against the advice of their unions, without maintaining emergency cover. Their willingness to do this may be due partly to the knowledge that adequately trained substitute labour is likely to be available. Recent changes in the distribution of union membership indicates that future disputes may receive less wholehearted support, and a proposed new salary structure may also lead to a reduction in militancy.

Nurses have not so far taken industrial action on any significant scale, and they are unlikely to do so in the forseeable future. The representation of nurses is split between the R.C.N., a professional organization whose rules forbid withdrawing services in furtherance of disputes, and trade unions affiliated to the T.U.C. During a major conflict with the Government in 1974, the R.C.N. threatened mass resignations from the N.H.S. and the provision of services on an agency basis unless nurses' demands were met, but disruptive action was restricted to members of C.O.H.S.E. Most nurses participated only in token protests during the 1982 dispute. The establishment of the Review Body for Nurses, Midwives and Professions Allied to Medicine makes it improbable that nurses will become actively involved in further campaigns of industrial action, at least while the Government continues to honour the Review Body's awards. The Government reserves the right to exclude from the Review Body's recommendations any groups which do have to resort to disruptive action.

Doctors have threatened to resign from the N.H.S. and establish an alternative fee-paying organization on a number of occasions. There have also been three major instances when they have provided only a limited service. In 1970 general practitioners refused to sign sickness notes, and in 1975 hospital consultants and junior doctors took part in separate protests which resulted in significant reductions in out-patient consultations and hospital admissions, although patients already in hospital or awaiting urgent treatment did not seem to be affected. The 1975 campaigns provoked considerable controversy within the medical profession and in 1979 a resolution was passed by the B.M.A.'s Annual Representative Meeting condemning the kind of industrial action which increases the sum of human suffering. Nevertheless, the B.M.A. does not wish to surrender the strike weapon.

APPROACHES TO INDUSTRIAL ACTION IN THE NATIONAL HEALTH SERVICE: A SURVEY OF HEALTH SERVICE ADMINISTRATORS.[51]

The code of practice proposed by the T.U.C. Health Services Committee for the conduct of disputes in the N.H.S. and the D.H.S.S. Circular 'If Industrial Relations Break Down', both of which are outlined in the section on ancillary workers earlier in this chapter, represent diametrically opposed approaches towards dealing with industrial action in an essential service. The former advocates the 'self-restraint/joint regulation' approach, whereby management and unions together arrange to maintain supplies and services essential for emergency services and services to high dependency patients. It carries the *quid pro quo* that management should not draw upon its full range of sanctions. The Circular affirms the managerial prerogative. This section describes the results of interviews with health service administrators (mainly District Administrators or District Personnel Officers)[52] carried out in 1983, which were designed to ascertain their responses to the 1982 national dispute and, more broadly, to investigate their attitudes towards the issues which each of these two approaches raise. The survey covered thirty-one health authorities in the south-east of England, in which the extent of industrial action varied from stoppages of one or two hours in order to join demonstration picket lines to prolonged disruption of key areas. It cannot claim to give a precise account of detailed management practice during the dispute; the handling of the action at different hospitals within districts may not have been entirely uniform and a small number of those interviewed only took up their posts after the dispute had already started. Its main interest lies in the range of attitudes towards dealing with industrial action which are revealed.

Conducting negotiations

All the administrators included in the survey supported the Circular's policy of leaving responses to industrial action to local discretion on the ground that successful management required detailed knowledge of the local industrial relations climate and the flexibility to respond quickly to changes in circumstances. Many were highly critical of the way the Government had handled the dispute at national level and were determined to minimize the disruption to industrial relations in their district.

In contrast to the 1972–3 ancillary workers' dispute, in every district covered by the survey discussions took place between management and staff before industrial action started. Generally these were at unit (hospital) level between unit managers and shop stewards or branch officials of the relevant unions, with the participation in a few cases of district managers who wanted to ensure a co-ordinated response throughout the district. In two cases there were meetings with the unions at both district and unit level, the district-level meetings covering broad policy issues and the units working out the details. In nearly all districts the unions gave sufficient notice of industrial action to allow managers to make adequate preparations to deal with it. In two cases, however, surprise became one of the unions' main weapons, and this forced managers to prepare for a range of contingencies.

In the vast majority of districts, administrators attempted to agree levels of emergency cover with the unions. In one district, however, trust between management and union representatives was eroded at an early stage of the dispute, and managers made up any shortfall in cover with internal volunteers. In two districts managers refused to negotiate on emergency cover in any way and simply stated their requirements. Again, volunteers met any shortfall. In a fourth district the level of industrial action was never sufficient to merit negotiations.

In eight districts where cover had been negotiated, administrators reported that agreed staffing levels were not always provided. In general they attributed this to inadequate control by the unions over their members rather than duplicity. Administrators in twenty-one districts considered the unions' code of practice helpful in establishing a reference point in negotiations on cover, but many saw the lack of enforcement machinery as a serious limitation on its usefulness. In their experience, if individual shop stewards or members refused to abide by the code's provisions, as had happened in a few districts, full-time union officials could (or would) do nothing about it.

In only four districts within the survey did the industrial action have no effect on admissions or out-patients clinics. In many districts an 'emergencies only' restriction applied only to the Days of Action, but some were officially down to emergencies only for much of the dispute. In nine districts administrators acknowledged that they had agreed to restrict admissions in return for the unions providing agreed levels of cover. In three cases this arrangement applied only to the Days of Action; in others, the 'deal' extended over a longer period. In three districts managers agreed not to admit private patients during the dispute. This was a 'tidy' way of satisfying the unions' need to demonstrate that their action was having an impact. In two of these, together with the remaining districts covered by 'deals', non-emergency cases were not admitted for some or all of the dispute. In every district where there was a 'deal' the unions accepted that the classification of a case as an 'emergency' was a matter of clinical judgement, although in all but two districts (where the restriction was only for Days of Action), some form of appeals machinery was established. In one district the Medical Executive Committee (M.E.C.) set up a three-man vetting committee to which medical staff agreed to refer any borderline cases. In another, the chairman and vice-chairman of the M.E.C. sat in on negotiations with the unions to confirm on behalf of their colleagues the cases which had been treated. In only one district (and on only two occasions) did the unions challenge a case before an operation rather than retrospectively.

Of the remaining districts where admissions were postponed or clinics cancelled, seven administrators said they had done this as a precaution, six because they were unable to cope, and the remainder fell into a grey area which could not be classified. In some of these latter districts, administrators denied making any 'deals', but there seems to have been some form of tacit understanding with the unions.

Administrators in twenty districts in the survey said that they could envisage circumstances in which they would agree with the unions to reduce services, although their enthusiasm for doing this varied greatly. A few gave unreserved support to this approach. They felt that, given that there would inevitably be a reduction in services, it was better to plan it jointly from the start to see where the reduced throughput would cause the least overall disruption. In one district there were discussions to identify workers who had rest days on the Days of Action who could therefore participate in the protest without losing pay, coupled with an agreement to limit admissions to emergencies. The remainder felt that a 'deal' was legitimate if the alternative was more drastic disruption of services, but would only make one if forced into it. Most of these managers saw a distinction between a national and a local dispute in this context, however. In a national dispute the parties had no direct control over the outcome, and the 'joint regulation' approach could be appropriate to limit disruption in their district. By contrast, in a local dispute, management would be concentrating on resolving it rather than planning how to lessen its impact. Entering into negotiations on cover could prolong the dispute and lead to new areas of confrontation.

A few administrators said that they would refuse to make a 'deal' in any circumstances. Three considered that, given that their task was to maximize patient services, they could not condone any action which interfered with that priority. They would never concede an emergency level however much services were reduced. One maintained that any reduction must be the sole responsibility of the unions, who would forfeit public sympathy if the situation became dangerous. Another considered that agreeing to limit services was doing the unions' job for them and might achieve a greater impact than industrial action could do. A third felt that if management demonstrated a hard-line response in a national dispute, there was a good chance that the unions would shift their attention elsewhere, whereas if they knew that managers were 'soft', they would concentrate on that district.

Publicity is a crucial factor in any dispute, and this is another area where unions and management may reach an understanding. The unions need their action to have a significant impact without being accused of irresponsibility. In nine districts in the survey (three of which had agreed to restrict admissions) there was an agreement, generally tacit, over publicity. On the union side, what this amounted to was 'if you say you're being hit, we won't hit you that hard'. As well as reaching the public at large, this arrangement also protected local union branches from external pressure to take more severe action. In two cases administrators agreed press statements with the unions. A couple of administrators connived at activities which would attract publicity. One allowed the unions to keep banners on hospital railings. In another district, where workers had refused to move rubbish bags, a 'deal' was struck that a contractor would be employed to remove them when they became a health hazard but before then the press would be called in to photograph the scene, so maximizing the impact of limited union action. Others told the press that action was 'having an impact' without specifying its nature.

In the remaining districts most administrators realized that to say industrial action was having little or no effect would probably provoke more severe disruption on the next occasion, and so did not in general set out to contradict the unions' version of events. In two districts, however, management wanted to reassure the public that it was 'business as usual'. The manipulation of publicity can make it hard to discover from media sources what actually happened during a dispute; it is significant that many administrators felt that they had been let off lightly by the unions as compared with neighbouring districts!

Implementing sanctions

The only mandatory sanction against participating in industrial action laid down in the D.H.S.S. Circular is that staff on strike should not be paid or receive allowances which have not been earned. All those interviewed in the survey said that they had complied with this provision in principle, although a couple suggested that due to problems of management recording, pay might not always have been deducted for one or two hour stoppages. In the case of restrictive working (working-to-rule, 'blacking' certain work, restricting production or refusing to co-operate with agency staff, contractors or volunteers), which the Circular states is usually a breach of contract,[53] managers are advised first to consider whether less than full service is acceptable to them. If not, the staff concerned could be sent home without pay after being given a warning notice at least two days before this sanction is implemented.[54] If they decide to accept restrictive working, managers could either offer staff, *ex gratia* and without negotiation, such proportion of normal payments as they consider reasonable for the proportion of normal duties performed[55] or they could offer to pay, on a full-time basis, only the number of staff required to maintain the level of service offered.

Fifteen of the districts included in the survey experienced some form of restrictive working during the 1982 dispute. In only three cases were deductions made from pay. In the first, where porters were refusing to cover operating theatres, the deduction was negotiated with the unions; the administrator considered that this prevented more drastic action being taken. In another district staff accepted 80 per cent of their normal wages during a ban on private patients; management felt that this was a sufficient reduction to put pressure on the employees to resume normal working but not enough to escalate the action. In the third district, a group of occupational therapists who elected to work only in their own department had their pay withheld for the time which they should have spent on the wards. In five of the fifteen districts management considered that the industrial action did not have sufficient impact to justify any deduction. In the remaining districts staff were either sent home or the threat of this sanction led to normal working being resumed. In the five where staff were actually sent home, this was only for a short period.

In twelve of the thirty-one districts in the survey, administrators said that they would prefer to send workers home rather than to impose deductions. A variety of reasons were given for this choice: that allowing workers to select their duties, even at a reduced rate of pay, could set a dangerous precedent; the difficulties of assessing the appropriate amount of pay; and that workers who were doing only part of their job were of little benefit. Seven thought part payment was a useful sanction, however. The remainder could envisage implementing one or other sanction in extreme circumstances but were concerned that this would provoke an escalation of the action. The replaceability of workers by volunteers appeared to be an important consideration in this context.

Another sanction which is referred to in the Circular is reducing annual leave; it states that entitlement will not accrue during periods of industrial action for which no payment is made (nor will superannuation entitlement accrue). In response to a query, the D.H.S.S. emphasized, however, that 'the fact that employees have no right to the benefits conferred by their contracts during. . . a period of industrial action does not legally oblige the employing authority to withhold those benefits'.[56] In only four districts in the survey was annual leave entitlement adjusted. In a fifth, threatening to do this led to a return to normal working. In the majority of other districts administrators felt that periods of absence had been too short to justify the labour involved in making adjustments.[57] Some said they would consider deducting annual leave if the absence was prolonged, but others felt that to impose a sanction which would probably operate long after the dispute was settled was unduly punitive and provocative.

Using volunteers

In general, health service unions tacitly accept the use of management volunteers to provide cover during disputes but strongly oppose the deployment of external volunteers. The Circular makes no such distinction. It encourages authorities to make 'such use of volunteers as they think fit', whether recruited from existing N.H.S. staff or from the general public. It adds the proviso that the position of regular volunteers who already work alongside paid staff may require special consideration, but it makes no reference to the guidelines issued by the Volunteer Centre, referred to earlier in the chapter. Volunteers were used in 1982 in twenty of the districts we visited but they were all drawn from existing staff, generally managers and nurses. Despite the N.A.L.G.O. instruction and R.C.N. advice to their respective members not to do strikers' jobs, in only one district did R.C.N. nurses refuse to exceed their normal duties; otherwise, membership of these organizations did not appear to prevent individuals from volunteering. In two districts known union members were not asked to volunteer.

In some cases the use of management volunteers was taken for granted by the unions in calculating emergency cover. One administrator objected to this practice; he made clear to the unions at the outset that managers would not be permitted to perform ancillary jobs and claimed that the unions modified their plans as a result. Most administrators said that they would call for external volunteers only as a desperate last resort; their deployment would escalate the action and they would be of little, if any, use. They would require training and supervision and any trade unionists who did remain at work would probably refuse to co-operate with them. Three administrators said they would prefer to close a hospital altogether rather than rely on their services.

Summary

On the evidence of this survey, there is a wide range of opinion among administrators at local level in the N.H.S. on the appropriate management response to industrial action. There was considerable support for the 'joint regulation' approach in national disputes where managers were convinced that not following it would mean greater disruption to services, and a few took a more positive attitude towards it. In local disputes, however, managers thought that their energies would be directed towards achieving a settlement. A small proportion of administrators were firmly opposed to the 'joint regulation' approach in any circumstances. As far as publicity for disruption is concerned, it seems that administrators may be prepared to condone an element of exaggeration in descriptions of its extent. In considering whether or not the various provisions of 'If Industrial Relations Break Down' should be implemented, the risk of escalating disruption was generally seen as an important factor, although a few took the line that if the unions chose to extend the action, they would have to answer for the consequences themselves. There was widespread reliance on internal volunteers to do strikers' jobs but little enthusiasm for calling on volunteers from outside the service. Finally, most administrators considered the unions' code of practice helpful in establishing a reference point in negotiating emergency cover, but many saw the lack of machinery for enforcing it as a serious limitation on its usefulness.

CONCLUSION: THE OPERATION OF THE 'QUEENSBERRY RULES' APPROACH

The account of the conduct of disputes in the five sectors discussed in this and the preceding chapter shows that trade unions have generally designed their campaigns of disruptive action to take account of public health and safety. Their self-restraint is usually made conditional, however, on employers exercising reciprocal self-restraint and not seeking to undermine the campaign in ways which are considered unacceptable. This 'Queensberry Rules' approach was spelt out expressly by the N.H.S. unions when they stated that observance of their code of practice depended upon a 'sensible local management response'.[58] The nature of the self-restraint required from management may not be identical in every sector; during the 1983 water strike, for example, the unions justified departures from the code of practice on the ground that white-collar workers had been performing strikers' jobs, whereas such conduct has frequently been condoned by unions in the health service. In some disputes management may have to agree to pay workers who maintain emergency cover their normal wages even though they are refusing to perform their full range of contractual duties. As the survey of health service administrators reveals, the 'Queensberry Rules' approach may also make employer representatives complicit in curtailing services or in furnishing them in accordance with union priorities.

It is not only employers, but also the Government, which may choose to subscribe to the 'Queensberry Rules' approach. This has been done on a number of occasions. In 1924 the MacDonald Labour Government planned to invite union members to transport essential foodstuffs and fuel, rather than to declare a state of emergency, during a dock strike on condition that no more men than necessary for this limited purpose would be enlisted.[59] The Heath Conservative Government advised health authorities not to call for volunteers during the 1972–3 ancillary workers' dispute unless the unions failed to maintain emergency services, and also sought union assistance in unloading perishable foodstuffs during dock strikes in 1970 and 1972. A clear articulation of this approach came from the Labour Government which followed. At the beginning of the 1979 N.H.S. dispute, the Secretary of State for Social Services, Dr David Ennals, said that it was 'the task of Government and of the unions who instituted the action to keep it within tolerable limits'.[60] As a *quid pro quo*, health authorities were requested not to implement sanctions against staff taking action, although this bargain broke down in the later stages of the dispute.

A similar strategy was following during the road haulage strike of that year, when the Government presented union leaders with a list of supplies which should not be impeded and the unions incorporated this list into a code of practice. Daily meetings were held between Government and union officials to monitor adherence to the code and to identify problem areas. Despite strong pressure in Parliament to declare a state of emergency or send in troops, and a less than uniform response from drivers to the code of practice, the Government defended its strategy as being 'the quickest and most efficient way of minimising the inevitable disturbance'.[61]

The 'Queensberry Rules' approach to disputes has certain advantages for unions, employers and the Government. For unions, it demonstrates the effectiveness of a campaign of industrial action whilst avoiding allegations of irresponsibility, and it may also protect those taking action against undue financial hardship. For employers, it defines and limits the scope of disruption and offers the continuation of a basic service. Where a dispute falls within the ambit of the 1920 Act, it may spare the Government the political and financial consequences of declaring a state of emergency. It may also avoid the need to send in troops. It can be argued, however, that such an approach involves unwarranted limitations on the management prerogative, dilutes the responsibility of the trade unions for the disruption and restricts the Government's freedom of manoeuvre. For some Governments the idea of liaising with trade unions to limit the impact of industrial action has been anathema. The Lloyd George Government opposed any such suggestion on the ground that this would prevent it from using 'the national resources for combating the strike,[62] and the Baldwin administration declined the T.U.C.'s offer of co-operation in distributing essential foodstuffs during the 1926 General Strike. Mr Winston Churchill explained this decision to the House of Commons by asking rhetorically:

> What Government in the world could enter into partnership with a rival Government, against which it is endeavouring to defend itself, and society, and allow that rival Government to sit in judgment on every train that runs and on every lorry on the road. . . We cannot by any means divest ourselves of the responsibility of maintaining the life of the nation in essential services and in public order.[63]

There have been no express statements on this subject by the present Conservative Government, beyond the kind of sentiments expressed in 'If Industrial Relations Break Down', but the hot-lines between Government departments and union headquarters which operated during the two previous administrations have not been in evidence.

The 'adversarial' approach to disputes which was articulated by Churchill can be implemented where the commodity which is subject to disruption can be rationed or stored or where there is an adequately trained substitute labour force available. Where, however, disruption affects a service which requires the continuous availability of skilled labour, such as areas of health care or the electricity or water industries, rejecting trade union co-operation may mean that the service is lost altogether.

Workers in essential services who observe a code of practice voluntarily accept a reduction in their bargaining power. By pledging themselves to comply with certain standards, they also risk attracting public condemnation for breaching their code, regardless of the circumstances in which these breaches occur. Ministers were not slow to draw attention to situations where participants in the 1982 N.H.S. dispute and 1983 water strike had deviated from their codes of practice. Furthermore, adherance to a code, by avoiding immediate crises, may prolong a dispute until the workers' will to fight on is exhausted. During the 1982 N.H.S. dispute, for example, the unions

> committed themselves to a lengthy and ultimately unsuccessful dispute with a government which saw itself as fighting for an essential element in its economic policy and which was unmoved by the hardship caused to the community by the withdrawal of non-essential medical services.[64]

The self-restraint approach can only be expected to operate successfully where the employer genuinely wants to negotiate a settlement rather than being prepared to sit out a dispute. It also requires commitment to self-restraint on both sides, a process which could be aided considerably by the provision of standing agreements which set out the scope of permissible action by unions and management during disputes. Further considerations of the form such agreements might take appears in Chapter 7. The 'Queensberry Rules' approach has often been applied in an informal, *ad hoc* manner in disputes in essential services in Britain. With clearer articulation of the principles which should govern the conduct of disputes in particular sectors, it could offer the cheapest and most efficacious method of securing the continuous provision of basic services.

NOTES

1. See Bob Hepple, 'Labour Law and Public Employees in Britain' in *Labour Law and the Community*, ed. Lord Wedderburn of Charlton and W.T. Murphy, Institute of Advanced Legal Studies, London, 1982, Ch. 7.

2. For commentaries on the operation of the system, see Lord McCarthy, *Making Whitley Work*, D.H.S.S., London, 1976; Royal Commission on the National Health Service, Cmnd. 7615 (1979); Trades Union Congress, *Improving Industrial Relations in the National Health Service: A Report by the T.U.C. Health Services Committee*, T.U.C., London, 1981.

3. National Health Service Act 1977, Sched. 5, para 10(1).

4. Roger Dyson and Katherine Spary, 'Professional Associations' in *Industrial Relations in the NHS: The Search for a System*, ed. Nick Bosenquet, King Edward's Hospital Fund for London, London, 1979, Ch. 7.

5. In 1948 the density of union membership in health services was 42.6 per cent.; in 1968 it was 37.9 per cent. By 1979 it had risen to 73.7 per cent: George Sayers Bain and Robert Price, 'Union Growth: Dimensions, Determinants, and Destiny' in *Industrial Relations in Britain*, ed. George Sayers Bain, Blackwell, Oxford, 1983, p. 15.

6. John Berridge, *A Suitable Case for Treatment*, Open University Press, Milton Keynes, 1976, p. 30.

7. Nick Bosenquet, 'The Search for a System' in *Industrial Relations in the NHS: The Search for a System*, King Edward's Hospital Fund for London, London, Ch. 1.

8. Roger Dyson, *Ancillary Staff Industrial Action Spring 1973*, A Survey and Report Prepared for the Leeds Regional Hospital Board, 1973.

9. *Ibid.*, p. 5.

10. Sir Keith Joseph, Secretary of State for Social Services, H.C. Deb., Vol. 853, col. 458 (March 21, 1973).

11. Tom Manson, 'Management, the Professions and the Unions: A Social Analysis of Change in the National Health Service' in *Health and the Division of Labour* ed. Margaret Stacey, Margaret Reid, Christian Heath and Robert Dingwall, Croom Helm, London, 1977, pp. 207–8.

12. Dr David Ennals, Secretary of State for Social Services, H.C. Deb., Vol. 961, col. 1214 (January 30, 1979).

13. Dr David Ennals, H.C. Deb., Vol. 962, col. 719 (February 5, 1979).

14. Dr David Ennals, H.C. Deb., Vol. 961, col. 1673 (February 1, 1979).

15. Guidelines for Relationships between Volunteers and Paid Non-Professional Workers, The Volunteer Centre, Berkhamsted, 1977.

16. Roger Dyson, 'Industrial Action 1979: What Can We Learn?', *British Medical Journal* May

26, 1979, p. 1435 at p. 1436.

17. For an example of such an agreement, see W. Duncan Dolton, 'Managing the Industrial Action', *Health Services Manpower Review* (1979), 25.

18. Dr David Ennals, H.C. Deb., Vol. 964, cols. 714–5 (March 15, 1979).

19. Dr David Ennals, H.C. Deb., Vol. 965, col. 559 (April 3, 1979) (written answer).

20. As above, note 2.

21. Trades Union Congress, *Improving Industrial Relations in the National Health Service: A Report by the T.U.C. Health Services Committee*, as above, note 2, para. 10.11.

22. The C.O.H.S.E. rule-book states that 'a reasonable standard of patient care' should be maintained and 'the respect of human dignity' observed. N.A.L.G.O. advises members to ensure the safety of life and limb of members of the public. A.S.T.M.S. instructs members to provide emergency cover for 'life and death cases' in consultation with the appropriate doctor. The E.E.T.P.U. tells its members to make arrangements to deal with 'genuine emergencies to protect the fundamental interest of patients'.

23. See Chapter 5.

24. As above, note 21, para. 10.9.

25. HC (79) 20.

26. Mr Norman Fowler, H.C. Deb., Vol. 25, col. 417 (June 10, 1982).

27. See Chapter 2.

28. Various newspaper publishers had been granted injunctions restraining union officials from instructing or advising employees to take part in the industrial action, which was unlawful secondary action under the Employment Act 1980. The Secretary of the Fleet Street Press Branch of the E.E.T.P.U. was fined £350 for breaching the order by not doing his best to revoke directions and advice already given to members of his union to withdraw their labour on that day: *Express Newspapers PLC and others* v. *Mitchell and others* [1982] I.R.L.R. 465.

29. *N.U.P.E. Journal* No. 1, 1983.

30. Some health service workers responded to the 1982 campaign by joining N.I.C.E., an organization created during the dispute to emphasize the 'caring' image of health service workers. In September 1985 it claimed to have in membership 900 workers, belonging to a variety of health service grades.

31. For objections to such a course, see Chapter 4.

32. Mr Hector Monro, Under-Secretary of State for Health and Education at the Scottish Office, H.C. Deb., Vol. 867, col. 3 (January 9, 1974).

33. In the year ending September 30, 1983, there were 394,620 nurses and midwives in England (excluding agency staff and nursing cadets).

34. Another organization open to all nursing grades, both qualified and unqualified, is the F.N.P., founded in 1973, which in September 1985 claimed to have 1,160 members. It is opposed to any form of industrial action which affects total patient care.

35. *What the R.C.N. stands for*, R.C.N., London, 1984, pp. 55–6.

36. In 1979, 2,639 voted for a change and 5,824 voted against it; in 1980, 13,982 voted in favour and 36,556 against; and in 1982, 3,144 voted in favour and 9,003 against.

37. For strikes in individual asylums immediately before and after the First World War, see Brian Abel-Smith, *A History of the Nursing Profession*, Heinemann, London, 1960, pp. 131–2, and Mick Carpenter, *All for One*, C.O.H.S.E., Surrey, 1980, pp. 22–6. Mental hospital nurses conducted an overtime ban in the mid-1950s.

38. *Report of the Committee of Inquiry into the Pay and Related Conditions of Service of Nurses and Midwives*, H.M.S.O., London, 1974.

39. Mick Carpenter, 'The Labour Movement in the National Health Service' in *Industrial Relations and Health Services*, ed. Amarjit Singh Sethi and Stuart J. Dimmock, Croom Helm, London, 1982, p. 77.

40. Roger Dyson, 'Under New Management', *Nursing Times*, October 27, 1982.

41. Mrs Margaret Thatcher, Prime Minister, H.C. Deb., Vol. 46, col. 462 (July 27, 1983) (written answer).

42. Mr Norman Fowler, H.C. Deb., Vol. 31, col. 431 (November 9, 1982).

43. *The Guardian*, June 7, 1985.

44. The remainder of the B.M.A.'s membership is accounted for by community physicians, civil service doctors, doctors working in the armed forces and occupational health, and medical

academics.

45. Susan Treloar, 'The Junior Hospital Doctors' Pay Dispute 1975–1976: An Analysis of Events, Issues and Conflicts', *Journal of Social Policy* 10 (1981), 1 at 19.

46. Department of Health and Social Security, Annual Report 1975, Cmnd. 6565 (1976), p. 27.

47. As above, note 45, p. 26.

48. See G. Dworkin, 'Strikes and the National Health Service: Some Legal and Ethical Issues', *Journal of Medical Ethics* 3 (1977), 76, and the commentary by Peter Zacharias at p. 83.

49. *The Handbook of Medical Ethics*, B.M.A., London, 1984, para. 66.

50. *British Medical Journal*, November 9, 1974, pp. 357–9.

51. These interviews were conducted by the author with the assistance of Stephen Rydzkowski. For a fuller description of the survey, see 'Anatomy of a Dispute', *Health and Social Service Journal*, April 12, 1984, and 'Approaches to Industrial Action in the National Health Service', *Industrial Law Journal* 13 (1984), 153.

52. In seventeen districts the District Administrator was interviewed, either alone or in conjunction with another administrator; in ten districts the District Personnel Officer was interviewed; and in four districts the Unit Administrator of the largest acute hospital in the district was interviewed. In a few cases district-level interviews were followed up by interviews at unit level.

53. A work-to-rule may not always be in breach of contract: see *Secretary of State for Employment* v. *A.S.L.E.F.* (No. 2) [1972] 2 Q.B. 455; Paul Davies and Mark Freedland, *Labour Law: Text and Materials*, 2nd edn., Weidenfeld and Nicolson, London, 1984, pp. 353–4. The advice given in the Circular is expressly based on the premise that the employee's conduct would have justified summary dismissal.

54. An employer's right to send employees home without pay if they refuse to comply with their contractual obligations, in the absence of any agreement restricting this right, was upheld in *Cresswell and others* v. *Board of Inland Revenue* [1984] I.R.L.R. 190.

55. Managers are urged to ensure that any payments made are not taken as an acceptance of or acquiescence in the employee's action. It is not clear that an employer can accept in practice imperfect performance of the contract without affirming it and so entitling the employee to sue for any unpaid wages due to him: *Royle* v. *Trafford Borough Council* [1984] I.R.L.R. 184; *Miles* v. *Wakefield Metropolitan District Council* [1985] I.C.R. 363, per Parker L.J; cf. *Henthorn and Taylor* v. *C.E.G.B.* [1980] I.R.L.R. 361 which states that an employee suing for unpaid wages must prove he was ready and willing to perform the contract. For principles for calculating the appropriate deduction of wages recently applied by the courts see *Royle* v. *Trafford Borough Council*, above, and *Sim* v. *Rotherham Metropolitan Borough Council, The Times*, May 30, 1986.

56. Quoted in a letter from the D.H.S.S. to the author, January 19, 1984.

57. It is unclear how any reduction in annual leave should be calculated; the Whitley agreements do not mention the impact of industrial action. The agreements talk in terms of completed months of service in calculating leave for employees who have not worked a full year. On one interpretation, a day's unauthorized absence means the entitlement earned by that month's service is discounted, and one Regional Health Authority in the area within the survey applied this to its own employees. The alternative view is that days of absence should be aggregated and the reduction calculated on a *pro rata* basis.

58. Trades Union Congress, *Improving Industrial Relations in the National Health Service: A Report by the T.U.C. Health Services Committee*, as above, note 2, para. 10.9.

59. See C14/24, Cab 23/47, February 18, 1924; C15/24(2), Cab 23/47, February 20, 1924.

60. H.C. Deb., Vol. 961, col. 1676 (February 1, 1979).

61. The Attorney-General, Mr Sam Silkin, H.C. Deb., Vol. 961, col. 719 (January 25, 1979). See also Chapter 3.

62. Note by the Secretary, Cab. meeting S.T.C., October 20, 1920, CP 199A, Cab 24/112.

63. H.C. Deb., Vol. 195, col. 123 (May 3, 1926).

64. Paul Davies and Mark Freedland, *Labour Law: Text and Materials*, 2nd edn., Weidenfeld and Nicolson, London, 1984, p. 886.

7

Prospects for the Future

The British approach to industrial action in essential services has traditionally centred upon taking measures to secure supplies which are threatened with disruption by alternative means rather than attempting to use the law to restrain workers in these areas from withdrawing their labour in the first place. Restrictions imposed upon particular groups (the police, the armed forces, merchant seamen and postal and telecommunications workers) were introduced in a piecemeal fashion for a variety of reasons rather than as the product of an integrated strategy, and a provision which in theory could restrict industrial action by many essential service groups (section 5 of the Conspiracy and Protection of Property Act 1875) has not been enforced. The primary focus of Government policy has been the development of effective administrative machinery to ameliorate the impact of stoppages, and since the end of the Second World War the maintenance of such machinery has been regarded by most members of the major political parties as a legitimate and necessary function of government. In recent years contingency planning has become increasingly sophisticated, and an elaborate organization, involving ministers, civil servants, the police and the military, is able to spring into action immediately should the situation so demand. If the measures to be taken require recourse to special powers, these can be made available quickly, without prior sanction by Parliament and, in the case of authority to use troops as substitute labour, without the need to obtain formal approval from Parliament at any stage.

On paper, the executive seems amply equipped to counter the effects of industrial action in essential services. There are practical constraints on its ability to do this, however. These stem largely from the lack of qualified labour with which to replace a striking work-force. The use of troops for this purpose has always been a crucial element in

Government contingency planning and it still remains important in many contexts. Nowadays, however, in areas which are technologically complex, such as electricity and water supply, troops can be deployed only with the co-operation of the white-collar staff in those industries, co-operation which is unlikely to be granted during official disputes. If highly trained professional groups withdraw their labour, the prospects of adequate replacement are even more remote. Troops are also severely limited in terms of numbers. In some recent disputes, most notably those involving ambulancemen, the police have rendered assistance, but their skills and availability, too, are limited, and their use as substitute labour prejudices their law enforcement role. The idea of recruiting civilian volunteers to replace strikers has been considered on several occasions, most recently in 1980, but this would be an extremely divisive and provocative step politically, and again, their efficacy in skilled occupations would probably be negligible. In certain key areas, therefore, continued provision of a service is dependent upon a minimum number of permanent staff remaining at work.

The limitations of the contingency planning process, which were highlighted by the public sector stoppages of the 1970s, and the growth in militancy among essential service workers, have made the problems presented by strikes in essential services a prominent issue of public debate. As Chapter 1 indicated, a variety of possible avenues of reform have been mooted. This chapter evaluates these strategies in the light of the British experience.

ALTERNATIVE STRATEGIES AND PROPOSALS FOR REFORM[1]

The strategies which have been advocated to deal with the problems caused by industrial action in essential services fall into four major groups:

(1) The restriction of industrial action in essential services by means of the criminal law.
(2) The restriction of industrial action in essential services by means of the civil law.
(3) The negotiation of 'no strike' agreements in essential services.
(4) The 'self-restraint/joint regulation' approach.

The implications of each of these strategies will be examined in turn.

(1) The restriction of industrial action in essential services by means of the criminal law

One apparently straightforward method of protecting essential services against disruption is to make industrial action by workers in those services a criminal offence. This is the approach put forward by the Centre for Policy Studies.[2] The implementation of this strategy requires the formulation of answers to three major questions: how should essential services be defined; how could the law be enforced; and how should disputes be resolved in the absence of a freedom to strike?

Defining essential services

The freedom of workers to withdraw their labour is recognized in international agreements to be a fundamental freedom which should be restricted only when strictly necessary.[3] As Chapter 1 indicated, acceptance of this proposition has not brought agreement among the countries of the world as to the sectors in which the public interest in securing an uninterrupted service justifies restricting the freedom. This is partly explained by the fact that the impact of disruption to a particular service will depend upon the geographical situation of a country, its economic structure and level of technological development, and the availability of alternative sources of supply. More fundamentally, however, it reflects a lack of consensus as to the appropriate criteria to be adopted in assessing whether a service is truly 'essential'. There is, therefore, no generally accepted 'model' which could be readily incorporated into British law.

Legal systems which prohibit industrial action in essential services divide broadly into those which specify the services in question and those which attach restrictions if disruption threatens to produce certain consequences. The enumeration method has two major advantages. It means the law is clear, and it avoids the need to decide in the heat of the moment whether individual campaigns should be proscribed. As Pankert notes, such decisions may be influenced more by political considerations and the pressure of public opinion than by the nature of the disruption. Such factors

> explain why it has frequently happened in almost all countries that the disputes procedure established for essential services has been applied in the case of relatively harmless disputes whilst it has not been in the case of other much more serious ones.[4]

Córdova makes the point that

> the reaction of public opinion is not necessarily commensurate with the essentialness of the service or services concerned, but rather with the degree of inconvenience caused by the strike. A strike in a hospital or ambulance service, for instance, arouses less hostility than a strike in the urban transport system, because many

regular users of the latter feel that they are not going to need the former services[5]

The enumeration method prevents these factors holding sway over the decision as to whether to proscribe a particular stoppage (although it clearly leaves open the possibility that the law will not be enforced in a uniform fashion). This method also allows the establishment of standing arrangements to compensate workers whose freedom to strike is curtailed, a system which may cause less resentment than subjecting disputes to compulsory resolution on an *ad hoc* basis. The major disadvantage of the enumeration method is its inability to distinguish between disputes which endanger essential services and those which do not. Even if restrictions are confined to services which are vital to 'life, personal safety or health', as required by the I.L.O.,[6] not all workers or activities are equally crucial to the continued operation of a service. Severing electricity supplies may endanger health or safety; failing to read electricity meters does not. A refusal by firemen to answer emergency calls clearly affects the public; refusing to perform routine duties may not. Sometimes the duration of action is material; a one-day strike by refuse collectors causes only inconvenience, a five-week strike is a major hazard to health. At the other end of the spectrum, a strike in a service which is not *per se* essential may deprive an essential service of vital supplies. A strike by oxygen suppliers could paralyse hospitals, a strike by chemical manufacturers could bring water purification to a halt. The Centre for Policy Studies caters for this problem by suggesting specific bans on industrial action in the fire, health and sewage services and the gas, water, electricity and nuclear power industries, combined with a power for the Secretary of State for Employment or some appropriate parliamentary body to extend these restrictions to auxiliary services or industries without whose labour or support an essential service cannot function. This proposal would reflect the practice in many countries which have adopted the enumeration method. It means, however, that large numbers of auxiliary or support workers, perhaps even the majority, could be caught within the net of prohibition.

Proscribing industrial action which produces specified consequences clearly allows much more flexibility than the enumeration method. It directs attention to the nature and scope of a campaign and enables most groups to take at least limited forms of action. There remains, of course, the problem of deciding upon the consequences which should attract prohibition. Danger to 'public health or safety' is the lowest common denominator of the definitions adopted by other countries, and this definition accords with standards set by the I.L.O. A wider definition becomes more difficult to apply. As stated in Chapter 1, some systems include damage to the national economy as a factor attracting prohibition, at which point it becomes hard to envisage any major disputes which could escape a strike ban.

The 'consequences' method also carries with it the problem of deciding at what stage a prohibition should be imposed and by whom. One approach is simply to make industrial action which leads to certain consequences a criminal offence; the legality or otherwise of a campaign then depends upon whether a prosecution is brought and whether it meets with success. This approach has the disadvantage of leaving the legality of a campaign uncertain until a court has pronounced upon the issue, a system which may prejudice unduly the work-force in dispute.

An alternative method is to allow a designated person or body the power to declare a campaign unlawful on their own initiative before the action starts. This power, however, may also be applied in an inconsistent fashion. If the decision to proscribe a dispute is left to the Government, political considerations of the kind discussed above may rule the day. To require endorsement of such a decision by Parliament would afford little protection when the Government has a working majority. Giving this task to the courts may give an illusion of objectivity, but the courts do not act of their own motion; the decision to seek a prohibition would remain a matter of political judgement. Moreover, experience of the 'emergency procedures' under the Taft-Hartley Act in the United States, and the brief experience in Britain of the Industrial Relations Act procedure, discussed in Chapter 3, indicate that the courts are reluctant to scrutinize the Government's case, particularly when time is of the essence. The courts may become little more than a rubber-stamp for the executive under this kind of procedure.

The Green Paper on Trade Union Immunities, issued by the Department of Employment in 1981, saw the problems of defining essential services as a major impediment to reforming the law. It concluded:

> there would be great difficulty in deciding which groups of workers should be chosen and on what criteria. There are clearly dangers in going too wide or appearing to be inequitable. There are many views on which groups should be restricted but very little agreement . . . [Indeed] the interdependent nature of industry means that a case can now be made for regarding a strike by most groups of workers as threatening essential services or supplies.[7]

Although the present Government has since put forward further proposals, which are discussed below, it has made no apparent progress in specifying the services to which they might apply. The task of defining essential services clearly involves enormous difficulties for any legislator.

A variant of the prohibition approach is to make the legality of campaigns dependent upon the maintenance of a minimum level of service by the work-force in dispute. The I.L.O. has accepted the legitimacy of imposing such requirements, provided that the minimum service is confined to 'operations that are strictly necessary to avoid endangering the life, personal safety or health of the whole or part of the population'. It also states that workers' organizations should participate in defining the minimum service in the same way as employers and the public authorities.[8] The considerations which are relevant to this approach are discussed in the section on self-restraint and joint regulation, below.

Enforcing the law

In a free society, the law cannot force people to work against their will; it can only penalize them if they fail to do so. It is a basic principle of British law that workers cannot be compelled to perform their contracts,[9] and any form of compulsory labour would mark a radical departure from this tradition. The problem is therefore one of devising an appropriate sanction for those who transgress a strike ban, a task which experience in Britain and elsewhere shows to be fraught with difficulty. The sanctions most commonly relied upon are fines, imprisonment and dismissal, but none of these meet the situation very satisfactorily. Fines are frequently too slight a deterrant, and problems are created if they remain unpaid. Mass dismissals are viable only if a work-force can be readily replaced; if the workers have necessary skills, this is unlikely to be possible, and in Britain the union movement would be bound to attempt to 'black' the vacant jobs. Mass imprisonment of strikers is a political and bureaucratic nightmare which does nothing to hasten resumption of the service; imprisoning dispute organizers is equally likely to retard a return to work, which may be made conditional upon an amnesty for those who have already been prosecuted. The administrative difficulties associated with mass prosecutions are also overwhelming; charges may take weeks or even months to process, and to continue pressing charges after a dispute has ended does not promote industrial harmony. A world-wide survey of strike laws in the public sector found that for reasons of this kind many administrations

> have refrained from enforcing the law and preferred to let strikes go

> unpunished. The judiciary has also tended to be lenient either because of the large numbers of public employees involved or because public servants were usually brought before the courts after the dispute had already been settled.[10]

An oft-quoted British example of the futility of prosecuting strikers arose from events at Betteshanger Colliery in Kent in 1941, when 4,000 miners went on strike in breach of wartime legislation. Summonses were served on 1,000 underground workers, but, as described to the Donovan Commission:

> Charges against 1,000 persons could only be handled satisfactorily if the men pleaded guilty. If each man pleaded 'not guilty' the proceedings might last for months. The Union was asked if they would instruct their members to plead guilty, and accept a decision on a few test cases. The Union obligingly did so.[11]

All the workers were fined and their leaders were imprisoned for terms of one or two months. This meant that

> the only men who could call off the strike were now in gaol. . . . The Secretary of Mines went down to Kent to see them accompanied by . . . [the union's national president]. Negotiations were re-opened and . . . an agreement was signed, in prison, between the colliery management and the Kent Miners' Union. Apart from some face-saving words, it gave the men what they wanted. Then the Secretary for Mines took a deputation to the Home Secretary asking for the immediate release of the three local officials. The men would not start work until their leaders were free. After eleven days in prison they were released.[12]

There remained the problem of collecting the fines, which only nine men had paid. The employers asked if they could pay them to avoid further trouble, but the Ministry of Labour vigorously opposed this course. Finally, the dilemma was resolved by the Court being advised against enforcing the unpaid fines.

For the Donovan Commission, this episode proved 'the fruitlessness of the use of penal sanctions for the purpose of enforcing industrial peace'.[13] It is hard to disagree with this conclusion.

Machinery for resolving disputes

The freedom of workers to take industrial action is generally regarded as an integral part of the right to bargain collectively; workers who cannot withdraw their labour are deprived of a crucial component of their bargaining power. For this reason the I.L.O. insists that workers who are subject to such a limitation must receive adequate guarantees to safeguard their position.[14] The difficulty comes in devising a system of dispute resolution which can satisfactorily protect the interests of workers, employers and the Government.

One method which is commonly adopted to settle essential service disputes is compulsory arbitration; that is, the submission of a dispute for settlement by a third party or parties without the necessity for consent by the parties concerned.[15] A variant of this process, which is used in some North American jurisdictions, is 'last-offer' or pendulum arbitration, by which arbitrators choose between the final offers of each side, either as a total package or on an issue-by-issue basis. Compulsory arbitration, with binding awards, has not been adopted for interest disputes in Britain outside times of war, although in many industries the parties agree voluntarily to refer disputes to arbitration as the final stage of their disputes procedure. (These agreements traditionally have not been legally enforceable). Compulsory arbitration would therefore represent a major departure from previous practice. To comply with I.L.O. standards, the Government would have to undertake to implement arbitral awards for workers deprived of the freedom to strike without exception; the Freedom of Association Committee of the Governing Body requires that

> restrictions on the right to strike should be accompanied by adequate, impartial and speedy conciliation and arbitration proceedings in which the parties concerned can take part at every stage and in which the awards, once made, are fully and promptly implemented. The reservation of budgetary powers to the legislative authority should not have the effect of preventing compliance with the terms of awards handed down by the compulsory arbitration tribunal.[16]

The British Government, however, has always reserved the right to veto arbitral awards and the recommendations of Review Bodies in the sectors for which it is responsible if it deems this necessary in the national interest, and Parliament, too, can exercise a right of veto.[17] Access to arbitration in the first place may also be denied on 'policy' grounds, as in 1981 when the Government refused to allow a civil service claim to go to arbitration, contrary to the Civil Service Arbitration Agreement of 1925. Recent Government proposals for a new system of pay determination in the civil service countenance arbitration only with the consent of both parties and within funding limits, and they reserve the right to suspend the operation of the agreement 'to safeguard the public purse or public policy'.[18] This restrictive approach reflects a general hostility to arbitration on the part of the present administration, which regards it as an inflationary method of dispute settlement which takes too little account of affordability.

The merits of arbitration as a method of dispute resolution, and its impact on collective bargaining, are beyond the scope of this book. It seems clear, however, that the Thatcher Government is unlikely to encourage it. The S.D.P. at one time advocated compulsory arbitration when industrial action threatens life and limb,[19] but its leader, Dr David Owen, has since put forward alternative suggestions, outlined below, based on no-strike undertakings. The Institute of Directors supports a restricted form of compulsory arbitration, the details of which are discussed in the section which follows.

An alternative method of protecting workers for whom industrial action is forbidden is to construct a system of indexation which links their pay to that of other groups which are not subject to such a limitation. This is currently done in the case of the police, whose pay follows changes in average earnings, and firemen. The argument which is commonly raised against formulae of this kind is that they are inflationary. Whether or not this is a price worth paying to avoid strikes in the public sector is a matter of political judgement; in 1982, the Conservative Government made clear its opposition to extending these arrangements to any other groups.[20]

Conclusion

The imposition of further restrictions on industrial action in essential services enforced through the mechanism of the criminal law is a strategy which is beset with problems. The A.C.A.S. Annual Report for 1983 concluded:

> Apart from the difficulties of identifying the essential services that would be covered by any legislation in this area, the major problem would be to find an acceptable means of determining the pay and conditions of employment of the workers concerned should direct collective bargaining fail to secure an agreement.[21]

Legislation of this nature would be unequivocally opposed by trade unions affiliated to the T.U.C., and it is hard to conceive of any arrangements for pay determination or dispute resolution which would persuade them to surrender entirely their members' freedom to withdraw their labour. A primary reason for this is distrust of the

Government. As Mr Jim Mortimer, a former chairman of A.C.A.S., has explained:

> The problem is that governments too frequently dishonour their obligations under arbitration. They are too ready to find some exceptional circumstances which, they say, compel them to refuse arbitration. An obligatory arbitration clause in an area of public employment has too often meant that the union was tied when it was strong, but the government was able to repudiate its obligations when it felt that the circumstances were exceptional. . . . The evidence is on the side of those who say that public authorities are disposed to break their word when the going gets rough.[22]

The same reasoning could be applied to other methods of dispute resolution. Whilst the Centre for Policy Studies argues that trade union opposition is irrelevant, experience world-wide confirms that 'legal prohibitions and restrictions have been powerless to prevent strikes' and that penal sanctions which remain on statute books are of 'theoretical, educational or residual' value.[23] At the time of writing there is no indication that the present Government intends to pursue this strategy.

(2) The restriction of industrial action in essential services by means of the civil law

As Chapter 2 describes, the freedom to strike in Great Britain rests on a system of immunities from specified heads of tortious liability. Immunity depends on industrial action being taken 'in contemplation or furtherance of a trade dispute'.[24] Industrial action which has no immunity will almost always attract liability in tort, and this enables the courts to halt a campaign by issuing an injunction, and to order dispute organizers to pay damages to employers who have suffered loss. Breach of an injunction is contempt of court for which the penalties are fines or imprisonment. Industrial action in essential services could be restricted by means of the civil law either by removing the immunities which currently protect it or by creating statutory wrongs which the immunities do not protect. The criteria which the judges adopt in deciding whether or not to grant an interlocutory injunction would favour the plaintiff where liability was in doubt.[25]

The 1983 Conservative election manifesto, which came in the wake of the water strike earlier that year, favoured the former approach. It stressed the need for essential services to be governed by 'adequate procedure agreements' and promised to conduct consultations on the idea of removing immunity from industrial action which was taken in breach of procedure. The influential Institute of Directors is a strong supporter of this approach.[26] As yet the Government has not said more about which services it envisages would be designated as 'essential' nor has it spelt out the nature of the procedure agreements it would like to see. The Institute of Directors advocates arbitration as the final stage of procedure in essential services on either a 'last-offer' basis or on the basis that the arbitrators would apply specified criteria, such as improved performance targets, in reaching their decisions. It considers that '[t]argets based on employment cost as a percentage of added value would help to ensure that increases were both affordable and non-inflationary'.[27]

In 1979, the Court of Appeal opened up the possibility of liability for organizing industrial action which hinders employers in the performance of their statutory duties,[28] a wrong which is unprotected by the immunities. If this head of liability were developed, it could put in jeopardy the lawfulness of industrial action by many public sector groups. As Chapter 2 explains, the ability of plaintiffs to sue for wrongs based on breach of a statutory duty or hinderance of its performance is now uncertain. There is, however, nothing to prevent legislation specifically granting the right to proceed against dispute organizers whose activities result in disruption to services supplied pursuant to a statutory duty. This has already been done in the telecommunications industry, where the Telecommunications Act 1984 allows any person affected by a telecommunications operator's non-compliance with an enforcement order which is caused by industrial action to sue the organizer for any act which, by inducing a breach of the operator's duty to obey the order or interfering with its performance, 'causes that person to sustain loss or damage and which is done wholly or partly for the purpose of achieving that result'.[29] Although Government spokesmen have claimed that this provision was designed to grant a remedy for selective industrial action against particular customers, and would not put in jeopardy strikes to improve pay and conditions which led incidentally to an enforcement order being breached, it is far from clear that the right to sue will be limited in practice in that way.[30] The Telecommunications Act could serve as a model for future legislation in other essential services, such as the gas, water and electricity industries. During the course of the water strike, ministers at one time seemed to favour this approach,[31] but subsequently the emphasis shifted to removing immunity for industrial action in breach of procedure. The possibility that the Government may wish to re-examine the idea of creating further statutory wrongs cannot, however, be excluded.

Restricting industrial action in essential services by means of the civil rather than the criminal law has two major advantages for the Government. First, it dispenses with the political and administrative problems raised by mass prosecution of strikers. If issuing an injunction fails to halt a dispute, the penalties are primarily financial; although individual dispute organizers could be imprisoned for contempt of court, where a dispute is official the penalty is likely to be a fine, with the possibility of sequestrating the union's assets if it refuses to pay. Such penalties are likely to arouse rather less public sympathy and controversy than the imprisonment of strike leaders. The second major advantage of the civil law approach is that the Government is officially distanced from the decision to proscribe a particular dispute and from the political odium which this may attract (although clearly the Government may make its views known to employers in the public sector on an unofficial basis). It means, however, that the decision as to whether a campaign is halted is left in the hands of private individuals. In the 1981 Green Paper on Trade Union Immunities, the Department of Employment considered that this aspect made the removal of immunity

> an inadequate remedy in the case of a national emergency. It would enable an employer to sue the organizers of the industrial action for an injunction or damages but the community as a whole would be protected only if an employer decided to bring such a private action. It would not provide the Government itself with any direct means of intervening to stop the strike or to protect the community.[32]

Since that document was produced there has been evidence of a greater willingness on the part of employers to seek redress against dispute organizers. The 1980 and 1982 Employment Acts narrowed the scope for lawful secondary action and picketing, and the Trade Union Act 1984 removed immunity from official industrial action taken without the support of the majority of those expected to take part in it being expressed in a secret ballot. The Employment Act 1982 also removed the immunity previously enjoyed by trade unions from liability in tort.[33] All these measures envisaged 'a more interventionist role for the civil law in industrial disputes' and '[e]mployers [now] appear to be less influenced by the possible harm that such litigation may do to their long-term industrial relations'.[34] Significantly, however, none of the public sector employers which suffered damage from the 1984–5 miners' strike, such as British Rail, the Central Electricity Generating Board and the British Steel Corporation, sought to invoke the law, and the employer in dispute, the National Coal Board, did not pursue contempt proceedings for breaches of injunctions obtained against pickets at an early stage of the dispute.

The non-use of the law by public sector employers during the 1984–5 miners' strike may well have been influenced by fears that working miners and other public sector workers would then have been drawn into the stoppage. It is possible that the prospect of provoking sympathetic action would have a similarly inhibiting effect in the context of essential service disputes. Nonetheless, if legislation is to be enacted in this area by the present Government, it will probably be based upon granting civil remedies against essential service stoppages, in line with the Government's general strategy. This approach means that there is no political accountability for the decision to institute proceedings in respect of a particular dispute. This is a major objection to it. The arguments for restricting industrial action in essential services rest upon protection of the 'community' rather than upon protection of the interests of employers. In the light of this, it is inappropriate to leave the decision as to whether or not a campaign should be enjoined to individuals who cannot be called to account and who have no direct responsibility for the welfare of the public.

(3) The negotiation of 'no strike' agreements

The 1981 Green Paper on Trade Union Immunities concluded that the problems involved in restricting industrial action in essential services by law made it

> possible to argue that the most effective way of making progress on this question . . . [was] through voluntary 'no strike' agreements between management and unions in those sectors of industry where strikes might threaten the national interest.[35]

There are now an increasing number of agreements in private sector high-technology industries, negotiated mainly by the E.E.T.P.U., which seek to minimize the possibility of industrial action by laying down disputes procedures of which the last stage is binding pendulum arbitration. These provisions are generally accompanied by statements to the effect that the parties recognize the need to ensure continuous production.[36] This practice has been criticized by many other unions with members in the public sector who fear it could encourage the Government to impose such terms on the public sector, and it was condemned in a motion proposed by the F.B.U. at the T.U.C.'s 1985 Congress.[37] There was also concern that the 'no disruption' agreement which the C.C.S.U. put forward for workers at G.C.H.Q., discussed in Chapter 2, could provide an unfortunate precedent, and the conferences of two of the Civil Service unions involved, the S.C.P.S. and the C.P.S.A., repudiated the offer.

A few smaller unions in the public sector have declared themselves in favour of 'no strike' agreements.[38] These include the Professional Association of Teachers, which is recognized at national level and has over 30,000 members, and the Ministry of Defence Staff Association, which has achieved limited departmental recognition. Their policies are based on the premise that the Government will agree to arrangements which would adequately protect their members' earnings and other conditions of employment. As argued earlier in this chapter, such guarantees are unlikely to be forthcoming, from the present Government at least, although the S.D.P. takes a different view of this issue. Its leader, Dr David Owen, has recently proposed that public sector groups which agree to no-strike undertakings should automatically be granted pay awards which equal the increase in private sector earnings over the previous year. Groups which rejected this arrangement would continue to bargain in the normal way. (The employer's offer should then be based upon the increase in private sector earnings adjusted for productivity).[39] As matters stand, the majority of large trade unions in the public sector are unlikely to be willing to surrender their members' freedom to withdraw their labour whatever the terms of the *quid pro quo* on offer.

In recent years a number of official inquiries have examined the possibility of restricting industrial action by particular groups of workers in return for specific pay determination procedures. They all rejected such schemes as unworkable. In the words of the 1982 Megaw Inquiry into Civil Service Pay:

> Neither side would be likely to be able to pledge itself to honour the bargain, nor would it be easy to reach a deal at a price acceptable to all parties, including the taxpayer.[40]

The Royal Commission on the National Health Service pointed out that

> Health workers, like other workers, will not find it necessary to take industrial action if they are satisfied with the arrangements for settling disputes over pay and conditions of service and if disputes which have arisen are seen to be fairly dealt with. If they are not so satisfied, it seems unlikely that the outlawing of industrial action could be made to stick. In the future, workers would not necessarily consider themselves bound by an

> agreement reached by their predecessors, possibly in different circumstances.[41]

The May Committee of Inquiry into the Prison Service considered that 'the inability to take action could, without an improvement in the general industrial relations climate, lead eventually to resentment and frustration'.[42]

Another factor which should be borne in mind is that the negotiation of 'no strike' agreements, without more, would not effect a change in the existing legal position of workers within their scope. Collective agreements are not, generally speaking, legally enforceable as between employers and trade unions,[43] and the insertion of a 'no strike' obligation into the contracts of employment of individual workers would make no practical difference to their situation;[44] most forms of industrial action, including strikes which are not preceded by notice of termination, already amount to a fundamental breach of contract which entitles the employer to dismiss the workers involved without notice.[45] The Government could, however, decide to introduce legislation which denied the application of the statutory immunities for industrial action taken in breach of a 'no strike' agreement. The arguments which apply to this line of approach have been discussed in the previous section.

Despite the terms of the 1983 election manifesto, at the time of writing the Government appears to have no immediate intention of further restricting industrial action in essential services by law. Rather, the present Employment Minister, Mr Kenneth Clarke, has said that the Government wishes to encourage 'sensible procedure agreements' which 'minimize' public sector stoppages.[46] As has already been stated, however, there is no indication that the Government is prepared to offer anything in return to secure these agreements nor, indeed, that any guarantees that might be offered would persuade the larger unions to seriously limit their members' freedom to withdraw their labour. The Government has attempted to introduce a 'no strike' arrangement for nurses and professions allied to medicine through the back door by reserving the right to exclude from the recommendations of their Review Body, established in the wake of the 1982 dispute, any groups which have resort to industrial action. This unilaterally imposed restriction would probably meet with greater resistance from workers in other areas of the public sector, and in any case, the Government shows no inclination to extend the review body system further. For the time being, it seems that the negotiation of 'no strike' agreements in the public sector is likely to remain in the realms of theoretical discussion.

(4) The 'self-restraint/joint regulation' approach

Self-restraint and joint regulation are the intertwined methods of approaching industrial action in essential services which are most favoured by the large trade unions with members in these areas. As Chapters 5 and 6 describe, trade unions traditionally have had regard to the exigencies of health and safety when planning their campaigns, and during the public sector stoppages of the 1970s it became common practice to issue codes of conduct which laid down broad guidelines as to the services which members should seek to protect. In 1979 the T.U.C. formalized the self-restraint approach when it issued its 'Guide to Affiliated Unions on the Conduct of Industrial Disputes'.[47] The Guide advises unions to 'make arrangements in advance and with due notice, in consultation and preferably by agreement with the employer, for the maintenance by their members of supplies and services essential to the health or safety of the community or otherwise required to avoid causing exceptional hardship or serious pollution'. The exercise of restraint is generally made conditional, expressly or impliedly, upon reciprocal self-restraint by management, and possibly also by the Government. As the two previous chapters have indicated, the precise nature of this self-restraint may vary between sectors, but it commonly involves employers agreeing to pay workers who maintain emergency cover their normal wages, even though they are refusing to perform their full range of contractual duties, or acknowledging that certain services cannot be provided during the dispute or that they should be furnished in accordance with union priorities. It may require that the Government does not send in troops or encourage the use of volunteers. If managers or the Government transgress these limits and seek to undermine the impact of limited industrial action, this may result in the work-force in dispute withdrawing their labour completely.

As Chapter 6 explains, the attitude of governments towards joint regulation has differed considerably. The Labour Government supported it strongly in 1979, and the Heath Government also sought union assistance in maintaining particular services during certain disputes. For the Baldwin Government in 1926, however, the idea of relying upon co-operation with the trade unions was anathema, and the present Conservative administration has not subscribed to this approach on an official level; rather, it has tended to encourage assertion of the managerial prerogative.[48]

The lack of official endorsement has not meant that the 'joint regulation' approach has been abandoned by employers, however, as shown by the conduct of the N.H.S. and water disputes in 1982 and 1983, respectively. What these disputes illustrated very clearly was the *ad hoc*, informal nature of the process. Representatives of unions and management negotiated the provision of emergency cover at local level, and although the unions provided guidance from the centre on the application of their codes to specific situations, there was no standing agreed framework of principles within which these negotiations could be conducted. The scope and terms of joint regulation in the N.H.S. was subject to wide variation between districts, as indicated by the survey of health service administrators which appears in Chapter 6, and during the water strike arrangements to maintain emergency cover broke down in several areas due to allegations of 'strikebreaking' and disputes over the definition of an 'emergency'. This kind of informality allows both sides to attempt to maximize their advantage according to the circumstances of the local situation. It also has major disadvantages for both sides. For the unions, departures from their self-imposed codes of conduct inevitably expose them to public criticism, regardless of the actions which have provoked them. From the other side, employers suddenly may find themselves without the labour they require to provide a basic level of service. Development of the 'joint regulation' approach requires clearer articulation of the scope of permissible action which may legitimately be taken both by unions and by management during the course of disputes.

The 'code of conduct' approach to disputes in essential services in Britain is part of a world-wide trend of 'growing efforts . . . by public service unions to exert a measure of self-discipline as regards the occurence and scope of strikes'.[49] In a few cases, this self-discipline has been incorporated into a legal framework. In the Federal Republic of Germany, where union self-discipline has a long history,[50] directives issued by the German Confederation of Trade Unions provide that in the event of a labour dispute the workers should continue to perform the tasks necessary for safeguarding industrial installations and for supplying the population with essential goods and services.[51] Trade union rule-books impose an obligation upon members to undertake emergency work of this nature. In Italy, a code of conduct devised by the three main union confederations has been incorporated into legally binding collective agreements.

In Canada, the notion of the 'controlled strike' is a product of legislation. This concept first appeared in the Public Service Staff Relations Act 1967, and it requires employees who have been designated by the tripartite Public Service Staff Relations Board to remain at work to provide essential services.[52] It is an offence for employees who have been designated not to continue working. Under the Act, 'the proportion of designated employees within a given bargaining unit has varied from under 1 per cent of employees in the case of postal workers to over 85 per cent in the case of fire fighters'.[53] This approach to strikes in public services has since been adopted (with certain variations) in a number of provinces in Canada, and Paul Weiler, a former chairman of the British Columbia Labour Relations Board, has given a vivid account of the difficulties which may surround the designation process in a description of a strike at the Vancouver General Hospital in 1976.[54] The hospital, the largest in the province, had 1,500 acute, and 300 extended-care, beds. The 2,000 non-professional staff at the hospital gave seventy-two hours' notice of a strike, whereupon the Board was called in to designate services which must continue to be offered to prevent 'immediate danger to life, health or public safety'. The management maintained that all the services came into this category and all 2,000 employees should be directed to work; the union maintained that none of its members should be required to 'scab on their own union's strike'.[55] Eventually, the Board decided that all the extended-care, but only 700 acute, beds should be kept open. It took the view, however that

> the basic labour in running the hospital – cleaning, cooking, laundry, practical nursing and administration – would have to be performed by . . . other staff members, not the workers who were exercising their legal right to strike. Indeed, if necessary, the hospital would have to draw on volunteers from its auxiliary organizations, or even upon the patient's (*sic*) relatives. Quite a few people might have to do tiring, dirty, and often distasteful work normally performed by the nonprofessional staff. After all, as the Union pointed out, a strike was not intended to be a garden party. At the same time there were a number of . . . [Union] members who had the skills or experience to perform specialized tasks or operate equipment which were indispensible for patient safety, and who, as a practical matter, were irreplaceable during the strike: renal technicians, operators of respiratory machines or hyperbaric chambers, medical records staff . . . and so on.[56]

Just under 100 union members were directed to stay at work. The merits of this scheme were hotly debated and it attracted a great deal of public hostility, but for the three weeks the strike lasted the hospital was able to provide safe patient care, albeit with a 'herculean' effort from other staff.[57] The strike convinced Weiler that it was 'feasible to maintain a carefully modulated strike of public safety employees' which also performed 'its role in the collective bargaining process'.[58] The resources of the administrative and medical staff were strained to the limit, most of the union members were losing pay, and after three weeks:

> The union and its members, the hospital administration and its government paymaster, all quickly appreciated that the position into which they had earlier entrenched themselves might not be so unshakeable after all.[59]

The transplantation of procedures from other legal systems into domestic industrial relations is fraught with danger, as the Industrial Relations Act 1971 amply demonstrated. Nevertheless, the Canadian experience is worthy of study because it indicates how some of the objections to the 'joint regulation' approach as it has operated in Britain could be met. In Paul Weiler's account, a predetermined body was ready to spring into action at short notice to determine which services and employees were truly essential. The union was then permitted to cause the maximum amount of inconvenience which was consistent with requirements of safety and could not be accused of recklessly putting patients at risk; indeed, in Weiler's words, the 'Labour Board proved to be the lightning rod which attracted the public flak'.[60] The management resources were stretched to the limit, and this meant that the dispute could not be 'ridden out' until the workers' will to fight on was exhausted, as seems to have happened in the N.H.S. dispute in 1982.

The compulsory regulation of disputes by an outside body is unlikely to find favour with either employers or trade unions in Britain. This does not mean, however, that the ground-rules for conducting disputes could not be laid down in voluntary agreements in individual sectors. At national level, agreements could specify the services which should always be maintained and the financial terms on which this should be done. These agreements should also impose specific limitations on the management response, breach of which would give the work-force just cause to escalate its action. Negotiators could then apply these principles at local level to determine exactly which employees should continue working. In the event of disagreement on this point, an independent ruling could be sought. This ruling and the reasons for it, would be made public.

A formalized approach of this nature is bound to attract opposition. Some trade unionists will regard it as an unjustifiable curb on the freedom to withdraw labour which fatally weakens trade union power. Equally, employers may see it as distorting the management role by implicating managers in curtailing services rather than encouraging them to circumvent disruption and defeat the stoppage by any means at their disposal. One must view this suggestion, however, in the light of the alternatives. It is not in the interests of trade unions for members to withdraw their services completely; they attract only condemnation and their own members suffer along with the rest. Equally, it is not in the interests of employers to risk provoking a complete withdrawal, particularly when workers are impossible or difficult to replace. The 'Queensberry Rules' approach to disputes has often been applied in practice in the sectors discussed in this book. What is now required is a clarification of these rules and an established procedure for applying them to specific situations.

CONCLUSION

This chapter has assessed the viability of four alternative strategies which have been advocated in recent years by particular groups to limit the extent of disruption to essential services. None of them is foolproof, but some are more problematic than others.

Restricting industrial action by means of the criminal law is extremely unlikely to achieve its object. It is difficult to devise a sanction which is a practicable and effective deterrant, and experience worldwide demonstrates that such prohibitory laws are rarely enforced. There are also problems of defining the groups to be restricted and of establishing methods of dispute resolution which can pay adequate regard to the interests of workers, employers and the Government. There is no indication that the present Government has any intention of pursuing this course. Restricting industrial action by means of the civil law also presents problems of definition and dispute resolution, and contains the fundamental defect that the decision to curtail a campaign is left in the hands of private individuals who are not politically accountable.

The Conservative manifesto for the last General Election promised consultations on removing immunity for industrial action in designated services which is taken in breach of procedure, but the Government has taken no steps to put this commitment into practice. A more likely development may be the extension of rights of action for consumers against those who organize the disruption of services supplied pursuant to a statutory duty. At the time of writing, however, the Government is playing down the prospect of legislation in favour of voluntary agreements to minimize the possibility of stoppages. The majority of trade unions are unlikely to accept this suggestion, particularly as the Government appears to be offering no guarantees in return. Official bodies which have investigated the viability of such schemes for particular groups have rejected them as unworkable.

In the light of these considerations, the last of the strategies, that of self-restraint and joint regulation, seems the most fruitful avenue to pursue. In recent years, trade unions and managers in a number of sectors have operated an informal, *ad hoc* system of joint regulation, according to which trade unions have maintained cover for emergencies, and management has refrained from taking measures which would undermine the action in an unacceptable manner. On some occasions, however, these 'understandings' have not been observed. On others, adherance to a code has enabled the authorities to 'ride out' a dispute, as happened in the case of the N.H.S campaign in 1982. What is required is a more formalized approach which enables industrial action to play its role in the collective bargaining process in essential services without putting the public unduly at risk. The ground-rules for disputes should be clearly articulated so the scope of permissible action for both sides is defined.

To those who subscribe to an adversarial approach to industrial disputes, the notion of joint regulation may seem laughable. To reject it out of hand, however, means that services which require the continuous availability of skilled personnel may be lost altogether in the absence of a sufficient number of adequately trained people to take them over. Contingency planning and emergency powers will always be required as a backstop. As a front-line approach, however, joint regulation can offer the cheapest and most efficacious method of securing the continued provision of basic services.

At the time of writing, the trade union movement appears weaker than it has done for many years past. The defeat of the miners in 1984 is bound to make other groups think carefully before they embark upon prolonged campaigns. Other developments have also undermined the strength of public sector unions. The Government has encouraged the contracting-out of certain health and local authority services to private enterprise, partly to reduce their vulnerability to disruption. Authorities may no longer restrict their contracting-out arrangements to suppliers who recognize trade unions.[61] The relaxation of monopolies in posts, telecommunications and electricity make possible the development of alternative sources of supply. The decentralization of collective bargaining has got underway in the water industry, where regional water authorities are no longer bound to observe nationally agreed conditions. Contingency planning has become highly sophisticated, and an elaborate administrative machine is ready to spring into action whenever essential services are under threat. None of these measures, however, can entirely ensure that essential services will never be subject to disruption. The breakdown of consensus among workers in these sectors that supplies and services should always be maintained means that the time has now come to make a choice between the alternative strategies which have been examined in this book. In a democratic society joint regulation is likely to be the most effective method of approaching the problems raised by industrial action in essential services.

NOTES

1. The discussion which follows does not attempt to consider every variety of restriction which may be imposed upon strikes in essential services; rather, it considers the major strategies which have been suggested by particular groups in Britain in recent years. Restrictions in the form of minimum-notice periods or cooling-off periods have not received strong support of late; many of the points made in section (1) which follows would apply to such provisions.

2. *The Right to Strike in a Free Society*, C.P.S., London, 1983.

3. European Social Charter, Articles 6(4), 31; decisions of the Freedom of Association Committee of the Governing Body of the I.L.O., *Freedom of Association*, 3rd edn., International Labour Office, Geneva, 1985.

4. A. Pankert, 'Settlement of Labour Disputes in Essential Services', *International Labour Review* 119 (1980), 723 at 731.

5. Efren Córdova, 'Strikes in the Public Service: Some Determinants and Trends', *International Labour Review* 124 (1985), 163 at 176.

6. As above, note 3, para. 387.

7. Cmnd. 8128 (1981), para. 334.

8. As above, note 3, para. 415.

9. This principle is now enshrined in s.16 of the Trade Union and Labour Relations Act 1974, which states that no court shall compel an employee to do any work or attend at any place for the doing of any work. The I.L.O. has ruled that workers should be requisitioned only to maintain 'essential services in circumstances of the utmost gravity during an acute national emergency': as above, note 3, para. 424.

10. Córdova, 'Strikes in the Public Service', as above, note 5, p. 173. Cf. s.210 of New York's Civil Service Law of 1967 (the 'Taylor law'), which provides as an automatic sanction that public employees will lose two days' pay for each day that they are on strike. For a critique of the severity of this penalty, see Andrew A. Peterson, 'Deterring Strikes by Public Employees: New York's Two-for-One Salary Penalty and the 1979 Prison Guard Strike', *Industrial and Labor Relations Review* 34. 4 (July 1981), p. 545.

11. Written Evidence of Sir Harold Emmerson, former Permanent Secretary of the Ministry of Labour, to the Royal Commission on Trade Unions and Employers' Associations 1965–1968, Cmnd. 3623 (1968), App. 6, para. 3. This account is taken from Sir Harold Emmerson's evidence.

12. *Ibid.*, para. 6.

13. Royal Commission on Trade Unions and Employers' Associations, *Ibid.*, para. 487.

14. As above, note 3, paras. 393–9.

15. See *Conciliation and Arbitration Procedures in Labour Disputes*, International Labour Office, Geneva, 1980, pp. 159–66.

16. As above, note 3, paras. 397–8.

17. Until recently there was a convention that the Government would not itself propose to Parliament that an arbitral award for civil servants should be overturned. In 1981, however, the Government refused civil servants access to arbitration on policy grounds. See Bob Hepple, 'Labour Law and Public Employees' in *Labour Law and the Community*, ed. Lord Wedderburn of Charlton and W.T. Murphy, Institute of Advanced Legal Studies, University of London, 1982, p. 76.

18. *The Financial Times*, October 17, 1985.

19. Social Democratic Party, *Reforming the Trade Unions*, S.D.P., 1982.

20. See, for example, Mr Kenneth Clarke, H.C. Deb., Vol. 24, col. 290 (May 25, 1982), written answer.

21. Para. 1.19.

22. J. Mortimer, 'Arbitration, the Public Interest and Labour Relations' in *Labour Law and the Community* ed. Lord Wedderburn of Charlton and W.T. Murphy, as above, note 17, p. 64.

23. Córdova, 'Strikes in the Public Service', as above, note 5, pp. 166, 174.

24. Trade Union and Labour Relations Act 1974 (as amended), ss. 13,29,30.

25. See Chapter 2.

26. *Democracy and Competitiveness: Further Steps Towards Trade Union Reform*, I.O.D., 1983.

27. *Ibid.*, para. 52.

28. *Meade* v. *Haringey London Borough Council* [1979] I.C.R. 494; *Associated Newspaper Groups Ltd* v. *Wade* [1979] I.C.R. 664. See Chapter 2.

29. S.18(6)(b).
30. See Chapter 2 for a more detailed discussion of this provision.
31. *The Guardian*, February 25, 1983.
32. Cmnd. 8128 (1981), para. 326.
33. Employment Act 1982, s.15.
34. Roger Benedictus, 'The Use of the Law of Tort in the Miners' Dispute', *Industrial Law Journal* 14 (1985), 176 at 176, 190.
35. Cmnd. 8128 (1981), para. 337.
36. See *Industrial Relations Review and Report* 324 (July 24, 1984), 7–11.
37. Agenda for the 1985 Congress, T.U.C., London, Motion 2.
38. In addition, the rules of the R.C.N., the largest organization representing nurses, forbid industrial action; see further, Chapter 6.
39. *The Guardian*, June 25, 1985.
40. Report of an Inquiry into the principles and the system by which the remuneration of the non-industrial Civil Service should be determined, Cmnd. 8590 (1982), para. 261.
41. Cmnd. 7615 (1979), para. 12.21.
42. Committee of Inquiry into the United Kingdom Prison Service, Cmnd. 7673 (1979), para. 10.49.
43. Trade Union and Labour Relations Act 1974, s.18(1) lays down a conclusive presumption to this effect for all agreements negotiated before December 1, 1971, and after September 16, 1974, unless the agreement is in writing and specifically states that the parties intend it to be a legally enforceable contract.
44. Any such obligation would have to have been entered into in compliance with conditions laid down in the Trade Union and Labour Relations Act 1974, s.18(4). For a discussion of the appropriateness of 'no strike' clauses for incorporation into individual contracts, see B.A. Hepple, *Employment Law*, 4th edn., Sweet and Maxwell, London, 1981, pp. 128–31.
45. *Simmons* v. *Hoover Ltd* [1977] I.C.R. 61. The exercise of this right may lead to claims for unfair dismissal from the workers dismissed if the employer discriminates between them: see the Employment Protection (Consolidation) Act 1978 (as amended), s.62.
46. *The Financial Times*, October 23, 1985.
47. Annex to the 'Social Concordat', *The Economy, the Government and Trade Union Responsibilities: Joint Statement by the T.U.C. and Government*, H.M.S.O., London, 1979.
48. See, for example, Circular H.C. 79(20), 'If Industrial Relations Break Down', issued by the D.H.S.S. in December 1979 and discussed in Chapter 6.
49. Córdova, 'Strikes in the Public Service', as above, note 5, p. 174.
50. See K.W. Wedderburn, 'Industrial Action, the State and the Public Interest' in *Industrial Conflict: A Comparative Legal Survey*, ed. B. Aaron and K.W. Wedderburn, Longman, London, 1972, pp. 348–50.
51. Quoted in A. Pankert, 'Settlement of Labour Disputes in Essential Services', as above, note 4, p. 725.
52. Alternatively, unions in sectors covered by the Act may elect, before negotiations begin, to go to arbitration in the event of negotiations breaking down.
53. Allan Ponak, 'Public-Sector Collective Bargaining' in *Union–Management Relations in Canada*, ed. John C. Anderson and Morely Gunderson, Addison-Wesley (Canada), Don Mills, Ontario, 1982, p. 369.
54. P. Weiler, *Reconcilable Differences*, Carswell, Toronto, 1980, Ch. 7.
55. *Ibid.*, p. 211.
56. *Ibid.*, p. 211.
57. *Ibid.*, p. 212.
58. *Ibid.*, p. 212, 236.
59. *Ibid.*, p. 236.
60. *Ibid.*, p. 212.
61. Employment Act 1982, ss.12, 13.

Bibliography

AARON, BENJAMIN, 'Strikes in Essential Services: Reflections on the Western Experience' in *Second Asian Regional Congress of Labor Law and Social Security, September 14–16, 1983*, Seoul, Korea, 1983, 17–28.

ABEL-SMITH, BRIAN, *A History of the Nursing Profession,* Heinemann, London, 1960.

ADVISORY, CONCILIATION and ARBITRATION SERVICE, *Report of a Committee of Inquiry into industrial relations in the London Fire Service*, A.C.A.S., London, 1977.

ALLEN, CARLTON KEMP, *Law and Orders*, 3rd ed., Stevens, London, 1965.

ALLEN, V.L., 'The National Union of Police and Prison Officers', *The Economic History Review* XI:1 (1958), 133–43.

BAIN, GEORGE SAYERS and ROBERT PRICE, 'Union Growth: Dimensions, Determinants, and Destiny' in *Industrial Relations in Britain* ed. George Sayers Bain, Blackwell, Oxford, 1983, 3–33.

BALFOUR, CAMPBELL, *Unions and the Law*, Saxon House, Farnborough and Lexington, 1973.

BARNES, DENIS and EILEEN REID, *Governments and Trade Unions: The British Experience 1964–79*, Heinemann, London, 1980.

BEAUMONT, P.A., and D.A. HEALD, 'Public Employment' in *Government Policy Initiatives 1979–80: Some Case Studies in Public Administration* ed. P.M. Jackson, 1981, 16–41.

BENEDICTUS, ROGER, 'The Use of the Law of Tort in the Miners' Dispute', *Industrial Law Journal* 14 (1985), 176–90.

BERRIDGE, JOHN, *A Suitable Case for Treatment*, Open University Press, Milton Keynes, 1976.

BONNER, DAVID, *Emergency Powers in Peacetime*, Sweet and Maxwell, London, 1985.

BOSENQUET, NICK, 'The Search for a system' in *Industrial Relations in the NHS: the search for a system*, King Edward's Hospital Fund for London, London, 1979, 1–22.

BRITISH MEDICAL ASSOCIATION, *The Handbook of Medical Ethics*, B.M.A., London, 1984.

CALDERON, CICERO D., 'Labour Relations in Essential Services' in *Second Asian Regional Congress of Labor Law and Social Security, September 14–16, 1983*, Seoul, Korea, 1983, 29–48.

CARPENTER, MICK, *All for One*, C.O.H.S.E., Surrey, 1980.
——, 'The Labour Movement in the National Health Service' in *Industrial Relations and Health Services* ed. Amarjit Singh Sethi and Stuart J. Dimmock, Croom Helm, London, 1982, 74–89.
CARTY, HAZEL, 'Telecommunications Act 1984' *Industrial Law Journal* 13 (1984), 165–7.
CENTRE for POLICY STUDIES, *Liberties and Liabilities: The Case for Trade Union Reform*, C.P.S., London, 1980.
——, *The Right to Strike in a Free Society*, C.P.S., London, 1983.
CITRINE, WALTER, *Men and Work – the Autobiography of Lord Citrine*, Hutchinson, London, 1964.
Clerk and Linsell on Torts, Sweet and Maxwell, London, 1982.
CLUTTERBUCK, RICHARD, *Britain in Agony*, Penguin, Harmondsworth, 1980.
COLE, G.D.H., *Labour in the Coal-Mining Industry (1914–1921)*, Clarendon Press, Oxford, 1923.
Committee of Inquiry into the United Kingdom Prison Service, Cmnd. 7673 (1979), H.M.S.O., London
Committee of Inquiry on the Police: Reports on Negotiating Machinery and Pay, Cmnd. 7283 (1978), H.M.S.O., London.
Committee on Ministers' Powers, Cmnd. 4060 (1932), H.M.S.O., London.
CÓRDOVA, EFREN, 'Strikes in the public service: some determinants and trends', *International Labour Review* 124: March-April (1985), 163–79.
CROOK, WILFRED HARRIS, *The General Strike*, University of North Carolina Press, Chapel Hill, 1931.
CROSSMAN, RICHARD, *The Diaries of a Cabinet Minister Volume One Minister of Housing 1964–66*, Hamish Hamilton and Jonathan Cape, London, 1975.

DAVIES, PAUL and MARK FREEDLAND, *Kahn-Freund's Labour and the Law*, 3rd edn., Stevens, London, 1983.
——, *Labour Law: Text and Materials*, 2nd. edn., Weidenfeld and Nicolson, London, 1984.
de SMITH, S.A., *Constitutional and Administrative Law*, 5th edn., ed. Harry Street and Rodney Brazier, Penguin, Harmondsworth, 1985.
DEPARTMENT of HEALTH and SOCIAL SECURITY, *Annual Report 1975*, Cmnd. 6565 (1976), H.M.S.O., London.
DOLTON, W. DUNCAN, 'Managing the Industrial Action', *Health Services Manpower Review* 5:3 (1980), 25.
DYSON, ROGER, *The Ancillary Staff Industrial Action Spring 1973*, A Survey and Report Prepared for the Leeds Regional Hospital Board, 1973.
——, 'Industrial Action 1979: What can we learn?', *British Medical Journal* 26 May 1979, 1435–7.
DYSON, ROGER and KATHERINE SPARY, 'Professional Associations', in *Industrial Relations in the NHS: the search for a system* ed. Nick Bosenquet, King Edward's Hospital Fund for London, London, 1979, 145–75.
DWORKIN, G., 'Strikes and the National Health Service: some legal and ethical issues', *Journal of Medical Ethics* (1977), 76–82.
The Economy, the Government and Trade Union Responsibilities: Joint Statement by the T.U.C. and

Government, H.M.S.O., London, 1979.

ENGLAND, GLYN, *Facing the Challenge*, Central Electricity Generating Board, London, 1982.

EVANS, J.M., *de Smith's Judicial Review of Administrative Action*, 4th edn., Stevens, London, 1980.

FARMAN, CHRISTOPHER, *The General Strike*, Rupert Hart-Davis, London, 1972.

First Report of the Court of Inquiry into certain matters concerning the shipping industry, Cmnd. 3025 (1966), H.M.S.O., London.

GEARY, ROGER, *Policing Industrial Disputes 1893 to 1985*, Cambridge University Press, Cambridge, 1985.

GLASGOW, GEORGE, *General Strikes and Road Transport*, Geoffrey Bles, London, 1927.

GOODHART, A.L., 'The Legality of the General Strike in England', *Yale Law Journal* XXXVI (1926–7), 464–85.

GREER, STEPHEN C., 'Military Intervention in Civil Disturbances: The Legal Basis Reconsidered', *Public Law* (1983), 573–99.

HENNESSY, PETER 'Whitehall Contingency Planning for Industrial Disputes' in *Military Intervention in Democratic Societies* ed. Peter J. Rowe and Christopher J. Whelan, Croom Helm, Beckenham, 1985.

HEPPLE, B.A., *Hepple and O'Higgins: Employment Law*, 4th edn., Sweet and Maxwell, London, 1981.

HEPPLE, BOB, 'Labour Law and Public Employees in Britain' in *Labour Law and the Community* ed. Lord Wedderburn of Charlton and W.T. Murphy, Institute of Advanced Legal Studies, London, 1982, 67–83.

HURD, ARCHIBALD, 'The Navy on "Active Service"', *Fortnightly Review* 120 N.S. (1926), 87–104.

INSTITUTE of DIRECTORS, *Democracy and Competitiveness: Further Steps Towards Trade Union Reform*, I.O.D., London, 1983.

——, *Settling Disputes Peacefully*, I.O.D., London, 1984.

Interim Report by a Court of Enquiry concerning the stoppage of the London Tramway and Omnibus Services, Cmd. 2087 (1924), H.M.S.O., London.

INTERNATIONAL LABOUR OFFICE, *Conciliation and Arbitration Procedures in Labour Disputes*, I.L.O., Geneva, 1980.

——, *Freedom of Association and Collective Bargaining*, I.L.O., Geneva, 1983.

——, *Freedom of Association*, 3rd edn., I.L.O., Geneva, 1985.

——, *Decisions of the Committee of Experts on the Application of Conventions and Recommendations*, I.L.O., Geneva, 1985.

JEFFERY, KEITH and PETER HENNESSY, *States of Emergency*, Routledge and Kegan Paul, London, 1983.

JONES, AUBREY, *The New Inflation*, Penguin, Harmondsworth, 1973.

JONES, THOMAS, *Whitehall Diary* Vols. 1 and 2, ed. Keith Middlemas, Oxford University Press, London, 1969.

Judicial Statistics for England and Wales 1926, Cmd. 3055 (1928), H.M.S.O., London.

KAHN, PEGGY, NORMAN LEWIS, ROWLAND LIVOCK and PAUL WILES, *Picketing: Industrial Disputes, Tactics, and the Law*, Routledge and Kegan Paul, London, 1983.

KAHN-FREUND, OTTO, *Labour and the Law*, Stevens, London, 1972.

KIDD, RONALD, *British Liberty in Danger*, Lawrence and Wishart, London, 1940.

KIDNER, RICHARD, *Trade Union Law*, 2nd edn. Stevens and Sons, London, 1983.

KLUGMANN, JAMES, *History of the Communist Party of Great Britain.* Vol. 1: *Formation and Early Years 1919–1924*, Lawrence and Wishart, London, 1968; Vol. 2: *The General Strike 1925–1926*, Lawrence and Wishart, London, 1969.

KNOWLES, K.G.J.C., *Strikes — A Study in Industrial Conflict*, Blackwell, Oxford, 1952.

LAW SOCIETY, THE, *A Guide to the Professional Conduct of Solicitors*, The Law Society, London, 1974.

LEWIS, ROY and BOB SIMPSON, *Striking a Balance? Employment Law after the 1980 Act*, Martin Robertson, Oxford, 1981.

LOCK, G.F., 'Labour Law, Parliamentary Staff and Parliamentary Privilege', *Industrial Law Journal* 12 (1983), 28–37.

LYMAN, RICHARD W., *The First Labour Government 1924*, Chapman and Hall, London, 1957.

MCCARTHY, LORD, *Making Whitley Work*, D.H.S.S., London, 1976.

MCCARTHY, WILLIAM, *Freedom at Work: Towards the Reform of Tory Employment Laws*, Fabian Society, London, 1986.

MANSON, TOM, 'Management, The Professions and the Unions: A Social analysis of change in the National Health Service' in *Health and the Division of Labour* ed. Margaret Stacey, Margaret Reid, Christian Heath and Robert Dingwall, Croom Helm, London, 1977, 196–214.

MARQUAND, DAVID, *Ramsey MacDonald*, Jonathan Cape, London, 1977.

MARSHALL, GEOFFREY, *Constitutional Conventions*, Clarendon Press, Oxford, 1984.

MASON, A., 'The Government and the General Strike', *International Review of Social History*, XIV:1 (1969), 1–16.

MORRIS, GILLIAN S., 'A Study of the Protection of Public and Essential Services in Labour Disputes 1920–1976', unpublished PhD. dissertation, University of Cambridge, 1978.

——, 'The Police and Industrial Emergencies', *Industrial Law Journal* 9 (1980), 1–12.

——, 'The Ban on Trade Unions at Government Communications Headquarters', *Public Law* (1985), 177–86.

——, and STEPHEN RYDZKOWSKI, 'Anatomy of a dispute', *Health and Social Service Journal*, April 12, 1984.

——, 'Approaches to Industrial Action in the National Health Service', *Industrial Law Journal* 13 (1984), 153–64.

MORTIMER, J., 'Arbitration, The Public Interest and Labour Relations' in *Labour Law and the Community* ed. Lord Wedderburn of Charlton and W.T. Murphy, Institute of Advanced Legal Studies, London, 1982.

MOWAT, CHARLES LOCH, *Britain between the Wars 1918–1940*, Methuen, London, 1966.

MUNRO, COLIN, 'The Separation of Powers: Not Such a Myth', *Public Law* (1981), 19–24.

NATIONAL ASSOCIATION FOR THE CARE AND RESETTLEMENT OF OFFENDERS, *Some effects of the Prison Officers' Dispute 6 October 1980 — 11 February 1981*, N.A.C.R.O., London, 1981.

PANKERT, A., 'Settlement of Labour Disputes in Essential Services', *International Labour Review* 119: November–December (1980), 723–37.

PEAK, STEVE, *Troops in Strikes*, The Cobden Trust, London, 1984.

PETERSEN, ANDREW A., 'Deterring Strikes by Public Employees: New York's Two-for-One Salary Penalty and the 1979 Prison Guard Strike', *Industrial and Labor Relations Review*, 34:4 (1981), 545–62.

PHILLIPS, G.A., *The General Strike: The Politics of Industrial Conflict*, Weidenfeld and Nicolson, London, 1976.

PLIATZKY, SIR LEO, 'Cash Limits and Pay Policy', *Political Quarterly* 53 (1982), 16–23.

PONAK, ALLAN, 'Public-Sector Collective Bargaining' in *Union-Management Relations in Canada* ed. John C. Anderson and Morley Gunderson, Addison-Wesley (Canada), Don Mills, Ontario, 1982, 343–78.

PRICE, ROBERT and GEORGE SAYERS BAIN, 'Union Growth Revisited: 1948–74 in Perspective', *British Journal of Industrial Relations* XIV (1976), 339–55.

REINER, ROBERT, *The Blue-Coated Worker*, Cambridge University Press, Cambridge, 1978.

RENSHAW, PATRICK, *The General Strike*, Eyre Methuen, London, 1975.

Report of the Committee on the Police Service, Part 1, Cmd. 253 (1919), H.M.S.O., London.

Report of the Committee of Inquiry into the Pay and Related Conditions of Service of Nurses and Midwives, H.M.S.O., London, 1974.

Report of the Cunningham Inquiry into the Work of the Fire Service, Cmnd. 4754 (1971), H.M.S.O., London.

Report of a Court of Inquiry into Unofficial Strikes in the London Docks. Cmd. 8236 (1951), H.M.S.O., London.

Report of a Court of Inquiry into a dispute between the parties represented on the National Joint Industrial Council for the Electricity Supply Industry, Cmnd. 4594 (1971), H.M.S.O., London.

Report of a Court of Inquiry into a dispute between the National Coal Board and the National Union of Mineworkers under the chairmanship of the Rt. Hon. Lord Wilberforce C.M.G., C.B.E., Cmnd. 4903 (1972), H.M.S.O., London.

Report of an Inquiry into the principles and the system by which the remuneration of the non-industrial Civil Service should be determined, Cmnd. 8590 (1982), H.M.S.O., London.

Report of Her Majesty's Chief Inspector of Fire Services for 1977, Cmnd. 7311 (1977), H.M.S.O., London.

Report of Her Majesty's Inspector of Fire Services for Scotland for 1951, Cmnd. 8524 (1952), H.M.S.O., London.

Report of the Royal Commission on the Coal Industry, Cmnd. 2600 (1926), H.M.S.O., London.

Review of the British Docks Strikes 1949, Cmd. 7851 (1949), H.M.S.O., London.

REYNOLDS, GERALD W. and ANTHONY JUDGE, *The Night the Police went on Strike*, Weidenfeld and Nicolson, London, 1968.

RODGERS, WILLIAM, 'Government Under Stress: Britain's Winter of Discontent 1979', *Political Quarterly* 55 (1984), 171–9.

ROSKILL, STEPHEN, *Hankey: Man of Secrets Vol. II 1919–31*, Collins, London, 1972.

ROYAL COLLEGE of NURSING, *What the R.C.N. stands for*, R.C.N., London, 1984.

Royal Commission on the National Health Service, Cmnd. 7615 (1979), H.M.S.O., London.

Royal Commission on Trade Unions and Employers' Associations 1965–1968: Report, Cmnd. 3623 (1968), H.M.S.O., London.

RUBIN, GERRY R., *War, Law and Labour, 1915–1921*, Oxford University Press, Oxford, forthcoming.

SMITH, J.C., and BRIAN HOGAN, *Criminal Law*, 5th edn., Butterworths, London, 1983.

SOCIAL DEMOCRATIC PARTY, *Reforming the Trade Unions*, S.D.P., London, 1982.

Staff Relations in the Civil Service, 4th edn., (5th imp.) H.M.S.O., London, 1978.

THOMSON, A.W.J., and P.B. BEAUMONT, *Public Sector Bargaining: a study of relative gain*, Saxon House, Farnborough, 1978.

Trade Union Immunities, Cmnd. 8128 (1981), H.M.S.O., London.

TRADES UNION CONGRESS, *Improving Industrial Relations in the National Health Service: A Report by the T.U.C. Health Services Committee*, T.U.C., London, 1981.

——, *Industrial Relations Legislation*, T.U.C., London, 1986.

TRELOAR, SUSAN, 'The Junior Hospital Doctors' Pay Dispute 1975–1976: An Analysis of Events, Issues and Conflicts', *Journal of Social Policy* 10 (1981), 1–30.

TRICE, J.E., 'Methods of and Attitudes to Picketing', *Criminal Law Review* (1975), 271–82.

UNDY, R., V. ELLIS, W.E.J. MCCARTHY, and A.M. HALMOS, *Change in Trade Unions: The Development of U.K. Unions since the 1960s*, Hutchinson, London, 1981.

UNITED KINGDOM CENTRAL COUNCIL, *Code of Professional Conduct for Nurses, Midwives and Health Visitors*, U.K.C.C., London, 1983.

VOLUNTEER CENTRE, The, *Guidelines for Relationships between Volunteers and Paid Non-Professional Workers*, The Volunteer Centre, Berkhamsted, 1977.

WADE, E.C.S., and A.W. BRADLEY, *Constitutional and Administrative Law*, 10th edn., Longmans, London, 1985.

WALLINGTON, PETER, 'Policing the Miners' Strike', *Industrial Law Journal* 14 (1985), 145–59.

WEDDERBURN, K.W., 'Industrial action, the State and the public interest' in *Industrial Conflict: A Comparative Legal Survey* ed. B. Aaron and K.W. Wedderburn, Longman, London, 1972, 319–83.

WEDDERBURN, LORD and W.T. MURPHY (eds.), *Labour Law and the Community: Perspectives for the 1980s*, Institute of Advanced Legal Studies, London, 1982.

W[EDDERBURN], 'Rocking the Torts', *Modern Law Review* 46 (1983), 224–31.

WEEKES, BRIAN, MICHAEL MELLISH, LINDA DICKENS, and JOHN LLOYD, *Industrial Relations and the Limits of Law: The Industrial Effects of the Industrial Relations Act 1971*, Blackwell, Oxford, 1975.

WEILER, P., *Reconcilable Differences*, Carswell, Toronto, 1980.

WHEELER-BENNETT, JOHN W., *John Anderson, Viscount Waverley*, Macmillan, London, 1962.

WHELAN, CHRISTOPHER J., 'Military Intervention in Industrial Disputes', *Industrial Law Journal* 8(1979), 222–34.

—, 'On Uses and Misuses of Comparative Labour Law: A Case Study', *Modern Law Review* 45 (1982), 285–300.

—, 'Armed Forces, Industrial Disputes and the Law in Great Britain' in *Military Intervention in Democratic Societies* ed. Peter J. Rowe and Christopher J. Whelan, Croom Helm, Beckenham, 1985.

WHITE, ROGER, 'Statistics of a strike', *Water Bulletin*, May 6 1983, 5–6.

WIGHAM, ERIC, *Strikes and the Government 1893–1981*, Macmillan, London, 1982.

WILLIAMS, DAVID, *Keeping the Peace*, Hutchinson, London, 1967.

WILSHER, PETER, DONALD MACINTYRE, and MICHAEL JONES, *Strike: Thatcher, Scargill and the Miners*, Andre Deutsch, London, 1985.

WILSON, HAROLD, *The Labour Government 1964–1970*, Weidenfeld and Nicolson and Michael Joseph, London, 1971.

WINCHESTER, DAVID, 'Industrial Relations in the Public Sector' in *Industrial Relations in Britain* ed. George Sayers Bain, Blackwell, Oxford, 1983, 155–78.

YOUNG, THOM, *Incitement to Disaffection*, The Cobden Trust, London, 1976.

Table of Cases

Index